CATCH THE VIBE

Building Revolutionary AI Applications That Connect

A Strategic Guide for Non-Technical Founders and Entrepreneurs

JUDSON VOSS

Harness the power of AI to build intuitive applications that resonate with users

THE VIBE CODE

The Art of Building Apps That Connect

First Edition: 2025

Published by Kuhle Word Consulting, LLC https://kuhlewordconsulting.com

Printed in the United States of America

THE VIBE CODE

Preface

The world of software development is undergoing a seismic shift. For years, the ability to bring a digital idea to life was gated behind the complex walls of traditional coding. If you weren't a developer, your vision often remained just that—a vision. But something exciting is happening. The rise of powerful AI tools and intuitive platforms is tearing down those walls, ushering in an era where passion, insight, and a clear understanding of a problem are becoming just as valuable, if not more so, than the ability to write intricate lines of code.

I've watched this transformation with fascination, seeing brilliant minds—entrepreneurs, artists, experts in countless fields—hesitate at the technical threshold. I saw the frustration of having a solution but lacking the traditional means to build it. Then came the "vibe"—this intuitive, intent-driven approach to creation, amplified by AI that could translate vision into function. Andrej Karpathy gave it a name in early 2025: "vibe coding." It resonated instantly. It wasn't just about new tools; it was a new philosophy, a democratization of digital creation.

This book was born from the desire to capture the essence of this revolution and provide a practical guide for anyone feeling the pull to create in this new landscape. Whether you're a non-technical visionary with a game-changing app idea, an entrepreneur needing to move faster, a product manager wanting to prototype concepts, or even a curious developer looking to leverage AI, the principles of vibe coding offer a new path forward.

"Catch the Vibe" is not just about harnessing AI to generate code; it's about embracing a user-first, intuition-driven mindset. It's about focusing on the *what* and the *why*—the core problem, the user experience, the market need—while letting intelligent tools handle more of the *how*. We'll journey together through the entire process, from validating your idea and designing with feeling, to building your first version, navigating the launch, and thinking about the future.

My hope is that this book demystifies the process, empowers you with actionable strategies, and inspires you to ride the wave of this incredible technological moment. The power to create is shifting, and the vibe is yours to catch. Let's build something amazing together.

Chapter 1: Welcome to the Vibe Coding Revolution

The Dawn of a New Era

Picture this: You have a brilliant app idea that could solve a real problem for thousands of people. In the past, your options were limited—learn to code (a multi-year journey), hire expensive developers, or abandon your vision. But what if there was another way? A way that lets you transform your idea into reality without writing a single line of traditional code?

Welcome to the vibe coding revolution—a transformative approach to app development that's changing who can build software and how they build it.

Vibe coding represents a fundamental shift in how we create digital products. Rather than meticulously crafting every line of code, vibe coding embraces the power of AI to handle the technical implementation while you focus on what truly matters: the vision, the user experience, and the market fit.

As Andrej Karpathy, a co-founder of OpenAI, described when he coined the term in February 2025, vibe coding means "fully giving in to the vibes, embracing exponentials, and forgetting that the code even exists." This approach transforms software development from a technical task into an intent-based conversation.

Why Vibe Coding Matters Now

We're standing at a unique moment in technological history. The barriers that once restricted app creation to a small subset of technically skilled individuals are crumbling. Just as desktop publishing democratized print media in the 1980s and website builders democratized web presence in the 2000s, vibe coding is now democratizing app development.

Here's why this matters right now:

The Democratization of Creation: With vibe coding, domain expertise becomes more valuable than programming expertise. The approach enables people without formal programming training to build functional software, allowing those who understand problems best to directly create solutions tailored to their needs.

Accelerated Innovation: When the time from idea to implementation shrinks dramatically, we can test more concepts, iterate faster, and deliver solutions that truly connect with users. Projects that once took days or weeks can now be completed in hours, fostering creativity and experimentation.

The Rise of AI Co-pilots: Modern AI tools don't just assist with coding—they transform the entire development process. Large language models can generate code based on natural language descriptions, handling technical details while you focus on strategic direction.

Lower Financial Barriers: Building minimum viable products no longer requires significant upfront investment in development teams. Development cycles can be drastically reduced, sometimes from months to days, with potential time savings up to 90% compared to traditional methods. This accelerates time-to-market for new ideas and MVPs, making entrepreneurship more accessible to everyone.

In Y Combinator's Winter 2025 batch, 25% of startups had codebases that were 95% AI-generated. This isn't a fringe movement—it's quickly becoming standard practice for innovative companies looking to move quickly and efficiently.

The Mindset Shift: From Code-First to User-First Thinking

Vibe coding isn't just about new tools—it's about a fundamental shift in how we approach problem-solving. At its core, vibe coding shifts the focus from the *how* of writing code (syntax, algorithms) to the *what* the software should do. This turns software development into more of an intent-based outcome specification.

This shift transforms your relationship with technology:

From How to What: Instead of focusing on how to implement features, you concentrate on what the app should do for users. Developers and even non-technical individuals can describe their intentions and let AI tools handle the technical implementation.

From Syntax to Intent: Rather than worrying about correct syntax, you communicate your intentions in natural language. The quality of the AI-generated code heavily depends on how effectively the "vibe" or desired outcome is communicated through natural language prompts.

From Technical Debt to Experience Excellence: Your energy goes into perfecting the user experience, not fighting technical limitations. With AI handling more of the implementation, the focus shifts to user needs, prioritizing features, and crafting a great user experience.

Think of vibe coding like having a team of expert developers at your disposal, ready to implement your vision—only more flexible, faster, and available 24/7.

The Vibe Coding Philosophy

At its core, vibe coding embraces several key principles:

1. Intuition Over Implementation Trust your understanding of what users need rather than technical conventions. The developer's role transforms from a meticulous implementer to a guide, tester, and refiner of the AI's output. Your intuition about what feels right for users often leads to better experiences than slavishly following development patterns.

2. Market Awareness Over Technical Perfection A "good enough" app that solves a real problem is infinitely more valuable than a technically perfect app nobody wants. Vibe coding prioritizes market fit over architectural elegance. Critics point out that code generated without careful planning can be prone to errors and difficult to maintain, but for many applications, especially early-stage prototypes, the benefits of speed and accessibility outweigh these concerns.

3. User Connection Over Code Complexity The measure of success isn't code quality but user experience quality. Does your app forge an emotional connection with users? Does it solve their problems in a way that feels natural and intuitive? With AI handling more of the implementation, "vibe design" underscores the increasing importance of focusing on user needs.

4. Continuous Evolution Over Fixed Requirements Vibe coding embraces the iterative nature of product development. Your app isn't a static entity but a living creation that evolves based on user feedback and changing market conditions. Vibe coding allows for rapid iteration and exploration, enabling the quick prototyping of features by simply telling the AI the intent.

The Tools of the Revolution

While the philosophical shift is important, vibe coding wouldn't be possible without powerful AI-driven tools that transform natural language into functional code. These tools are evolving rapidly, but several stand out as pioneers in the vibe coding ecosystem:

Cursor: An AI-powered code editor based on VS Code, considered a flagship for vibe coding with features like its composer chat for instructions, "Fix with AI" button, and both normal and Agent modes.

Replit: An online IDE where 75% of users don't write code, relying on Ghostwriter AI. It requires no setup and supports rapid prototyping.

GitHub Copilot: An AI pair-programmer integrated with VS Code that autocompletes code, turns comments into code, and includes Copilot Chat.

ChatGPT/Claude: LLM chatbots for generating and explaining code that support multiple programming languages and are enhanced by community plugins.

Windsurf AI: An AI tool with agentic mode for automatic changes that keeps users "in the flow" and differs from Cursor in its automation philosophy.

The reality is that these tools will continue to evolve, but the principles of vibe coding will remain constant: using natural language to guide AI in creating the technical implementation of your vision.

The Promise and the Pitfalls

Like any revolutionary approach, vibe coding comes with both tremendous promise and potential pitfalls. Let's be honest about both:

The Promise:

- Transform ideas into working prototypes in hours instead of weeks, enabling rapid prototyping and experimentation
- Test multiple approaches quickly to find what resonates with users, accelerating the development process
- Focus your energy on strategy and experience, not technical details, shifting your role to guide, test, and refine the AI's output
- Create apps that would be impossible with your technical skills alone, opening up software creation to non-engineers and domain experts

The Pitfalls:

- Generating code without understanding can lead to maintenance challenges. AI-generated code can be bloated, slow, or difficult to maintain, particularly for complex projects.
- Security and performance may suffer without proper testing and refinement. Vibe-coders may lack awareness of security exploits, risking vulnerabilities in applications, especially those handling sensitive data.
- Over-reliance on AI can limit your growth and learning. Unlike traditional coders, vibe-coders may not understand the risks of flawed systems, increasing the likelihood of errors going unnoticed.
- "Vibe coded" applications might require professional

intervention for maintenance, likened to hiring contractors for DIY projects gone awry.

This book doesn't advocate blind acceptance of AI-generated code without review ("blind coding"), which is considered risky. Instead, we'll show you how to harness vibe coding responsibly—combining the speed and accessibility of AI with thoughtful testing, refinement, and user-centered design.

Who This Book Is For

This book is written for several types of readers:

The Visionary Non-Developer: You have brilliant ideas but lack technical skills to implement them. Vibe coding enables people without formal programming training to build functional software, allowing you to create without learning to code.

The Time-Constrained Entrepreneur: You need to move quickly, testing concepts and getting to market before your competition. Vibe coding allows for rapid iteration and exploration, enabling the quick prototyping of features by simply telling the AI the intent.

The Curious Developer: You already know how to code but want to leverage AI to boost your productivity and focus on higher-level problems. Some engineers see vibe coding as a way to learn new languages and technologies by leveraging AI to generate initial code and understand how different components work.

The Product Manager: You want to create quick prototypes to validate concepts before investing in full development. The developer's role transforms from a meticulous implementer to a guide, tester, and refiner of the AI's output, with some even describing the vibe coder as a product manager orchestrating the AI.

No matter which category you fall into, this book will provide practical guidance for turning your ideas into reality using the vibe coding approach.

How to Use This Book

This book is designed as a practical journey through the entire app development process using vibe coding principles. Each chapter builds on the previous one, but feel free to skip to sections most relevant to your current challenges.

For maximum benefit:

1. Read the chapters in order to understand the complete vibe coding workflow
2. Complete the exercises at the end of each chapter to apply what you've learned
3. Use the templates and resources provided to accelerate your progress
4. Join our online community to share your experiences and learn from others

Throughout the book, you'll find:

- **Real-World Examples**: Case studies of successful apps built using vibe coding principles, like Mytender (an AI tool for contract bids), Coverdoc (an AI-powered platform for job seekers), My AskAI (an AI customer support chatbot), and Coachvox AI (an AI platform for creators).

- **Action Steps**: Concrete tasks to move your project forward
- **Vibe Tips**: Insider advice for getting the most from AI coding tools, such as how to craft effective "vibe prompts" that communicate your intentions clearly
- **Caution Zones**: Areas where extra attention is needed to avoid common pitfalls, like testing for security vulnerabilities, performance issues, and maintenance challenges

Your Vibe Coding Journey Starts Now

The app economy is waiting for your contribution. With vibe coding, you have the tools to transform your ideas into reality faster than ever before. Whether you're building a side project, launching a startup, or innovating within an existing company, vibe coding can help you create apps that truly connect with users.

In the next chapter, we'll explore the current state of the app economy and why now is the perfect moment to leverage vibe coding for your projects. But before we move on, let's take a moment to reflect on what you've learned and the exciting possibilities ahead.

Chapter Summary

- **Vibe coding** is a revolutionary approach that uses AI to handle technical implementation while you focus on vision and user experience
- The approach was coined by Andrej Karpathy in February 2025, describing it as "fully giving in to the vibes, embracing exponentials, and forgetting that the code even exists"
- This approach **democratizes app development**, making it accessible to non-developers by lowering barriers to entry
- Vibe coding represents a mindset shift from code-first to user-first thinking, focusing on the *what* rather than the *how*
- The philosophy prioritizes intuition, market awareness, user connection, and continuous evolution
- Tools like Cursor, Replit, GitHub Copilot, ChatGPT, Claude, and Windsurf AI enable the vibe coding approach
- While powerful, vibe coding comes with both promises and pitfalls that must be navigated thoughtfully through proper testing and refinement

Action Steps

1. **Reflect on your app idea**: Write down the core problem your app will solve and the specific value it delivers to the customer. Start with a problem-first orientation rather than "Let's use AI for X."
2. **Assess your current approach**: Are you thinking code-

first or user-first? Consider how shifting from focusing on the *how* to the *what* might change your development process.

3. **Explore vibe coding tools**: Create accounts on platforms like Cursor, Replit, or try ChatGPT/Claude to start exploring the capabilities of AI-assisted development.
4. **Practice vibe prompting**: Try crafting clear and precise instructions for AI. Instead of saying "Make a login system," use a more effective vibe prompt like "Create a Flask route that serves a login form with email and password fields, and validate the inputs using WTForms."
5. **Set your vibe coding goal**: Define one specific project you'll tackle using vibe coding principles as you work through this book. Focus on building the core features that deliver immediate value and test key assumptions.

Are you ready to transform how you build apps? Let's continue our journey into the new app economy and discover why right now is the perfect moment to embrace vibe coding.

Chapter 2: The New App Economy: Opportunities for Everyone

The Gold Rush Moment

We're living through a remarkable moment in technological history. The barriers that once kept app development exclusive to a small club of technical experts are crumbling rapidly. What we're witnessing is nothing short of a gold rush in the app economy, and the exciting news is that **you don't need to be a seasoned coder to stake your claim**.

Think about this: in early 2025, Y Combinator—the prestigious startup accelerator that launched giants like Airbnb and Dropbox—reported that 25% of their startups had codebases that were 95% AI-generated. This isn't a future prediction; it's happening right now. We're entering an era where your vision and market understanding can be more valuable than traditional coding skills.

The democratization of app development is being driven by the convergence of several powerful forces: increasingly capable AI tools, sophisticated low-code/no-code platforms, and the emergence of what Andrej Karpathy (co-founder of OpenAI and former Tesla AI director) calls "vibe coding." In February 2025, Karpathy described this new paradigm as a process where programmers rely entirely on AI to handle coding tasks using conversational prompts. As he put it, "It's not really coding - I just see things, say things, run things, and copy-paste things, and it mostly works."

This isn't just about making life easier for existing developers—it's about opening the door to people who've never written a line of code but have brilliant ideas for solving real problems.

Why Now is the Perfect Moment to Enter App Development

The Democratization Revolution

The tools available today have fundamentally changed the game. AI-assisted development and no-code platforms are removing the technical barriers that once kept many innovative minds on the sidelines. Let's look at what makes this moment so unique:

1. **AI-Powered Development Tools**: Tools like GitHub Copilot, Cursor, and Replit's Ghostwriter can now generate substantial portions of code from simple natural language descriptions. You describe what you want, and AI handles the technical implementation.
2. **No-Code/Low-Code Maturity**: Platforms like Bubble, FlutterFlow, and Microsoft Power Apps have evolved from simple website builders to sophisticated app development environments. Gartner predicts that by 2025, these technologies will be responsible for developing 70% of new applications in enterprise organizations.
3. **AI Integration Built-In**: Many of these platforms now come with AI capabilities embedded directly in the tools—from AI-assisted development suggestions to natural language processing features you can add to your app with a few clicks.
4. **Reduced Development Time**: Projects that previously

took months can now be completed in days or weeks. According to industry research, development cycles can be reduced by up to 90% compared to traditional methods.

The result? The playing field has been leveled. The person with the best understanding of a market problem and the most compelling solution can now compete with established players, regardless of technical background.

The Rise of Successful Non-Technical Founders

The evidence for this shift isn't just theoretical—it's playing out in the market with real companies founded by people with limited or no coding backgrounds. Let me share a few examples:

From Excel Prototype to Viable Business

One founder described starting with nothing more than an Excel model as their prototype. They collaborated with a designer for basic mockups, validated the concept with potential customers, and then resourcefully hired initial part-time engineers found on Reddit. This lean, iterative approach allowed them to test their concept without significant technical skills or venture capital.

The Power of Visual Communication

Alex Turnbull, the non-technical founder of Groove HQ, initially used hand-drawn sketches and then learned basic Photoshop to create mockups of his app idea. These visuals were crucial in persuading talented engineers to join and build the backend. His ability to communicate his vision visually compensated for his lack of coding skills.

No-Code to $1,000 MRR

Ambar Shrivastava utilized the no-code platform Softr to build Coverdoc, an AI-powered platform for job seekers, achieving $1,000 in Monthly Recurring Revenue (MRR). This demonstrates that no-code tools can be sufficient to build and monetize a SaaS product in the AI space without traditional development skills.

AI-Powered Customer Support from Finance Background

A founder with a finance background, after experimenting with GPT-3 technology, created My AskAI, an AI customer support chatbot for SaaS businesses. Starting with minimal cost ($99), the venture reached $25,000/month ($300,000/year) by applying AI technology to a specific, valuable business problem.

What these success stories reveal is consistent: successful non-technical founders excel at translating a clear business vision into an actionable plan. This translation might occur through direct manipulation of no-code tools or via effective communication with technical partners using tools like mockups, prototypes, and clear requirement definitions.

The Common Factors in Non-Technical Founder Success

Analyzing these trailblazers reveals several recurring success factors:

1. Problem Obsession

These founders invariably started with a deep understanding of a specific problem and the needs of their target audience, rather than starting with the technology itself. They recognized that technology is just a means to an end—solving a real pain point for real people.

2. Strategic Tool Utilization

Whether leveraging no-code platforms for rapid MVP development or employing strong visual communication tools (sketches, wireframes, mockups) to bridge the gap with technical teams, these founders made effective use of the tools available to them.

3. Effective Collaboration & Role Clarity

Success often hinged on building strong partnerships with technical experts (co-founders, employees, agencies). This required clear communication of the vision, well-defined roles, and establishing trust. Non-technical founders understood their primary role was often outside the code itself—focusing on market understanding, user experience, and business strategy.

4. Validation-Driven Approach

Many adopted an iterative approach: building minimally, launching quickly, measuring results, and using customer feedback to guide the next steps. This lean methodology helped de-risk development and ensure product-market fit before committing significant resources.

5. Business Acumen as the Differentiator

Skills in areas like marketing, sales, networking, storytelling, and overall business strategy frequently proved more critical to success than the founder's ability to code. They understood the crucial "now what?" phase after a product is initially built—how to get it into users' hands and grow from there.

Case Study: Mytender

A compelling example comes from two undergraduate students from Southampton University who developed Mytender, an AI tool to assist companies in writing bids for contracts in sectors like construction. Despite their likely limited technical backgrounds, their focus on solving a specific industry problem attracted £250,000 in seed funding from Fuel Ventures.

What made Mytender successful wasn't revolutionary technology—it was their identification of a painful, time-consuming process that affected many businesses. They recognized that AI could dramatically improve the efficiency of bid writing, saving companies significant time and resources while increasing win rates.

Their approach demonstrates that a clear problem focus and leveraging available AI tools can attract early-stage investment, even without deep technical founding expertise. By focusing on a vertical-specific solution rather than a general-purpose tool, they created a compelling value proposition that resonated with both users and investors.

How Modern Tools Have Lowered the Barrier to Entry

Let's get specific about the tools that are enabling this revolution. The modern app development toolkit has evolved dramatically, offering multiple pathways for non-technical founders:

AI-Assisted Coding Tools

Tools like Cursor (an AI-powered code editor based on VS Code) and GitHub Copilot (an AI pair-programmer) can take natural language descriptions and convert them into functional code. Even better, they can explain the code they generate, helping you learn as you build.

No-Code Application Builders

Platforms like Bubble and Webflow allow you to build sophisticated applications through visual interfaces. Remarkably, 75% of Replit users don't write code, relying instead on their Ghostwriter AI. These platforms have evolved to support complex functionality including:

- Database management
- User authentication
- Payment processing
- Third-party integrations
- Responsive designs
- Complex business logic

AI Model Integration Platforms

Services from companies like OpenAI, Anthropic, Google, and Microsoft now offer APIs that let you add sophisticated AI capabilities to your app with minimal technical work. Want to add natural language processing, image recognition, or content generation? There are now simple interfaces for that.

Component Libraries and Templates

Pre-built UI components and app templates dramatically reduce the design and development workload. These give you professional-looking, functional elements that can be customized to your needs.

The Shift in Startup Dynamics

This technological evolution isn't just changing how apps are built—it's changing the entire startup ecosystem. We're seeing several profound shifts:

1. Faster Time-to-Market

Development cycles that once took months can now be completed in weeks or even days. This acceleration allows for quicker testing of ideas and faster iteration based on user feedback.

2. Lower Capital Requirements

The reduced need for large development teams means startups can launch with significantly less initial capital. This opens entrepreneurship to a wider range of people who may not have access to substantial funding.

3. Emphasis on Business Model Innovation

With technical implementation becoming more accessible, competitive advantage increasingly comes from innovative business models, unique market insights, and exceptional execution rather than technical complexity.

4. The Rise of Solo Founders and Small Teams

We're seeing more successful ventures launched by individuals or very small teams, enabled by AI and no-code tools that multiply their productive capacity.

5. Increased Experimentation

The lower cost of building allows for more experimentation and market testing. Founders can try multiple approaches before committing to a direction, increasing the chances of finding product-market fit.

What This Means For You

If you're reading this book, you're likely intrigued by the possibilities of creating your own app. Here's what this new landscape means for you:

1. **Your Domain Expertise is Valuable**: Your specific knowledge of an industry, problem space, or user group is now more valuable than ever. The technical aspects of building can be augmented by AI and no-code tools.
2. **Start With What You Know**: The most successful non-technical founders typically build solutions for problems they've personally experienced or observed closely. This insight gives them an intuitive understanding of user needs.
3. **Focus on the "Vibe"**: As vibe coding suggests, focus on the intent and user experience—what you want your app to do and how it should feel to users—rather than getting lost in technical details.
4. **Build, Measure, Learn**: Adopt an iterative approach. Launch something simple to test your core idea, gather user feedback, and refine based on what you learn.

5. **Don't Go It Alone**: While modern tools can reduce dependence on technical teams, successful products often involve collaboration. Consider partnerships, advisors, or consultants who can complement your skills.

Case Study: Apps That Succeeded Through Vibe Coding Principles

Let's look at Coachvox AI, created by Jodie Cook. With a background in content and social media agency ownership, Cook leveraged her extensive existing content (books, articles, podcasts) to build an AI platform that allows creators to build AI versions of themselves for coaching and engagement.

The key insight wasn't technical innovation—it was recognizing that creators have valuable knowledge locked in their content that could be made interactive through AI. By focusing on this user need and leveraging her unique, non-technical assets (proprietary content), Cook created a successful niche product that achieved six-figure Annual Recurring Revenue (ARR) even before its official launch.

This exemplifies vibe coding principles in action: identifying a valuable user problem, focusing on the intended outcome rather than technical details, and leveraging existing strengths rather than technical expertise.

Chapter Summary: Key Takeaways

- We're experiencing a democratization of app development driven by AI and no-code tools that is lowering barriers to entry for non-technical founders.
- Successful non-technical founders focus on problem understanding, strategic tool use, effective collaboration, validation-driven approaches, and strong business acumen.
- Modern development tools—from AI-assisted coding to no-code platforms—provide multiple pathways to build sophisticated applications without traditional coding skills.
- The startup landscape is changing, with faster time-to-market, lower capital requirements, and increased opportunity for experimentation.
- Domain expertise and market understanding are becoming more valuable relative to technical skills in the early stages of product development.

Action Steps

1. **Identify Your Domain**: List 3-5 areas where you have deep knowledge or experience. What problems in these domains could be solved with an app?
2. **Explore the Toolbox**: Create free accounts on 2-3 no-code platforms (like Bubble, FlutterFlow, or Webflow) and spend an hour with each to understand their capabilities.
3. **Start a Problem Journal**: For one week, document friction points, inefficiencies, or frustrations you

encounter that could potentially be solved with an app.
4. **Visualize Your Idea**: Create a simple mockup of your app idea using a tool like Figma or even pen and paper. Focus on the key user flows and core value.
5. **Find Your Community**: Join at least one online community related to no-code development, AI, or your specific domain to start building your network.

Looking Ahead

In the next chapter, we'll dive into developing your "app radar"—training yourself to spot app-worthy problems in everyday life and evaluating which ideas have the most potential. We'll explore techniques for strengthening your idea muscle and identifying problems with genuine market potential.

The democratization of app development doesn't mean everyone will automatically succeed. It means that the limiting factor is no longer technical knowledge but rather your ability to identify real problems and craft compelling solutions. That's exactly what we'll focus on developing as we continue our vibe coding journey.

Chapter 2: The New App Economy: Opportunities for Everyone

The Gold Rush Moment

We're living through a remarkable moment in technological history. The barriers that once kept app development exclusive to a small club of technical experts are crumbling rapidly. What we're witnessing is nothing short of a gold rush in the app economy, and the exciting news is that **you don't need to be a seasoned coder to stake your claim**.

Think about this: in early 2025, Y Combinator—the prestigious startup accelerator that launched giants like Airbnb and Dropbox—reported that 25% of their startups had codebases that were 95% AI-generated. This isn't a future prediction; it's happening right now. We're entering an era where your vision and market understanding can be more valuable than traditional coding skills.

The democratization of app development is being driven by the convergence of several powerful forces: increasingly capable AI tools, sophisticated low-code/no-code platforms, and the emergence of what Andrej Karpathy (co-founder of OpenAI and former Tesla AI director) calls "vibe coding." In February 2025, Karpathy described this new paradigm as a process where programmers rely entirely on AI to handle coding tasks using conversational prompts. As he put it, "It's not really coding - I just see things, say things, run things, and copy-paste things, and it mostly works."

This isn't just about making life easier for existing developers—it's about opening the door to people who've never written a line of code but have brilliant ideas for solving real problems.

Why Now is the Perfect Moment to Enter App Development

The Democratization Revolution

The tools available today have fundamentally changed the game. AI-assisted development and no-code platforms are removing the technical barriers that once kept many innovative minds on the sidelines. Let's look at what makes this moment so unique:

1. **AI-Powered Development Tools**: Tools like GitHub Copilot, Cursor, and Replit's Ghostwriter can now generate substantial portions of code from simple natural language descriptions. You describe what you want, and AI handles the technical implementation.
2. **No-Code/Low-Code Maturity**: Platforms like Bubble, FlutterFlow, and Microsoft Power Apps have evolved from simple website builders to sophisticated app development environments. Gartner predicts that by 2025, these technologies will be responsible for developing 70% of new applications in enterprise organizations.
3. **AI Integration Built-In**: Many of these platforms now come with AI capabilities embedded directly in the tools—from AI-assisted development suggestions to natural language processing features you can add to your app with a few clicks.
4. **Reduced Development Time**: Projects that previously

took months can now be completed in days or weeks. According to industry research, development cycles can be reduced by up to 90% compared to traditional methods.

The result? The playing field has been leveled. The person with the best understanding of a market problem and the most compelling solution can now compete with established players, regardless of technical background.

The Rise of Successful Non-Technical Founders

The evidence for this shift isn't just theoretical—it's playing out in the market with real companies founded by people with limited or no coding backgrounds. Let me share a few examples:

From Excel Prototype to Viable Business

One founder described starting with nothing more than an Excel model as their prototype. They collaborated with a designer for basic mockups, validated the concept with potential customers, and then resourcefully hired initial part-time engineers found on Reddit. This lean, iterative approach allowed them to test their concept without significant technical skills or venture capital.

The Power of Visual Communication

Alex Turnbull, the non-technical founder of Groove HQ, initially used hand-drawn sketches and then learned basic Photoshop to create mockups of his app idea. These visuals were crucial in persuading talented engineers to join and build the backend. His ability to communicate his vision visually compensated for his lack of coding skills.

No-Code to $1,000 MRR

Ambar Shrivastava utilized the no-code platform Softr to build Coverdoc, an AI-powered platform for job seekers, achieving $1,000 in Monthly Recurring Revenue (MRR). This demonstrates that no-code tools can be sufficient to build and monetize a SaaS product in the AI space without traditional development skills.

AI-Powered Customer Support from Finance Background

A founder with a finance background, after experimenting with GPT-3 technology, created My AskAI, an AI customer support chatbot for SaaS businesses. Starting with minimal cost ($99), the venture reached $25,000/month ($300,000/year) by applying AI technology to a specific, valuable business problem.

What these success stories reveal is consistent: successful non-technical founders excel at translating a clear business vision into an actionable plan. This translation might occur through direct manipulation of no-code tools or via effective communication with technical partners using tools like mockups, prototypes, and clear requirement definitions.

The Common Factors in Non-Technical Founder Success

Analyzing these trailblazers reveals several recurring success factors:

1. Problem Obsession

These founders invariably started with a deep understanding of a specific problem and the needs of their target audience, rather than starting with the technology itself. They recognized that technology is just a means to an end—solving a real pain point for real people.

2. Strategic Tool Utilization

Whether leveraging no-code platforms for rapid MVP development or employing strong visual communication tools (sketches, wireframes, mockups) to bridge the gap with technical teams, these founders made effective use of the tools available to them.

3. Effective Collaboration & Role Clarity

Success often hinged on building strong partnerships with technical experts (co-founders, employees, agencies). This required clear communication of the vision, well-defined roles, and establishing trust. Non-technical founders understood their primary role was often outside the code itself—focusing on market understanding, user experience, and business strategy.

4. Validation-Driven Approach

Many adopted an iterative approach: building minimally, launching quickly, measuring results, and using customer feedback to guide the next steps. This lean methodology helped de-risk development and ensure product-market fit before committing significant resources.

5. Business Acumen as the Differentiator

Skills in areas like marketing, sales, networking, storytelling, and overall business strategy frequently proved more critical to success than the founder's ability to code. They understood the crucial "now what?" phase after a product is initially built—how to get it into users' hands and grow from there.

Case Study: Mytender

A compelling example comes from two undergraduate students from Southampton University who developed Mytender, an AI tool to assist companies in writing bids for contracts in sectors like construction. Despite their likely limited technical backgrounds, their focus on solving a specific industry problem attracted £250,000 in seed funding from Fuel Ventures.

What made Mytender successful wasn't revolutionary technology—it was their identification of a painful, time-consuming process that affected many businesses. They recognized that AI could dramatically improve the efficiency of bid writing, saving companies significant time and resources while increasing win rates.

Their approach demonstrates that a clear problem focus and leveraging available AI tools can attract early-stage investment, even without deep technical founding expertise. By focusing on a vertical-specific solution rather than a general-purpose tool, they created a compelling value proposition that resonated with both users and investors.

How Modern Tools Have Lowered the Barrier to Entry

Let's get specific about the tools that are enabling this revolution. The modern app development toolkit has evolved dramatically, offering multiple pathways for non-technical founders:

AI-Assisted Coding Tools

Tools like Cursor (an AI-powered code editor based on VS Code) and GitHub Copilot (an AI pair-programmer) can take natural language descriptions and convert them into functional code. Even better, they can explain the code they generate, helping you learn as you build.

No-Code Application Builders

Platforms like Bubble and Webflow allow you to build sophisticated applications through visual interfaces. Remarkably, 75% of Replit users don't write code, relying instead on their Ghostwriter AI. These platforms have evolved to support complex functionality including:

- Database management
- User authentication
- Payment processing
- Third-party integrations
- Responsive designs
- Complex business logic

AI Model Integration Platforms

Services from companies like OpenAI, Anthropic, Google, and Microsoft now offer APIs that let you add sophisticated AI capabilities to your app with minimal technical work. Want to add natural language processing, image recognition, or content generation? There are now simple interfaces for that.

Component Libraries and Templates

Pre-built UI components and app templates dramatically reduce the design and development workload. These give you professional-looking, functional elements that can be customized to your needs.

The Shift in Startup Dynamics

This technological evolution isn't just changing how apps are built—it's changing the entire startup ecosystem. We're seeing several profound shifts:

1. Faster Time-to-Market

Development cycles that once took months can now be completed in weeks or even days. This acceleration allows for quicker testing of ideas and faster iteration based on user feedback.

2. Lower Capital Requirements

The reduced need for large development teams means startups can launch with significantly less initial capital. This opens entrepreneurship to a wider range of people who may not have access to substantial funding.

3. Emphasis on Business Model Innovation

With technical implementation becoming more accessible, competitive advantage increasingly comes from innovative business models, unique market insights, and exceptional execution rather than technical complexity.

4. The Rise of Solo Founders and Small Teams

We're seeing more successful ventures launched by individuals or very small teams, enabled by AI and no-code tools that multiply their productive capacity.

5. Increased Experimentation

The lower cost of building allows for more experimentation and market testing. Founders can try multiple approaches before committing to a direction, increasing the chances of finding product-market fit.

What This Means For You

If you're reading this book, you're likely intrigued by the possibilities of creating your own app. Here's what this new landscape means for you:

1. **Your Domain Expertise is Valuable**: Your specific knowledge of an industry, problem space, or user group is now more valuable than ever. The technical aspects of building can be augmented by AI and no-code tools.
2. **Start With What You Know**: The most successful non-technical founders typically build solutions for problems they've personally experienced or observed closely. This insight gives them an intuitive understanding of user needs.
3. **Focus on the "Vibe"**: As vibe coding suggests, focus on the intent and user experience—what you want your app to do and how it should feel to users—rather than getting lost in technical details.
4. **Build, Measure, Learn**: Adopt an iterative approach. Launch something simple to test your core idea, gather user feedback, and refine based on what you learn.

5. **Don't Go It Alone**: While modern tools can reduce dependence on technical teams, successful products often involve collaboration. Consider partnerships, advisors, or consultants who can complement your skills.

Case Study: Apps That Succeeded Through Vibe Coding Principles

Let's look at Coachvox AI, created by Jodie Cook. With a background in content and social media agency ownership, Cook leveraged her extensive existing content (books, articles, podcasts) to build an AI platform that allows creators to build AI versions of themselves for coaching and engagement.

The key insight wasn't technical innovation—it was recognizing that creators have valuable knowledge locked in their content that could be made interactive through AI. By focusing on this user need and leveraging her unique, non-technical assets (proprietary content), Cook created a successful niche product that achieved six-figure Annual Recurring Revenue (ARR) even before its official launch.

This exemplifies vibe coding principles in action: identifying a valuable user problem, focusing on the intended outcome rather than technical details, and leveraging existing strengths rather than technical expertise.

Chapter Summary: Key Takeaways

- We're experiencing a democratization of app development driven by AI and no-code tools that is lowering barriers to entry for non-technical founders.
- Successful non-technical founders focus on problem understanding, strategic tool use, effective collaboration, validation-driven approaches, and strong business acumen.
- Modern development tools—from AI-assisted coding to no-code platforms—provide multiple pathways to build sophisticated applications without traditional coding skills.
- The startup landscape is changing, with faster time-to-market, lower capital requirements, and increased opportunity for experimentation.
- Domain expertise and market understanding are becoming more valuable relative to technical skills in the early stages of product development.

Action Steps

1. **Identify Your Domain**: List 3-5 areas where you have deep knowledge or experience. What problems in these domains could be solved with an app?
2. **Explore the Toolbox**: Create free accounts on 2-3 no-code platforms (like Bubble, FlutterFlow, or Webflow) and spend an hour with each to understand their capabilities.
3. **Start a Problem Journal**: For one week, document friction points, inefficiencies, or frustrations you

encounter that could potentially be solved with an app.

4. **Visualize Your Idea**: Create a simple mockup of your app idea using a tool like Figma or even pen and paper. Focus on the key user flows and core value.
5. **Find Your Community**: Join at least one online community related to no-code development, AI, or your specific domain to start building your network.

Looking Ahead

In the next chapter, we'll dive into developing your "app radar"—training yourself to spot app-worthy problems in everyday life and evaluating which ideas have the most potential. We'll explore techniques for strengthening your idea muscle and identifying problems with genuine market potential.

The democratization of app development doesn't mean everyone will automatically succeed. It means that the limiting factor is no longer technical knowledge but rather your ability to identify real problems and craft compelling solutions. That's exactly what we'll focus on developing as we continue our vibe coding journey.

Chapter 3: Developing Your App Radar

Training Yourself to Spot App-Worthy Problems in Daily Life

In a world saturated with apps, the difference between creating just another download and building something people genuinely need comes down to one critical skill: developing your "app radar." This is your ability to detect problems begging for solutions—problems that aren't just minor inconveniences but genuine friction points in people's lives.

Think of your app radar as a specialized sense—like how a chef develops a refined palate or how a musician trains their ear. It's about training yourself to notice opportunities hiding in plain sight. The best app ideas rarely come from brainstorming sessions staring at a blank wall; they emerge from observing real problems in everyday life.

The Observational Mindset

Karpathy's concept of vibe coding isn't just about using AI to generate code—it's about approaching development with a new mindset that prioritizes intuition and market awareness. The foundation of this approach is learning to observe the world with fresh eyes.

"The hottest new programming language is English," as Karpathy noted. This shift means your ability to articulate problems clearly becomes more valuable than writing code. Your app radar starts with how you observe and describe the friction points you encounter.

Practice Exercise: The Daily Friction Journal

For one week, carry a small notebook or use a notes app on your phone. Document every friction point you encounter:

- Tasks that take longer than they should
- Processes that feel unnecessarily complex
- Moments of frustration in your daily routine
- Problems you solve repeatedly
- Workarounds you've created

At the end of the week, review your entries and look for patterns. The most frequent frustrations often represent the most promising app opportunities.

From Personal Pain to Market Opportunity

Your personal frustrations are often excellent starting points for app ideas, but developing a strong app radar means going beyond your own experience to identify problems with market potential.

Case Study: MyTender

Two undergraduate students from Southampton University built MyTender, an AI tool that helps companies write bids for contracts in sectors like construction. Despite their limited technical backgrounds, their focus on solving a specific industry problem attracted £250,000 in seed funding from Fuel Ventures.

What made this app idea successful wasn't technical brilliance—it was the founders' identification of a specific pain point with clear business value. Their app radar detected a process that was time-consuming, complicated, and had direct financial implications for businesses.

The Market Validation Test

When your app radar detects a potential problem, ask:

1. Is this a problem many people experience? (frequency)
2. Does solving it deliver significant value? (impact)
3. Are people currently solving this problem in suboptimal ways? (opportunity)
4. Would people pay to have this problem solved? (monetization)

An idea that checks all four boxes warrants further exploration.

Techniques for Generating Ideas with Market Potential

While observation is the foundation of your app radar, several techniques can help you refine and amplify this skill, helping you generate ideas with genuine market potential.

1. The Reverse Engineering Approach

Study successful apps and reverse engineer why they work. The most successful apps generally solve one of these core problems:

- They save time
- They reduce complexity
- They connect people
- They provide insights or information
- They entertain or reduce boredom

Exercise: App Dissection Choose three apps you use daily and answer:

- What core problem does each solve?
- How did they identify that problem?
- Why did their solution succeed where others failed?

This analysis trains your app radar to recognize the patterns of successful problem-solution fits.

2. The Conversation Mining Technique

People constantly reveal app-worthy problems in conversation—you just need to listen for them. Pay attention when you hear phrases like:

- "I wish there was a better way to..."
- "The most annoying thing about _____ is..."
- "It drives me crazy when..."
- "I waste so much time on..."
- "Why hasn't anyone figured out how to..."

These statements are gold for your app radar. They signal unmet needs and frustrations that could translate into valuable app ideas.

Exercise: Conversation Capture During social gatherings or work meetings, note when people express frustrations. Follow up with questions to understand the problem more deeply: "How often does that happen?" "What have you tried to solve it?" "How would you ideally solve that?"

3. The Industry Gap Analysis

Every industry has inefficiencies and gaps that represent app opportunities. Focusing on specific industries can help you identify valuable, targeted problems to solve.

Exercise: Industry Deep Dive Select an industry you have experience in or are interested in. Research:

- Common complaints from customers
- Repetitive tasks professionals perform
- Areas where the industry lags in technology adoption
- Recent regulatory changes creating new compliance needs
- Processes that still rely on outdated methods or paper

Industries undergoing digital transformation often present the richest opportunity landscape for new apps.

Finding the Sweet Spot: Passion, Expertise, and Market Needs

The most successful app ideas typically exist at the intersection of three factors: your passion, your expertise, and market needs. This "sweet spot" is where your app radar should ultimately focus.

The Passion Factor

Building an app requires sustained effort and enthusiasm. When you're genuinely passionate about solving a particular problem, you'll have the motivation to push through challenges. Your app radar will naturally be more attuned to problems in areas you care about.

Ask yourself: What topics, activities, or challenges am I genuinely interested in? What problems would I be excited to solve even if it were difficult?

The Expertise Component

Your knowledge and experience give you insights others might miss. Your app radar is naturally stronger in domains where you have expertise because you understand the nuances of problems in those areas.

Ask yourself: In what areas do I have specialized knowledge? What insights do I have that others might not? What problems am I uniquely positioned to understand?

The Market Need Verification

Passion and expertise must align with actual market needs for a viable app idea. Your app radar must filter for problems that enough people experience and are willing to pay to solve.

Exercise: The Sweet Spot Matrix

Create a three-circle Venn diagram with:

- Circle 1: Topics/areas you're passionate about
- Circle 2: Domains where you have expertise
- Circle 3: Problems with clear market demand

List potential ideas in each circle, then look for those that appear in the overlap of all three. These "sweet spot" ideas deserve your closest attention.

Exercises to Strengthen Your "Idea Muscle"

Like any skill, your app radar improves with deliberate practice. Here are exercises designed to strengthen your ability to identify valuable app opportunities:

The "Ten Ideas a Day" Challenge

For 30 days, challenge yourself to list ten potential app ideas daily. They don't need to be revolutionary—the point is to train your mind to constantly look for problems and solutions. By day 30, you'll have generated 300 ideas and significantly strengthened your "idea muscle."

What typically happens:

- Days 1-5: Easy ideas flow
- Days 6-15: You struggle and ideas feel forced
- Days 16-30: Your mind adapts and starts automatically spotting opportunities

This exercise conditions your brain to continuously scan for problems worth solving.

The "What If" Game

Innovation often comes from challenging assumptions. Pick an everyday process and ask:

- "What if this process were 10x faster?"
- "What if this could be done without [current requirement]?"
- "What if [constraint] didn't exist?"
- "What if [technology X] could be applied here?"

Example: "What if restaurant ordering didn't require interacting with a server?" This question led to tableside ordering apps that have revolutionized restaurant operations.

The "Big to Small" Technique

Major technological shifts create cascading opportunities for apps. Identify a significant tech trend, then work your way down to specific app ideas that leverage that trend.

Example:

- Big Trend: AI-powered voice interfaces
- Industry Application: Healthcare
- Specific Problem: Documentation during patient visits distracts doctors
- App Idea: An AI assistant that transcribes, organizes, and highlights key information from patient conversations

This technique connects your app radar to larger technological currents, helping you identify ideas with momentum behind them.

From Observation to Action: Validating Your App Radar's Findings

Having a keen app radar is just the beginning. Once you've identified a potential opportunity, you need to validate it before investing significant resources.

The Low-Cost Validation Approach

When your app radar detects a promising problem:

1. **Define it precisely:** Write a clear problem statement.
2. **Test your assumptions:** Talk to at least 10 potential

users about the problem.

3. **Analyze existing solutions:** How are people currently solving this problem? What's lacking?
4. **Create a minimal solution concept:** Describe how your app would solve the problem differently or better.
5. **Get feedback on your concept:** Present your solution idea to potential users.

This validation process helps confirm that your app radar has detected a genuine opportunity rather than a mirage.

Leveraging AI for Validation

With the emergence of vibe coding, validation has become faster and more accessible. AI tools can help you:

- Analyze market trends and search patterns related to your problem
- Generate quick prototypes to test assumptions
- Create surveys and analyze responses
- Research existing solutions and their limitations

Tools like ValidatorAI, CheckMyIdea, or even general AI assistants can accelerate your validation process, helping you quickly determine if your app radar has identified a truly valuable opportunity.

The App Radar Mindset: Becoming a Problem-Spotting Machine

Developing your app radar isn't just about spotting a single good idea—it's about cultivating a mindset that continuously identifies opportunities. The most successful app entrepreneurs don't just build one app; they develop a portfolio of solutions because their app radar is always active.

The Five Habits of Strong App Radar Thinkers:

1. **They question default processes:** They constantly ask, "Why is it done this way? Could it be better?"
2. **They listen intently:** They pay attention to complaints and frustrations expressed by others.
3. **They connect dots across industries:** They apply solutions from one domain to problems in another.
4. **They track their ideas:** They document potential opportunities as they arise.
5. **They remain user-focused:** They prioritize solving real problems over showcasing technology.

By developing these habits, you transform your app radar from an occasional flash of insight into a reliable system for identifying valuable opportunities.

App Radar in Action: Real-World Success Stories

Let's examine how real entrepreneurs used their app radar to detect problems and build successful solutions:

Coachvox AI: Founder Jodie Cook leveraged her extensive content (books, articles, podcasts) to build an AI platform allowing creators to build AI versions of themselves for coaching and engagement. Her app radar detected a unique opportunity at the intersection of content creation, coaching, and AI. The venture achieved six-figure Annual Recurring Revenue even before its official launch.

Coverdoc: Ambar Shrivastava used the no-code platform Softr to build Coverdoc, an AI-powered platform for job seekers. By achieving $1,000 Monthly Recurring Revenue, he demonstrated how non-technical founders can use LC/NC tools to capitalize on opportunities spotted by their app radar.

My AskAI: A founder with a finance background experimented with GPT-3 technology before pivoting to create My AskAI, an AI customer support chatbot for SaaS businesses. Starting with minimal cost ($99), the venture reached $25,000/month. This success came from applying AI to a specific, valuable business problem identified through their app radar.

Applying Your App Radar: Action Steps

1. **Start your observation practice today:** Begin documenting friction points and frustrations you encounter.
2. **Create your sweet spot map:** Identify where your passion, expertise, and market needs overlap.
3. **Begin the Ten Ideas a Day challenge:** Commit to generating ten potential app ideas daily for the next 30 days.
4. **Validate your top three ideas:** Talk to potential users about the problems your ideas would solve.
5. **Join communities in your target market:** Immerse yourself in environments where your potential users discuss their challenges.

Remember, developing your app radar is a continuous process. The more you practice observing and identifying problems, the more naturally you'll spot valuable opportunities that others miss.

Chapter Summary: Key Takeaways

- Your app radar is your ability to detect problems with genuine app potential
- The best app ideas emerge from observing real-world friction points
- Focus on the sweet spot where passion, expertise, and market needs intersect
- Validate your app ideas through conversations with potential users
- Strengthen your idea muscle through consistent practice and observation
- Successful vibe coders maintain an active app radar, constantly identifying new opportunities

---

In the next chapter, we'll explore how to evaluate the market viability of the opportunities your app radar identifies, helping you determine which ideas are worth pursuing.

Chapter 4: Market Vibes: Identifying Waves Worth Riding ◈

The Art of Catching Perfect Waves

Imagine standing on the shores of the vast digital ocean, watching waves of opportunity rise and fall. Some are gentle ripples that barely reach the sand. Others are massive swells with enough power to propel you forward at thrilling speeds—if you can catch them at the right moment.

In the world of vibe coding, your success isn't just about building something cool—it's about identifying and riding waves of market opportunity that can carry your app to success. The most brilliant app idea might sink without a trace if launched into calm waters, while even a simple concept can soar when carried by a powerful market wave.

"The best entrepreneurs are like skilled surfers," says Sam Altman, CEO of OpenAI. "They don't create the waves—they become experts at spotting them, positioning themselves correctly, and riding them to shore."

This chapter is your field guide to becoming that skilled surfer, helping you develop what I call your "wave radar"—the ability to sense promising market opportunities before they become obvious to everyone else.

The Market Research Revolution

Traditional market research used to be expensive, time-consuming, and often accessible only to well-funded startups or established companies. But we're living through a remarkable shift. AI tools have democratized high-quality market intelligence, giving solo founders and small teams access to insights that would have cost tens of thousands of dollars just a few years ago.

As a vibe coder, this is a game-changing advantage. You can now:

- Analyze vast datasets to identify emerging trends
- Track competitors' online presence and strategies
- Conduct sentiment analysis on customer feedback
- Detect emerging market signals often missed by manual analysis
- Segment markets based on complex demographic and behavioral data

Tools like ValidatorAI, Checkmyidea, Speak AI, Brandwatch, Perplexity AI, and GWI Spark have transformed what's possible for independent app creators. Market intelligence that once required a dedicated team can now be accessed with a few prompts.

But having access to these tools is just the beginning. The real skill lies in knowing what signals to look for and how to interpret them—the art of reading market vibes.

Four Market Signals Every Vibe Coder Should Track

1. Pain Points at Scale

The most reliable market waves are driven by widespread pain. When large groups of people or businesses share the same problem, there's inherent energy in the market that can propel your solution forward.

How to spot it: Look for consistent complaints, workarounds, or expressions of frustration across multiple channels:

- Social media conversations and sentiment
- Support tickets and forums
- Review sections of existing solutions
- Industry surveys and reports
- Direct customer interviews

Example: The founder of Loom spotted a consistent pain point when working remotely—the inefficiency of writing long emails to explain visual concepts. This pain intensified dramatically during the pandemic, creating a powerful wave that Loom was perfectly positioned to ride with its video messaging solution.

2. Technological Inflection Points

When core technologies advance significantly, they create ripple effects of opportunity across multiple industries. These inflection points often signal the perfect moment to build something new.

How to spot it: Monitor:

- Research breakthroughs being commercialized
- New APIs, platforms, or frameworks becoming available
- Computing power/cost ratios crossing key thresholds
- Existing technology reaching new levels of consumer adoption

Example: The release of GPT-3 and subsequent large language models created a massive inflection point, enabling a wave of new AI applications that were previously impossible. Companies like Jasper, Copy.ai, and Notion jumped on this wave early, building successful businesses around these new capabilities.

3. Behavioral Shifts

Changes in how people live, work, or interact create openings for new solutions that better fit these emerging behaviors.

How to spot it: Look for:

- Pandemic-accelerated changes becoming permanent
- Generational preferences entering the mainstream
- Workplace transformations
- New daily habits forming at scale
- Shifting expectations around existing experiences

Example: Mytender, founded by two undergraduate students, recognized the shifting behavior in how companies approached bidding for contracts. Their AI tool for assisting companies in writing bids for contracts attracted £250,000 in seed funding, despite their likely limited technical backgrounds, because they identified and addressed this behavioral shift effectively.

4. Regulatory and Economic Catalysts

Changes in regulations, economic conditions, or industry standards can suddenly create new requirements or capabilities that weren't viable before.

How to spot it: Monitor:

- Upcoming legislation and compliance deadlines
- Industry standards adoption
- Economic trends affecting business priorities
- Privacy and security requirement changes
- Cross-border commerce regulations

Example: The introduction of GDPR in Europe created an immediate need for compliance solutions, spawning numerous successful privacy-focused startups. Similarly, the rapid adoption of Zero Trust security frameworks created an opening for new authentication and security products.

The Sweet Spot Analysis Framework

The most promising market opportunities exist at the intersection of four key elements:

Market Opportunity = (Pain Intensity × Market Size) + Timing Advantage + Competitive Position

Let's break this down:

Pain Intensity (1-10)

How acutely is the pain felt? Is it:

- A minor annoyance (1-3)
- A significant frustration (4-7)
- A mission-critical problem (8-10)

Higher pain intensity means customers will be more motivated to try new solutions and more willing to pay for them.

Market Size

How many potential customers experience this pain? Consider both:

- Total addressable market (TAM): The total universe of potential customers
- Serviceable obtainable market (SOM): The portion you

can realistically capture

Remember that a small market with intense pain can be more valuable than a large market with mild interest.

Timing Advantage

Are you:

- Too early (market not ready)
- Too late (market saturated)
- Just right (market awakening)

The "just right" timing—where awareness of the problem is growing but solutions are still limited—creates a significant advantage.

Competitive Position

What unique advantage do you bring? This might be:

- Domain expertise in the problem area
- Access to unique data or resources
- A novel approach to solving the problem
- A distribution or go-to-market advantage

Verticalization: The Vibe Coder's Strategic Advantage

One of the most powerful trends in AI application development is verticalization—focusing deeply on a specific industry or niche rather than building general-purpose tools.

The market is shifting away from generic, one-size-fits-all AI models towards solutions tailored for specific industries and niches. Companies are increasingly developing domain-specific AI, and "thick wrappers"—AI applications built on foundational models but deeply integrated with industry-specific workflows and data—are providing significant competitive edges.

As a vibe coder, this trend creates a perfect opportunity to leverage your own industry knowledge, experience, or connections. You don't need to out-engineer the tech giants—you just need to understand a specific vertical better than they do.

Verticalization Success Patterns

Look for niches that have:

1. **Specialized vocabulary and workflows**: Industries with unique terminology, data types, or processes benefit most from custom solutions.
2. **High-value outcomes**: Focus on verticals where improvements directly impact revenue, cost-reduction, or compliance.
3. **Data advantages**: Industries with unique or proprietary data that can be leveraged for better AI performance.
4. **Underserved technical needs**: Sectors where existing solutions aren't tailored to their specific requirements.
5. **Your insider knowledge**: Your personal experience or network in an industry dramatically increases your chances of success.

Example: Jodie Cook, with a background in content and social media agency ownership, leveraged her extensive existing content (books, articles, podcasts) to build Coachvox AI. This platform allows creators to build AI versions of themselves for coaching and engagement. The venture achieved six-figure Annual Recurring Revenue (ARR) even before its official launch because it addressed a specific vertical where Cook had deep expertise.

The Anti-Portfolio: Markets to Approach with Caution

Just as important as identifying promising markets is recognizing those that might be challenging for vibe coders to enter successfully:

1. **Heavily regulated industries without compliance expertise**: Healthcare, finance, and legal applications require deep domain expertise and often face significant regulatory hurdles.
2. **Enterprise solutions requiring lengthy sales cycles**: These typically demand substantial resources for sales teams and long runways for funding.
3. **Commodity features easily replicated by platforms**: If your core idea could be implemented as a feature by existing platforms, proceed with caution.
4. **Consumer markets requiring massive scale**: Markets where success depends on acquiring millions of users before monetization.
5. **Hardware-dependent solutions**: Apps requiring specialized hardware development introduce additional complexity.

This doesn't mean these markets are impossible—just that they require additional resources, specialized knowledge, or strategic partnerships beyond the typical vibe coding approach.

Validation Before Commitment

Before fully committing to a market opportunity, savvy vibe coders validate their insights with minimal investment:

1. **Low-Cost Market Testing**:
   - Create simple landing pages to gauge interest before development
   - Run targeted ad campaigns to test messaging and problem statements
   - Use no-code tools to build interactive prototypes
2. **Strategic Customer Conversations**:
   - Conduct structured interviews with potential users
   - Focus on understanding their current workflow and pain points
   - Ask about willingness to pay and adoption barriers
3. **Competitive Intelligence**:
   - Analyze competitor offerings, pricing, and positioning
   - Identify gaps and unserved segments
   - Study customer reviews for pain points not being addressed
4. **Regulatory and Compliance Assessment**:
   - Verify any regulatory requirements affecting your solution
   - Consider data privacy implications
   - Assess potential ethical considerations, especially for AI applications

The goal is to gather real-world evidence that confirms your market hypothesis before investing significant time and resources in development.

The Vibe Validation Matrix

To help systematically assess market opportunities, use the Vibe Validation Matrix. This tool helps track the validation status of key assumptions underlying your app idea:

Assumption Area	Key Assumption	Validation Method	Evidence Gathered	Confidence Score	Next Steps
Problem/ Need	[Specific problem statement]	Customer interviews, AI market research	[Summary of findings]	Low/ Medium/ High	[Action plan]
Target Audience	[Specific audience need]	Landing page test, LinkedIn outreach	[Summary of findings]	Low/ Medium/ High	[Action plan]
Market Viability	[Market size/growth]	Market research, competitor analysis	[Summary of findings]	Low/ Medium/ High	[Action plan]
Technical Feasibility	[AI capabilities needed]	SME consultation, API review	[Summary of findings]	Low/ Medium/ High	[Action plan]
MVE Components	[Key experience elements]	User testing, prototype feedback	[Summary of findings]	Low/ Medium/ High	[Action plan]
Monetization	[Pricing model viability]	Customer feedback, A/B testing	[Summary of findings]	Low/ Medium/ High	[Action plan]

Use this matrix to identify the assumptions with the lowest confidence scores (highest risk) and focus your validation efforts there first.

Case Study: Catching the Perfect Wave

Ambar Shrivastava had no technical background when he spotted a market opportunity: job seekers struggling to create effective cover letters tailored to specific positions. Using the no-code platform Softr, he built Coverdoc, an AI-powered platform for job seekers.

What made this a perfect market wave to ride?

1. **Universal pain point**: Nearly every job seeker faces this recurring challenge
2. **Technological opportunity**: New AI language models made personalized writing assistance possible
3. **Timing advantage**: The rise of remote work increased job application volume
4. **Vertical focus**: Rather than building a general writing tool, he focused specifically on the job application process
5. **MVP feasibility**: He could build a valuable solution using no-code tools and AI APIs

Within months of launch, Coverdoc was generating $1,000 in monthly recurring revenue—all built by a non-technical founder who spotted and rode the perfect market wave.

Wave Spotting in Action: Current Market Opportunities

As of 2025, several promising market waves are forming that align particularly well with the vibe coding approach:

1. **AI-Enhanced Workflow Tools**: Industry-specific tools that integrate with existing workflows to boost productivity through AI assistance.
2. **Knowledge Transformation**: Solutions that convert unstructured organizational knowledge into actionable insights and decision support.

3. **Human-AI Collaboration**: Tools that leverage AI as a partner rather than a replacement, augmenting human capabilities rather than automating them away.
4. **Decision Intelligence**: Applications that help with complex decision-making by synthesizing multiple data sources and providing contextualized recommendations.
5. **Custom AI Agents**: Specialized autonomous agents focused on specific business functions or industry needs.

Each of these areas offers rich opportunities for vibe coders who can identify specific vertical applications and leverage the growing ecosystem of AI tools and platforms.

WAVE RIDER'S CHECKLIST

✓ **Identify Pain Points at Scale**

□ Search social media for consistent complaints

□ Review competitor app reviews for unmet needs

□ Interview potential users about their biggest challenges

□ Use AI tools to analyze sentiment around existing solutions

✓ **Assess Market Size and Growth**

□ Determine your total addressable market (TAM)

□ Calculate your serviceable obtainable market (SOM)

□ Verify growth trends in your target sector

□ Identify market segments with highest pain intensity

✓ **Evaluate Timing Advantage**

☐ Research adoption curves for related technologies

☐ Identify trigger events that may accelerate adoption

☐ Assess existing solution maturity

☐ Consider regulatory or economic factors affecting timing

✓ **Develop Vertical Focus**

☐ List industries where you have domain expertise

☐ Research verticals with specialized workflows

☐ Identify niches with high-value outcomes

☐ Evaluate data advantages in potential verticals

✓ **Validate Before Building**

☐ Create simple landing pages to test interest

☐ Conduct structured customer interviews

☐ Analyze competitive landscape

☐ Complete your Vibe Validation Matrix

MARKET WAVE READER TOOLKIT

Essential Market Research Tools:

- **VibeSense™**: Our proprietary market opportunity assessment tool (available at vibecoding.com/tools)
- **Perplexity AI**: AI-powered research tool for market insights
- **Speak AI**: For sentiment analysis and trend detection

- **SimilarWeb**: Analyze traffic and engagement for competitor websites
- **SparkToro**: Discover where your audience spends time online
- **ValidatorAI**: Analyze market demand for your concept

Recommended Resources:

- **Trend Reports**: CB Insights State of AI Report, Gartner Hype Cycle
- **Communities**: IndieHackers, ProductHunt, relevant industry forums
- **Datasets**: Kaggle, Google Dataset Search, industry-specific repositories
- **Analytics**: Google Trends, industry benchmark reports

Chapter Summary: The Wave Spotter's Mindset

The most successful vibe coders aren't just skilled at building—they're exceptional at spotting market opportunities. They develop a sixth sense for identifying pain points that are reaching critical mass, technologies crossing key thresholds, and behavioral shifts creating new openings.

The market research revolution has democratized access to these insights, giving independent app creators unprecedented visibility into emerging trends and opportunities. By focusing on four key market signals—pain points at scale, technological inflection points, behavioral shifts, and regulatory catalysts—you can identify waves worth riding.

The most promising markets often lie at the intersection of intense pain, adequate market size, perfect timing, and your unique competitive advantage. For vibe coders in particular, vertical specialization offers a strategic edge, allowing you to leverage domain expertise rather than competing on technical sophistication alone.

Before committing significant resources, validate your market insights through landing page tests, customer conversations, competitive analysis, and your Vibe Validation Matrix. Remember that choosing the right market wave is often more important than the specific implementation details of your solution.

As Sam Altman noted, "The best entrepreneurs don't create waves—they become expert at spotting them early and positioning themselves perfectly to ride them to shore."

In the next chapter, we'll explore how to validate these market insights through customer conversations and low-cost experiments before investing in full-scale development.

Chapter 5: The Resonance Test: Finding Ideas That Connect

The Emotional Core of App Success ⍰

The most successful apps in today's crowded marketplace share a common quality that transcends features, functionality, and even utility. They resonate on an emotional level with their users. This resonance—this deep connection—transforms a mere tool into something people actively want in their lives.

In this chapter, we'll explore how to evaluate your app ideas through what I call the "Resonance Test." This is the critical filter that separates technically viable ideas from truly compelling ones that will attract and retain users in a crowded digital landscape.

"People don't buy what you do; they buy why you do it. And what you do simply proves what you believe." — Simon Sinek

This resonance isn't accidental. It can be deliberately designed, tested, and refined. As a vibe coder—someone focused on intuition, market awareness, and user connection over technical details—your ability to evaluate and enhance this emotional impact may be your greatest competitive advantage.

Evaluating Ideas Based on Their Emotional Impact

The Emotional Spectrum of Successful Apps

Behind every successful app is an emotional promise. Consider these examples:

- **Relief from pain or frustration**: Apps that eliminate friction points in daily life
- **Enhanced capability**: Apps that make users feel more powerful or competent
- **Status and belonging**: Apps that connect users to desirable communities
- **Joy and delight**: Apps that bring unexpected moments of happiness
- **Security and peace of mind**: Apps that reduce anxiety or uncertainty

The first step in applying the Resonance Test is identifying which emotional promises your app concept makes—explicitly or implicitly—and evaluating how strongly it delivers on them.

Conducting Emotional Impact Interviews

To assess emotional impact effectively, go beyond standard market research to conduct "emotional impact interviews." These differ from typical user interviews by focusing specifically on emotional responses:

1. **Start with stories, not questions**: Ask potential users to share stories about their frustrations, desires, and experiences related to your app's domain.
2. **Listen for emotional language**: Pay close attention to emotionally charged words ("frustrated," "delighted," "worried," "excited") that indicate pain points or desires.
3. **Explore the "before and after"**: Ask users to imagine their life before using your app concept and after. What emotions characterize each state?
4. **Test intensity**: Rate emotional reactions on a scale from "mild interest" to "can't live without it." The stronger the

reaction, the better your concept scores on the Resonance Test.

5. **Watch for unprompted enthusiasm**: When describing your concept, do people immediately want to tell others? This unprompted sharing impulse is one of the strongest indicators of resonance.

Case Study: The "Aha Moment" Pattern

Many of the most successful apps create a memorable "aha moment"—that instant when users first experience the core emotional value of the app. For example:

- Dropbox's "aha moment" comes when users realize their files are instantly available across devices
- Instagram's "aha moment" is when users see their ordinary photo transformed by a filter
- Uber's "aha moment" happens when a car appears on the map, moving toward the user

When evaluating your app concept, identify its potential "aha moment." If you can't clearly define one, you may need to refine your idea until this pivotal experience emerges.

Understanding the Psychology of App Adoption

To create apps that connect deeply with users, we need to understand the psychological factors that drive adoption and continued use.

The Six Key Psychological Drivers

Research on user psychology reveals six primary factors that influence app adoption and loyalty:

1. **Perceived Value**: How clearly users see the benefit relative to the effort required
2. **Social Proof**: Evidence that others (particularly those in the user's aspirational circle) find the app valuable
3. **Loss Aversion**: The fear of missing out on benefits if they don't adopt
4. **Habit Formation**: How easily the app integrates into existing routines or creates new ones
5. **Identity Alignment**: How using the app reinforces or enhances the user's self-image
6. **Autonomy and Control**: The sense that the app empowers rather than constrains the user

Understanding these drivers allows you to deliberately incorporate them into your app concept, dramatically increasing its chances of adoption and retention.

The Cognitive Load Factor

A critical aspect of app adoption psychology is cognitive load—the mental effort required to understand and use your app. The vibe coding approach acknowledges an important truth: users have a limited cognitive budget.

Lower cognitive load by:

- Focusing on a single, clear value proposition
- Eliminating unnecessary features and choices
- Creating intuitive, familiar interaction patterns
- Breaking complex tasks into manageable steps

As you evaluate app ideas, score them on cognitive load. The lower the cognitive burden, the higher the likelihood of adoption.

The Emotional Investment Curve

Users' emotional investment in apps typically follows a curve:

1. **Initial Interest**: Sparked by curiosity or a specific need
2. **Trial Adoption**: Tentative exploration with minimal investment
3. **Value Recognition**: The "aha moment" when value becomes clear
4. **Habit Formation**: Integration into routine with increased dependency
5. **Identity Integration**: The app becomes part of how users see themselves

A strong app concept accounts for this entire journey, with specific strategies for moving users through each phase. Does your idea have clear pathways to guide users along this curve? If not, consider how to refine it.

Creating Concepts with "Sticky" User Appeal

"Stickiness" is that quality that keeps users coming back. The best app ideas have built-in mechanisms that naturally generate ongoing engagement.

The Seven Elements of Sticky Ideas

Building on the work of Chip and Dan Heath in "Made to Stick," we can identify seven elements that make app concepts naturally sticky:

1. **Simplicity**: A core idea that can be expressed in a single sentence
2. **Unexpectedness**: An element of surprise or novelty that captivates attention
3. **Concreteness**: Tangible benefits that users can easily visualize
4. **Credibility**: Built-in reasons for users to trust the concept
5. **Emotion**: A clear emotional appeal that resonates with target users
6. **Stories**: A narrative that helps users imagine themselves using the app
7. **Utility**: Practical usefulness that solves real problems

As you evaluate your app concepts, score them against each of these elements. The strongest ideas will hit multiple points on this list without feeling forced or contrived.

Applying the "Vibe" Philosophy to Stickiness

The essence of the vibe coding philosophy—prioritizing intuition, market awareness, and user connection—aligns perfectly with creating sticky app concepts. Instead of beginning with technical feasibility, start with the vibe:

1. **Vibe Identification**: What feeling or atmosphere do you want your app to evoke?
2. **Vibe Consistency**: How will this feeling infuse every aspect of the experience?

3. **Vibe Communication**: How will you convey this feeling in your marketing and onboarding?
4. **Vibe Evolution**: How will the feeling grow and deepen as users engage over time?

A strong concept maintains a consistent vibe across all touchpoints, creating a cohesive emotional experience that users can instantly recognize and connect with.

The Retention Loop: Building Stickiness Into Your Concept

The most sticky app concepts incorporate what growth experts call a "retention loop"—a built-in mechanism that naturally brings users back. Common patterns include:

- **Collection loops**: Users build collections over time (photos, achievements, content)
- **Mastery loops**: Users improve skills through continued use
- **Social loops**: Users maintain connections with others through the app
- **Utility loops**: The app becomes more valuable the more it's used
- **Content loops**: Fresh content keeps users returning for more

When evaluating your app concepts, identify which retention loops could be natural fits. The strongest ideas will have multiple, mutually reinforcing loops that don't feel forced or manipulative.

Worksheets for Ranking and Refining App Ideas

Now let's turn theory into practice with concrete tools for evaluating and improving your app concepts.

The Resonance Scoring Matrix

Use this worksheet to score each app idea on a scale of 1-5 across the key dimensions of resonance:

Dimension	Questions to Ask	Score (1-5)
Emotional Impact	How strongly does it evoke emotion? Which emotions?	
Problem Clarity	How clear and significant is the problem solved?	
Solution Elegance	How elegant and satisfying is the solution?	
"Aha Moment" Power	How memorable is the core revelation?	
Cognitive Load	How easily can users understand and adopt it? (lower is better)	
Retention Mechanics	How naturally does it encourage return visits?	
Sharing Impulse	How likely are users to tell others?	
Vibe Consistency	How cohesive is the emotional experience?	

Add up the total score for each app idea, then compare. While this numerical approach isn't definitive, it provides a structured framework for comparison and highlights specific areas for improvement.

The User Journey Emotion Map

For your top concepts, create an emotion map that traces the user's emotional journey:

1. Draw a timeline representing the user journey from discovery to regular use
2. Identify key touchpoints along this journey
3. For each touchpoint, note:
    - The user's likely emotional state
    - The desired emotional transition
    - Specific features or interactions that facilitate this transition

This visualization reveals emotional gaps or inconsistencies in your concept, highlighting opportunities for refinement.

The Concept Refinement Canvas

For ideas with promise but weaknesses in certain areas, use this refinement canvas:

Area for Improvement	Current State	Potential Enhancements
Value Clarity		
Emotional Impact		
"Aha Moment"		
Cognitive Load		
Retention Mechanics		
Sharing Triggers		
Vibe Consistency		

Work through each area methodically, brainstorming specific improvements that could strengthen your concept's resonance with users.

The Competitive Resonance Analysis

Understanding how your concept emotionally compares to alternatives provides valuable insight:

1. List your top 3-5 competitors or alternative solutions
2. For each (including your concept), identify:
    - The primary emotional need addressed
    - The unique emotional advantage
    - The key emotional weakness

This analysis often reveals untapped emotional territory that could differentiate your app in meaningful ways.

The Vibe Coder's Approach to Concept Testing

The traditional approach to validating app ideas focuses heavily on market size, technical feasibility, and business models. While these factors matter, the vibe coding philosophy prioritizes resonance testing as the first and most critical filter.

Minimum Viable Vibe (MVV)

Before building even a minimal viable product, consider creating what I call a "Minimum Viable Vibe"—the simplest expression of your app's emotional core. This might be:

- A simulated walkthrough using simple sketches

- A video portraying the user experience
- A storyboard highlighting emotional transitions
- A landing page that communicates the core feeling

Testing this MVV with potential users provides invaluable feedback on resonance before investing in actual development.

Resonance Testing in the Wild

Take your concepts beyond controlled testing environments:

1. **Coffee Shop Testing**: Share your concept (via simple visuals) with strangers in public settings
2. **Social Media Concept Testing**: Post concept teasers to gauge reaction
3. **Emotional Response Surveys**: Use online tools to gather quick emotional responses to your concept
4. **Community Feedback Loops**: Share concepts in relevant online communities

The most valuable feedback often comes from spontaneous, unguarded reactions in natural settings.

When to Pivot, When to Persevere

After resonance testing, you'll face the critical decision: Should you pivot to a different concept or persevere with refinements to your current one?

Signs to pivot:

- Consistently lukewarm emotional responses
- Confusion about the core value
- Lack of spontaneous enthusiasm

- Better emotional response to a tangential aspect of your concept

Signs to persevere:

- Strong emotional reactions, even if to only part of your concept
- Unprompted sharing and evangelism
- Users immediately imagining how they would use it
- Clear, specific feedback for improvements that maintain the core vibe

Remember that resonance can be refined. If the emotional core is strong but execution needs work, perseverance with targeted improvements is often the right path.

Case Study: The Evolution of Resonance

Let's examine how one app concept evolved through multiple iterations of resonance testing.

Initial Concept: A meditation app with AI-guided personalized sessions

- Resonance testing revealed: Users were interested but felt the AI concept was cold and impersonal for something as human as meditation

Refined Concept: A meditation app where real teachers create personalized sequences based on user needs

- Resonance testing revealed: Stronger emotional response, but concerns about cost and accessibility

Final Concept: A meditation app where users access a library of recorded sessions, with AI matching their specific needs to the right teacher and approach

- Resonance testing revealed: Strong emotional response combining the human connection of real teachers with the personalization of technology

This evolution demonstrates how resonance testing can guide concept refinement toward stronger emotional connection while maintaining technical and business viability.

Chapter Summary: Finding Your Resonant Idea

The Resonance Test evaluates app ideas based on their ability to create meaningful emotional connections with users. By understanding the psychology of app adoption, crafting concepts with sticky user appeal, and using structured tools to refine your ideas, you can identify and develop app concepts with the greatest potential for success.

Remember these key principles:

- Emotional impact often trumps technical innovation in determining app success
- Understanding the psychological drivers of adoption helps create naturally appealing concepts
- "Sticky" ideas incorporate specific elements that keep users engaged
- Structured evaluation tools provide objective frameworks for comparing and refining concepts
- Testing for resonance should precede significant investments in development

The most successful apps in today's market don't just solve problems—they create emotional connections with their users. As a vibe coder, your sensitivity to these emotional dimensions gives you a significant advantage in conceptualizing apps that truly connect.

Action Steps

1. **Evaluate Your Current Ideas**: Use the Resonance

Scoring Matrix to assess each of your current app concepts. Identify the strongest and weakest aspects of each.

2. **Conduct Emotional Impact Interviews**: Talk to at least five potential users, focusing specifically on emotional responses to your concept.
3. **Create an Emotion Map**: For your top concept, map the user's emotional journey from discovery through regular use.
4. **Develop a Minimum Viable Vibe**: Create the simplest expression of your app's emotional core and test it with potential users.
5. **Plan Concept Refinements**: Using the Concept Refinement Canvas, identify specific improvements to strengthen your concept's resonance.
6. **Competitive Resonance Analysis**: Compare the emotional impact of your concept to alternatives, looking for untapped emotional territory.
7. **Field Testing**: Take your concept into uncontrolled environments to gather spontaneous feedback on its emotional impact.

In the next chapter, we'll explore how to validate your resonant idea with minimal resources, ensuring you're building something people truly want before investing significant time and effort in development.

Chapter 6: Low-Cost Validation Strategies

"Ideas are cheap. Execution is expensive. Validation bridges the gap between inspiration and success." — Anonymous Entrepreneur

You've got an incredible app idea. Your mind is racing with features, designs, and the potential impact your creation could have. The vibe is strong, and you're eager to dive into coding—or rather, vibe coding—to bring your vision to life. But hold on.

Before you invest your precious time, energy, and resources into building something that might not resonate with your intended audience, let's talk about one of the most underrated yet critical phases in the app development journey: validation.

In this chapter, we'll explore how strategic validation not only saves you from potentially expensive mistakes but also strengthens your app concept. You'll discover practical, low-cost approaches to test your ideas, connect with early users, and gather the insights needed to refine your vision before full-scale development.

Saving Time and Resources Through Strategic Validation

The Validation Mindset

Imagine spending six months building an app, only to launch it and hear crickets. No downloads. No engagement. No traction. This nightmare scenario happens more often than you might think, and it's almost always preventable with proper validation.

Strategic validation is fundamentally about learning before building. It's the art of testing your assumptions and hypotheses about your app idea with minimal investment to determine if it's worth pursuing further. This approach follows the core principle of modern entrepreneurship: start small, learn fast, and adapt quickly.

"Validation is like using a map before embarking on a journey," says Maya Hernandez, founder of TaskFlow, a productivity app that reached 500,000 users within its first year. "You wouldn't drive across the country without some directions. Similarly, you shouldn't build an app without validating that you're heading in the right direction."

The True Cost of Skipping Validation

The real expense of bypassing validation isn't just financial—it's the opportunity cost. Every hour spent building features nobody wants is an hour not spent on creating something people would love and use.

Consider these hidden costs of inadequate validation:

- **Development resources wasted** on features that don't address real user needs
- **Market launch momentum lost** when your product fails to gain initial traction
- **Emotional burnout** from pouring your heart into something that doesn't connect
- **Reputation impact** that could affect future projects or fundraising efforts
- **Delayed time-to-market** as you scramble to pivot after release

Contrast this with the strategic validation approach where you might spend a few weeks and minimal resources to discover early on if your concept has merit. This allows you to either:

1. Proceed with confidence, knowing there's genuine interest in your solution
2. Pivot to a different approach based on feedback before significant investment
3. Abandon the idea entirely and move on to a more promising opportunity

As one entrepreneur in our research noted, with vibe coding, "bugfixing crazy code is still faster" than traditional coding—but fixing the wrong product idea is infinitely more expensive than validating first, regardless of your development approach.

The Build-Measure-Learn Loop

At the heart of strategic validation is the Build-Measure-Learn loop, popularized by Eric Ries in The Lean Startup. This iterative process helps you validate your assumptions with minimal resource expenditure:

1. **Build** the simplest version of your idea (often not even a functional product)
2. **Measure** how potential users interact with and respond to it
3. **Learn** from their feedback and behavior to inform your next steps

The key is keeping the "build" phase as lightweight as possible. With vibe coding, you can potentially create simple prototypes or demos faster than ever before—but resist the temptation to build out full features. Instead, focus on creating just enough to test your core assumptions.

Building Landing Pages to Gauge Interest Before Development

One of the most cost-effective validation tools at your disposal is the simple landing page. This digital outpost for your app idea lets you test market interest before writing a single line of code.

The Anatomy of an Effective Validation Landing Page

Your landing page doesn't need to be elaborate. Focus on these key elements:

- **Clear value proposition:** A concise statement of what your app does and why it matters
- **Key features/benefits:** The 3-5 most compelling aspects of your solution
- **Visual representation:** Simple mockups or illustrations of your concept
- **Email capture:** A way for interested visitors to sign up for updates or early access
- **Call-to-action (CTA):** A clear next step for visitors who are interested

"The beauty of a validation landing page is its simplicity," explains digital strategist Leila Washington. "You're not trying to sell anything yet—you're testing if your message resonates and if people care enough to take action."

Setting Up Your Landing Page in Hours, Not Days

With modern tools, creating a professional-looking landing page requires minimal technical skills:

1. **Choose a platform:** Services like Unbounce, Carrd, or even Webflow offer templates designed specifically for app validation
2. **Craft your message:** Focus on the core problem you're solving and how your app addresses it
3. **Add visual elements:** Simple mockups (which you can create using vibe design principles) help visitors visualize your concept
4. **Implement analytics:** Set up basic tracking to measure visitor behavior
5. **Create a signup form:** Capture emails of interested users for future testing and updates

For example, when Ricardo Sanchez was validating his language learning app concept, he spent just four hours creating a landing page that outlined the app's unique approach to vocabulary acquisition. "I didn't have any functioning product to show," Ricardo recalls. "Just some basic wireframes and a compelling description of what I wanted to build. But that was enough to get 350 signups in the first week, confirming there was genuine interest."

Driving Targeted Traffic to Your Landing Page

A landing page without visitors won't validate anything. Here are low-cost approaches to driving relevant traffic:

- **Micro-targeted social ads:** Spend a small budget ($50-200) on highly targeted Facebook, Instagram, or Twitter ads

- **Relevant communities:** Share your landing page in online communities where your potential users gather (with permission from moderators)
- **Personal network:** Leverage your existing contacts who fit your user profile or might know people who do
- **Content marketing:** Write a blog post about the problem you're solving and direct readers to your landing page
- **Online forums:** Participate in discussions related to your app's purpose and mention your solution when relevant

Interpreting Landing Page Results

What constitutes "validation" through a landing page? While there's no universal benchmark, here are general guidelines:

- **Conversion rate:** If 10-15% or more of visitors are signing up, that's a strong positive signal
- **Engagement metrics:** Time spent on page and scroll depth indicate interest level
- **Direct feedback:** Comments, questions, and emails from visitors provide qualitative insights
- **Social sharing:** Unprompted sharing of your landing page suggests genuine excitement

Remember that validation isn't binary. Low conversion doesn't necessarily mean a failed concept—it might indicate a messaging problem, wrong audience targeting, or a need to adjust your approach.

Conducting Effective User Interviews

While quantitative data from landing pages is valuable, nothing beats direct conversations with potential users. User interviews provide rich, nuanced insights that numbers alone can't reveal.

Finding the Right Interview Candidates

The quality of your insights depends heavily on speaking with the right people:

- **Target actual potential users:** Focus on individuals who represent your target audience
- **Seek problem-awareness:** Prioritize those who experience the problem you're solving
- **Aim for diversity:** Include various perspectives within your target demographic
- **Beware of courtesy bias:** Friends and family might give overly positive feedback; seek honest opinions

"When conducting user interviews, you're looking for candid insights, not validation of your ego," advises UX researcher Morgan Chen. "The most valuable interviews often come from people who challenge your assumptions."

Structuring Your Interview for Maximum Insight

An effective user interview follows a clear structure while allowing for organic conversation:

1. **Introduction and rapport-building** (2-3 minutes)
    - Thank them for their time
    - Explain the purpose of the conversation
    - Emphasize that honest feedback is most helpful
2. **Problem exploration** (10-15 minutes)

    - Understand their current experience with the problem
    - Explore existing solutions they've tried
    - Identify pain points and frustrations
3. **Solution discussion** (10-15 minutes)
    - Present your concept (verbally or with simple visuals)
    - Observe initial reactions
    - Explore how they might use it
4. **Wrap-up and next steps** (3-5 minutes)
    - Ask if they'd be interested in testing early versions
    - Thank them for their insights
    - Explain how you'll keep them updated

Critical Questions to Ask During User Interviews

The right questions can unlock invaluable insights:

- **Problem validation:** "How do you currently handle [problem your app addresses]?"
- **Pain point discovery:** "What's the most frustrating part of this process for you?"
- **Solution fit:** "How would you feel if you could no longer use our solution?"
- **Value perception:** "What would make this worth paying for?"
- **Feature prioritization:** "Of these potential features, which would be most important to you and why?"

Common User Interview Mistakes to Avoid

Even well-intentioned interviews can go astray. Watch out for these pitfalls:

- **Leading questions:** "Don't you think this feature would be helpful?" instead of "What do you think about this feature?"
- **Overselling:** Presenting your idea as flawless rather than seeking honest feedback
- **Defending instead of listening:** Reacting defensively to criticism rather than exploring it
- **Assuming understanding:** Failing to ask follow-up questions when responses are vague
- **Confirmation bias:** Only acknowledging feedback that supports your existing beliefs

"The goal of user interviews isn't to hear people say your idea is great," says product developer Jamie Wilson. "It's to discover if and how your solution fits into their lives, and what might make it even better. Negative feedback is often the most valuable."

Case Study: How Validation Prevented Expensive Mistakes

To illustrate the power of validation, let's look at the journey of Alex Rivera, a non-technical founder with a vision for Mindscape, an AI-powered meditation app with personalized guidance.

The Initial Vision

Alex was passionate about meditation and saw an opportunity to create an app that would use AI to analyze user feedback and biometric data (through smartphone sensors) to tailor meditation sessions to individual needs. The initial concept included:

- AI-generated meditation scripts based on user mood and goals
- Voice analysis to detect stress levels and adjust guidance accordingly
- Progress tracking with detailed metrics and insights
- Social features for community support and accountability

Excited about the potential, Alex was ready to dive into development using vibe coding approaches. The estimated development budget was $75,000, with a timeline of 7 months.

The Validation Process

Instead of immediately starting development, Alex decided to implement a strategic validation process:

1. Landing Page Test

Alex created a simple landing page describing Mindscape's concept and features, with mockups showing the proposed user interface. The page included a sign-up form for early access and a brief survey about meditation habits.

After driving traffic through targeted social media ads ($300 budget) and relevant online communities, the results were mixed:

- Good sign-up rate (12% of visitors)
- Strong interest in personalized meditation
- Low interest in the social and voice analysis features
- Concerns about privacy and data usage

2. User Interviews

Alex conducted 15 interviews with regular meditators who had signed up through the landing page. These conversations revealed:

- Users valued simplicity and calm interfaces over feature richness
- Privacy concerns were significant—many didn't want their voice analyzed
- The social component was seen as potentially distracting
- Price sensitivity was higher than expected ($3-5/month vs. the planned $12)
- Most users meditated in short sessions (<10 minutes) rather than the longer sessions (20+ minutes) the app was designed around

3. Competitor Analysis

Alex also analyzed user reviews of existing meditation apps, discovering:

- Frequent complaints about complexity in feature-rich apps
- Strong preference for quality of content over technological features
- High abandonment of apps that required too much setup or learning

The Pivot

Based on this validation data, Alex made several critical adjustments:

1. **Simplified the concept** to focus only on AI-personalized

meditation content without the voice analysis component
2. **Removed the social features** from the initial release
3. **Redesigned the user experience** to emphasize simplicity and quick starts
4. **Adjusted the pricing model** to a freemium approach with a lower subscription price
5. **Shortened the default meditation sessions** to align with actual user behavior

The Result

The revised app concept was developed for $32,000 (less than half the original budget) and launched in just 4 months. Within six months of launch, Mindscape had:

- 50,000+ downloads
- 7,500 paying subscribers
- 4.7/5 average rating in app stores
- Lower customer acquisition costs than industry average

"If I hadn't validated my initial concept, I would have built an expensive app that missed the mark," Alex reflects. "The validation process not only saved me money but led to a much better product that actually met user needs."

Alex estimates that without validation, the original concept would have required at least one major post-launch redesign, costing an additional $40,000-60,000 and potentially losing early market momentum.

The Validation Toolkit: Essential Resources

To implement effective validation strategies for your own app concept, consider these tools and resources:

Landing Page Platforms:

- Carrd.co - Simple, inexpensive one-page sites
- Unbounce - More features for testing variations
- Webflow - Higher flexibility for more complex needs

User Interview Tools:

- Calendly - For scheduling interviews
- Zoom or Google Meet - For remote interviews
- Otter.ai - For transcribing conversations
- Miro - For collaborative visual exercises during interviews

Analytics and Tracking:

- Google Analytics - Free website analytics
- Hotjar - Heatmaps and recording visitor behavior
- Mixpanel - Event-based user analytics

Traffic Generation:

- Google Ads - Search-based advertising
- Facebook/Instagram Ads - Demographic targeting
- ProductHunt - For tech product launches
- Relevant subreddits - Community engagement
- Medium articles - Content marketing

Key Takeaways: Validation Principles for Vibe Coders

The vibe coding approach—using AI to rapidly translate ideas into functional code—makes validation even more crucial. When development becomes faster and more accessible, the temptation to skip validation grows. Resist this urge by remembering these principles:

1. **Validate the problem first, then the solution**. Ensure you're addressing a real need before building anything.
2. **Embrace "embarrassing" early versions**. Your first landing page or prototype doesn't need to be perfect—it just needs to communicate your core concept.
3. **Listen more than you talk**. During user interviews, aim to have the participant speaking 80% of the time.
4. **Quantify to decide, qualify to design**. Use numbers to determine if there's interest, but use conversations to shape what you build.
5. **Be willing to pivot or abandon**. The goal isn't to validate your original idea but to find a path to a successful product.
6. **Documentation drives insight**. Record and organize your validation findings systematically to identify patterns.
7. **Validation never truly ends**. Even after launch, continue testing assumptions and gathering feedback.
8. **Speed beats perfection**. A quick, simple validation test today provides more value than a comprehensive one next month.

Action Steps: Implementing Your Validation Strategy

Ready to validate your app idea? Here's your roadmap:

This Week:

- [ ] Define the core problem your app solves in one clear sentence
- [ ] Identify 3-5 specific assumptions about your users and solution that need validation
- [ ] Create a simple landing page focused on your core value proposition
- [ ] Set up basic analytics to track visitor behavior

Next Week:

- [ ] Drive targeted traffic to your landing page (aim for at least 200 relevant visitors)
- [ ] Reach out to 10-15 people who signed up, inviting them to interviews
- [ ] Prepare your interview script with open-ended questions
- [ ] Conduct 5+ user interviews, recording insights systematically

Within 30 Days:

- [ ] Analyze your validation data and document key findings
- [ ] Make go/no-go/pivot decisions based on validation results

- [ ] If proceeding, create a development plan that addresses insights from validation
- [ ] If pivoting, design new validation tests for your revised concept

The Validation Mindset: Final Thoughts

Validation is not merely a phase in app development—it's a mindset that successful app creators carry throughout their journey. Every feature, every design choice, every marketing message is a hypothesis that deserves testing.

As you move forward with your vibe coding adventure, remember that validation doesn't constrain creativity—it channels it toward creating something people will genuinely value. The most innovative apps aren't just technically impressive or visually stunning; they're deeply aligned with real user needs.

By embracing low-cost validation strategies, you're not just saving resources—you're dramatically increasing your chances of building something that finds its place in people's lives. And ultimately, isn't that the true measure of success?

In the next chapter, we'll explore how to take your validated concept and create compelling prototypes that further refine your vision. You'll discover how to leverage vibe coding to rapidly create interactive demonstrations of your app idea, even without traditional design or development skills.

Chapter 7: Prototype Your Vision

"Vision without execution is just hallucination." - Thomas Edison

In the world of vibe coding, your ability to transform ideas into tangible, testable experiences will set you apart from the countless would-be entrepreneurs with "great ideas" that never materialize. Prototyping is where the magic begins to take shape - where abstract concepts become interactive experiences that users can touch, feel, and respond to.

Creating Visual Representations Without Coding Skills

Gone are the days when turning an idea into a visual prototype required extensive design skills or coding knowledge. The democratization of technology through AI tools has created a new paradigm where your ability to clearly articulate your vision becomes the primary skill.

The Power of Description-Based Design

Vibe design, a natural extension of vibe coding, allows you to describe what you want in plain language, letting AI translate your words into visual elements. This approach focuses on communicating the desired feel, functionality, and purpose rather than technical specifications.

Instead of: "Create a blue gradient button with 15px border-radius and 20px padding"

Try: "Design a friendly, approachable button that feels modern and stands out as the main call-to-action"

This description-focused approach aligns perfectly with how non-technical founders naturally think about their products. You're liberated to focus on the experience you want to create rather than the technical details of implementation.

From Text to Visual: The AI Translation

Modern AI tools can interpret descriptions and generate corresponding visual elements. For example, you might describe a dashboard for your fitness app:

"Create a clean, motivating dashboard showing daily step count with a circular progress indicator, weekly activity summary with bar charts using a blue-to-green color scheme, and prominent water intake tracker that makes it easy to log glasses throughout the day."

The AI can then generate a visual representation based on these instructions, giving you something concrete to evaluate and refine. This iterative process of description and generation creates a feedback loop that helps refine both your vision and its implementation.

Thinking in Experiences, Not Features

When creating visual representations through vibe design, focus on describing the experience rather than individual features. Consider:

- How should users feel when using your application?
- What problem are they solving in that moment?
- What is their emotional state before, during, and after using the feature?
- What visual metaphors or familiar patterns would make the experience intuitive?

By anchoring your descriptions in user experiences, you generate prototypes that communicate not just functionality but also emotional resonance and usability.

Tools for Wireframing and Prototyping for Non-Designers

The toolkit for non-technical founders has expanded dramatically in recent years, with a range of options that accommodate different levels of visual thinking and technical comfort.

AI-Powered Design Tools

Several platforms now specifically cater to the vibe coding approach, enabling you to create functioning prototypes through natural language instructions:

1. Integrated Vibe Design Platforms

- **Replit**: Allows you to describe features and functionality in conversational language, then generates working prototypes you can immediately test.
- **Cursor**: An AI-powered code editor that can interpret natural language instructions and generate corresponding UI elements and functionality.
- **Lovable**: Focuses on turning plain English descriptions into functional applications with an emphasis on appealing design.

2. Visual AI Prototyping Tools

- **Figma + AI plugins**: Combines industry-standard design capabilities with emerging AI features that can generate designs from descriptions.

- **Uizard**: Transforms rough sketches and descriptions into polished UI designs.
- **Galileo AI**: Generates UI designs from text descriptions with a focus on modern design principles.

3. No-Code Platforms with AI Assistance

- **Bubble**: A powerful no-code platform that's incorporating more AI-assisted design and development features.
- **Webflow**: Combines visual design with growing AI capabilities to help non-designers create professional websites.
- **Softr**: Simplifies application building with ready-made components that can be assembled and customized without coding.

Traditional Wireframing Tools with Low Learning Curves

If you prefer more control or are working with designers, these tools offer user-friendly interfaces for creating wireframes:

- **Balsamiq**: Deliberately simple, sketch-like wireframing that keeps focus on structure and functionality.
- **Whimsical**: Intuitive wireframing with a clean, minimal interface and easy collaboration features.
- **Miro**: A versatile whiteboard tool that includes wireframing capabilities and facilitates collaborative design thinking.

Choosing the Right Tool for Your Stage

The best tool depends on your specific stage in the development process:

- **Early ideation**: Start with simple tools like pen and paper sketches or digital whiteboards like Miro.
- **Concept validation**: Move to basic wireframing tools or AI-generated designs to visualize core flows.
- **User testing**: Graduate to more interactive prototypes using vibe coding platforms or no-code tools.
- **Pre-development**: Create higher-fidelity prototypes that can serve as blueprints for development.

Remember, the goal isn't to create perfect designs but to visualize your ideas quickly enough to gather feedback and iterate. As one founder put it, "I'm prototyping and building tools for myself, not writing production code, so need to chuck in new features willy nilly as I go."

User Flow Mapping for Intuitive Experiences

Before diving into detailed design, mapping the user journey through your application creates a foundation for intuitive experiences.

The Importance of Flow Thinking

User flows are the paths users take to accomplish their goals within your application. Clear, thoughtful flows create intuitive experiences, while confusing or convoluted ones lead to frustration and abandonment.

As a non-technical founder, you have an advantage: you're not constrained by thinking about implementation details. You can focus purely on creating the most natural and efficient path for users.

Mapping Flows Without Technical Knowledge

You don't need specialized tools to create effective user flows. Start with these simple approaches:

1. Narrative Mapping Write out step-by-step descriptions of how a user would accomplish each core task:

1. User opens app and sees daily meditation options
2. User taps "Quick Focus" meditation
3. User sets timer duration (default: 10 minutes)
4. User chooses optional background sounds
5. User begins meditation with gentle start sequence
6. Timer counts down with minimalist interface
7. Gentle ending sequence signals completion
8. User sees summary screen with streak information and option to share

2. Simple Visual Flows Create basic flowcharts showing the key screens and decision points using tools like:

- Whimsical
- Miro
- Draw.io
- Even PowerPoint or Google Slides

3. Customer Journey Mapping Expand beyond screens to include the user's emotional state, questions, and needs at each step:

STEP: Discovering meditation app

EMOTION: Stressed, skeptical but hopeful

NEEDS: Quick understanding of benefits, social proof

QUESTIONS: "Will this actually help me?" "How much time does it take?"

STEP: First meditation session

EMOTION: Slightly anxious, unsure

NEEDS: Simple instructions, distraction-free experience

QUESTIONS: "Am I doing this right?" "How long should I go?"

Using AI to Validate User Flows

Vibe coding tools can help validate your flow thinking by quickly implementing prototype versions of your mapped journeys. Describe each step in the flow, then ask the AI to generate a simple working prototype following that sequence.

This allows you to quickly test if the flow makes sense when implemented, identifying potential gaps or confusion points before investing in detailed design.

Flow Patterns to Consider

When mapping user flows, incorporate these proven patterns for intuitive experiences:

- **Progressive Disclosure**: Reveal information and options gradually as needed
- **Recognition Over Recall**: Use visual cues and familiar patterns rather than requiring users to remember

information

- **Consistency**: Maintain consistent navigation and interaction patterns
- **Feedback**: Provide clear feedback for all user actions
- **Error Prevention**: Design flows that prevent errors before they happen
- **Clear Exits**: Ensure users always have a clear way to go back or cancel actions

Getting Meaningful Feedback from Basic Prototypes

A prototype's true value comes from the feedback it generates. Even the most basic prototypes can yield invaluable insights if approached strategically.

The Power of Early Feedback

Getting feedback early in the development process has several advantages:

- **Course Correction**: Identify fundamental flaws in your concept before investing significant resources
- **Feature Prioritization**: Gain clarity on which features matter most to users
- **Language Refinement**: Discover the terminology users naturally use to describe your solution
- **Unexpected Use Cases**: Learn how users might use your product in ways you hadn't anticipated

As one practitioner noted, "I'm prototyping and building tools for myself, not writing production code, so need to chuck in new features willy nilly as I go." This iterative approach, guided by user feedback, leads to more successful products.

Preparing Your Prototype for Feedback

Before sharing your prototype, prepare it to generate maximum insights:

1. Focus on Core Functionality Ensure your prototype demonstrates the key value proposition, even if other elements are simplified or missing. Users should be able to experience the main problem-solving aspect of your product.

2. Create Contextual Scenarios Develop specific scenarios that put your prototype in context. Instead of asking "What do you think?", try "Imagine you're trying to quickly find a meditation for stress relief - show me how you'd use this."

3. Establish Clear Limitations Set appropriate expectations by explaining what aspects are not yet functional or finalized. This focuses feedback on your core questions rather than irrelevant details.

Structuring Effective Feedback Sessions

Follow these guidelines to get actionable insights from prototype testing:

1. Ask Open-Ended Questions

- "What do you think this feature is for?"
- "How would you accomplish [specific task]?"
- "What questions come to mind as you look at this screen?"

2. Observe More Than You Ask Watch how users interact with your prototype. Their natural behaviors often reveal more than their stated opinions.

3. Listen for Problems, Not Solutions When users suggest solutions ("You should add a button here"), focus on understanding the underlying problem they're trying to solve.

4. Capture Emotional Responses Note frustration, confusion, delight, or surprise - these emotional reactions are powerful indicators of your design's effectiveness.

5. Seek the "Why" Behind Feedback When users express opinions about your prototype, dig deeper to understand their reasoning. "You mentioned this feels confusing - what specifically made you feel that way?"

Getting a "Vibe Check" from Experts

While end-user feedback is invaluable, also consider getting a professional "vibe check" from someone with more experience before wider release. Experienced developers or designers can spot potential issues that novice users might miss, particularly regarding:

- Technical feasibility
- Scaling challenges
- Security concerns
- Accessibility issues
- Industry best practices

Using Feedback to Iterate

Feedback is only valuable if it drives improvement. After collecting insights:

1. **Categorize feedback** into immediate concerns, future enhancements, and comments that might indicate fundamental conceptual issues
2. **Prioritize changes** based on frequency of mentioned issues and their impact on core functionality
3. **Update your prototype** addressing the most critical issues first
4. **Test again** to validate your changes and uncover any new issues

The speed of vibe coding allows for rapid iterations based on feedback, accelerating your path to product-market fit.

Case Study: From Concept to Functional Prototype in Two Days

Alex had a brilliant idea for an AI-powered recipe app that would suggest meals based on ingredients already in a user's kitchen. With no coding experience, he expected months of development work ahead - until he discovered vibe coding.

Instead of hiring a developer, Alex created a simple user flow map showing the core journey: ingredient input, recipe suggestions, and detailed instructions. Using Cursor, an AI-powered development platform, he described each screen in detail:

"Create a clean, welcoming home screen with a search bar at the top labeled 'What ingredients do you have?' Below, show colorful category bubbles for common ingredients like 'Vegetables,' 'Proteins,' 'Grains,' etc. Each category should expand to show specific ingredients to select."

The platform generated a basic but functional UI. Alex continued describing each screen in the flow, and within hours had a navigable prototype. He shared it with a small group of friends who loved cooking.

Their feedback was immediate and actionable:

- *Users wanted to filter by dietary restrictions*
- *The ingredient selection process felt tedious*
- *People wanted to save favorite recipes*

Rather than starting from scratch, Alex simply described these changes to the AI, which updated the prototype accordingly. In just two days, he had evolved from a vague concept to a functional prototype that demonstrated his core value proposition.

"What would have taken months with traditional development took just days," Alex shared. "Even better, I was able to validate that people actually wanted this solution before investing significant resources."

Action Steps: Prototype Your Vision

1. **Start with hand sketches** of your core user journey - don't worry about artistic quality, focus on the flow
2. **Choose an appropriate prototyping tool** based on your comfort level - AI-assisted platforms like Cursor or Replit for a vibe coding approach, or user-friendly design tools like Figma or Balsamiq
3. **Create a narrative description** of each key screen and interaction in your application
4. **Generate a basic prototype** using your chosen tool, focusing on demonstrating core functionality rather than perfect design

5. **Identify 5-10 potential users** in your target audience willing to provide honest feedback
6. **Prepare specific scenarios** to guide users through testing your prototype
7. **Conduct feedback sessions**, observing how users interact with your prototype and asking open-ended questions
8. **Get a "vibe check"** from someone with technical or design expertise for another perspective
9. **Categorize and prioritize** the feedback you've received
10. **Iterate quickly**, updating your prototype based on critical feedback before testing again

Chapter Summary: The Prototype Advantage

Prototyping transforms abstract concepts into tangible experiences, allowing you to validate assumptions and refine your vision before significant investment. Through vibe coding and modern design tools, non-technical founders can now rapidly create functional prototypes without coding skills.

The key insights from this chapter:

- **Description-based design** lets you focus on communicating the desired experience rather than technical details
- **AI-powered tools** can translate your natural language descriptions into visual and functional prototypes
- **User flow mapping** creates the foundation for intuitive experiences, even without technical knowledge
- **Structured feedback sessions** with basic prototypes provide invaluable insights for iteration
- **Rapid iteration** based on feedback dramatically increases your chances of creating a product users actually want

Remember, the goal isn't perfection but learning. Each prototype brings you closer to product-market fit through validated learning rather than assumptions. In the vibe coding paradigm, prototyping isn't just a phase in the development process - it's an ongoing conversation between your vision and user reality.

As you move forward to the next chapter, keep this mantra in mind: prototype to learn, not to impress. Your ability to quickly visualize ideas, gather feedback, and adapt will be one of your greatest competitive advantages as a non-technical founder in the AI era.

Chapter 8: Finding Your Tribe: Early Adopters and Feedback Loops

"The best founders don't just build products—they build communities that believe in their vision. Finding your tribe isn't just about getting users; it's about finding the people who will champion your journey."

The Power of Your First Followers

In the rapidly evolving world of app development, having a great idea and even a functioning prototype is only part of the battle. The true magic happens when you connect with the right people—those early adopters who not only use your creation but become its evangelists. These pioneers form the foundation of your community, provide invaluable feedback, and create the momentum that transforms a fledgling app into a movement.

As a vibe coder, your approach to building is intuitive and user-focused. This same mindset should extend to how you identify, connect with, and nurture relationships with your early users. The community you build around your app can become one of your strongest competitive advantages—one that even the largest tech companies with unlimited resources cannot easily replicate.

Identifying Your Ideal Early Adopters

Not all early users are created equal. The right early adopters don't just test your app; they become partners in its evolution. Here's how to find them:

Define Your User Persona with Precision

Before you can find your tribe, you need to know exactly who you're looking for. Create detailed user personas that go beyond basic demographics to include:

- **Pain Points**: What specific problems are they trying to solve?
- **Current Solutions**: What are they using now, and why isn't it working?
- **Tech Comfort Level**: Are they early adopters of technology or more conservative?
- **Values & Motivations**: What drives their decisions and behaviors?
- **Online Behaviors**: Where do they spend their time digitally?

The more specific your personas, the easier it will be to find and connect with people who match them. For example, rather than targeting "productivity app users," you might focus on "freelance designers who struggle with time tracking across multiple client projects and currently cobble together solutions using spreadsheets and timers."

Go Where Your Users Already Gather

Once you know who you're looking for, find where they already congregate online and offline:

- **Niche Online Communities**: Reddit subreddits, Discord servers, Slack channels, and Facebook groups relevant to your app's purpose
- **Forums & Discussion Boards**: Industry-specific forums where people discuss problems your app solves
- **Professional Organizations**: Trade associations and

professional networks
- **Conferences & Events**: Industry gatherings where potential users network
- **Social Media Groups**: LinkedIn groups, Twitter communities, or Instagram hashtags where your audience engages

For example, if you're building an app for independent coffee shop owners, you might join forums like Coffee Geek, relevant subreddits, Facebook groups for indie cafe owners, and attend regional barista competitions or coffee conventions.

Listen Before You Speak

Before promoting your app, spend time listening and observing. This "digital ethnography" helps you understand:

- The language your potential users use to describe their problems
- The specific features they wish existing solutions had
- The objections or hesitations they might have about new tools
- The values that matter most to this community

This intelligence is gold for both product development and marketing. When you eventually introduce your app, you'll be able to speak their language and address their concerns directly.

Building a Community Around Your Concept

Communities don't just happen; they require intentional cultivation. Here's how to build a thriving community around your app:

Start With a Clear Purpose and Values

Communities form around shared purposes and values. Define and communicate:

- **Why your app exists** beyond making money
- **What values guide** your development decisions
- **How your community** makes members' lives better

For example, Notion built its community around values of flexibility, creativity, and productivity, while emphasizing how shared templates and workflows make everyone more effective.

Choose the Right Platform for Your Community

Different platforms foster different types of interactions. Select one that aligns with your community's needs:

- **Discord/Slack**: Great for real-time discussions and closer-knit communities
- **Circle/Mighty Networks**: Structured paid communities with courses or programs
- **Reddit**: Public forums with threaded discussions
- **Facebook Groups**: Accessible for less tech-savvy users
- **Twitter Spaces/Clubhouse**: Audio discussions and Q&As
- **Your Own Platform**: Custom forums or community features within your app

Consider where your users already spend time and their comfort level with different platforms. Sometimes the best approach is meeting them where they are rather than asking them to adopt yet another tool.

Create Content That Nurtures Community

Content serves as both the foundation and fuel for your community:

- **Educational Resources**: Tutorials, guides, and explanations
- **Discussion Starters**: Thought-provoking questions and scenarios
- **User Spotlights**: Highlighting community members and their work
- **Behind-the-Scenes**: Sharing your development process and decisions
- **Interactive Sessions**: Live Q&As, workshops, and demos

The key is creating content that invites participation rather than passive consumption. Every piece should include an invitation to engage, whether through comments, contributions, or conversation.

Establish Clear Community Guidelines

Healthy communities need boundaries. Create and enforce community guidelines that:

- Clarify what behaviors are encouraged and discouraged
- Establish how conflicts or issues will be addressed
- Set expectations for participation and contribution

- Reflect your app's values and purpose

When guidelines are clear and consistently enforced, members feel safer participating fully.

Creating Effective Feedback Loops

Feedback is the lifeblood of app development, especially for vibe coders who prioritize user experience over technical perfection. Here's how to create feedback systems that actually improve your idea:

Design Multiple Feedback Channels

Different users prefer different ways of sharing feedback:

- **In-App Feedback**: Direct reporting of bugs or feature requests
- **User Interviews**: One-on-one conversations about the experience
- **Surveys**: Structured questionnaires targeting specific aspects
- **Community Forums**: Open discussions where users can share ideas
- **Usage Analytics**: Data on how users actually use your app
- **Social Media Monitoring**: Tracking mentions and discussions

By offering multiple channels, you capture feedback from various user types and contexts.

Ask the Right Questions

The quality of feedback depends on the questions you ask. Focus on:

- **Problem-Centered Questions**: "What task were you trying to accomplish when you encountered this issue?"
- **Outcome-Focused Queries**: "What would success look like for you with this feature?"
- **Specific Rather Than General**: "How did the new calendar view affect your scheduling process?" versus "Do you like the new calendar?"
- **Open-Ended Exploration**: "If you could change anything about this process, what would it be?"

Avoid questions that simply confirm what you want to hear. The most valuable feedback often challenges your assumptions.

Create a Feedback Processing System

Collecting feedback is just the beginning. You need a system to:

1. **Capture** all feedback in a central repository
2. **Categorize** by type, feature, user segment, etc.
3. **Prioritize** based on alignment with vision, difficulty, and impact
4. **Action** by implementing changes or planning future development
5. **Close the Loop** by informing users how their feedback influenced the product

This systematic approach prevents feedback from becoming overwhelming or contradictory.

Close the Feedback Loop

When users provide feedback, they want to know it was heard and considered. Always close the loop by:

- Acknowledging receipt of their feedback
- Explaining how it fits into your development priorities
- Sharing when and how it influenced changes
- Inviting further input on implemented solutions

Users who see their feedback making a difference become even more invested in your success.

Leveraging Social Proof for Pre-Launch Momentum

Social proof—evidence that others value your app—is powerful in building pre-launch momentum. Here's how to leverage it effectively:

Document Early User Wins

Capture success stories from your beta testers and early adopters:

- **Testimonials**: Short quotes about specific benefits
- **Case Studies**: Detailed stories of transformation
- **Before-and-After Metrics**: Quantifiable improvements
- **User-Generated Content**: Screenshots, videos, or posts from users

These stories serve as proof points for new potential users and validation for your approach.

Create Exclusivity Through Staged Access

People want what they can't have. Consider a staged rollout that creates buzz:

- **Private Alpha**: Invitation-only for your inner circle
- **Closed Beta**: Application-based for selected users
- **Waitlist**: Open sign-up with gradual admittance
- **Public Launch**: Open to all, but with "founding member" benefits for early joiners

This approach not only makes your app more desirable but also allows you to scale your community management effectively.

Leverage Micro-Influencers in Your Niche

Major influencers might have broad reach, but niche micro-influencers often have deeper, more engaged followings. Look for people who:

- Have established credibility in your app's domain
- Reach your specific target audience
- Engage authentically with their followers
- Share values aligned with your app's purpose

A thoughtful partnership with the right micro-influencer can be more effective than mass marketing approaches.

Implementing Early Adopter Strategies: A Case Study

Let's examine how these principles might apply in practice through a fictional case study:

Marina was developing "StudioFlow," an app to help independent photographers manage their client workflows. Rather than building in isolation, she implemented a strategic early adopter program.

She began by creating detailed personas of her ideal users, including specific pain points like manual booking processes and disjointed communication with clients. Then, she joined several photography forums and Facebook groups, spending two weeks simply observing discussions about workflow challenges.

Using these insights, Marina created a landing page describing StudioFlow in photographers' language and invited interested photographers to join a private Facebook group for early access. She required applicants to answer three questions about their specific challenges, ensuring only genuinely interested users joined.

Within this group, Marina shared weekly progress updates, posted polls about feature priorities, and conducted monthly Zoom calls where photographers could see the evolving app. She created a structured feedback process where users could submit issues and vote on potential solutions.

When photographers reported success using StudioFlow's client communication features, Marina created polished case studies and testimonials. She also identified three active members who had substantial Instagram followings in the photography community and offered them extended free access in exchange for authentic sharing of their experience.

By launch day, StudioFlow had not only a solid product but 250 passionate early adopters who immediately generated word-of-mouth referrals, creating momentum that would have been impossible with a traditional launch approach.

This case demonstrates how finding your tribe isn't just about marketing—it's about co-creation and relationship building that makes your app stronger and its launch more successful.

Common Pitfalls to Avoid

As you build your community and feedback systems, watch out for these common missteps:

The Echo Chamber Effect

When you have a small but enthusiastic group of early adopters, it's easy to mistake their preferences for those of your broader target market. Prevent echo chamber effects by:

- Continuously recruiting fresh perspectives
- Comparing feedback against usage data
- Testing assumptions with users outside your core community
- Actively seeking contradictory viewpoints

Feedback Fatigue

Constantly asking for feedback can exhaust even your most dedicated users. Avoid fatigue by:

- Focusing feedback requests on specific aspects rather than the entire experience
- Spacing requests appropriately
- Making providing feedback enjoyable and low-effort
- Clearly demonstrating how previous feedback made a difference

The Feature Creep Trap

Not all feedback should lead to new features. Protect against feature creep by:

- Evaluating all requests against your core value proposition
- Looking for patterns rather than responding to individual requests
- Considering whether problems can be solved through improving existing features
- Being transparent about what's in and out of scope for your vision

Mistaking Politeness for Validation

Friends, family, and even some early users may give positive feedback to be encouraging rather than because they truly value your solution. Combat this by:

- Looking for behavioral evidence (actual usage) over verbal feedback
- Asking about problems more than solutions
- Observing users interacting with your app without guidance
- Measuring willingness to pay or refer as true indicators of value

Finding Your Tribe Action Plan

Let's translate these concepts into concrete steps:

1. **Week 1-2: Define and Locate**

- Create detailed user personas
- Identify 3-5 online communities where your ideal users gather
- Join these communities and begin listening actively

2. **Week 3-4: Engage and Invite**
    - Start participating authentically in community discussions
    - Create a simple landing page with email capture
    - Develop a screening process for early adopters
3. **Week 5-6: Structure Your Community**
    - Set up your community platform with clear guidelines
    - Create an onboarding process for new members
    - Establish regular touchpoints (weekly updates, monthly calls)
4. **Week 7-8: Implement Feedback Systems**
    - Design your feedback collection tools
    - Create a process for organizing and prioritizing feedback
    - Establish the cadence for feedback requests
5. **Week 9-10: Cultivate Champions**
    - Identify potential champions among your early adopters
    - Create opportunities for them to contribute meaningfully
    - Develop assets they can use to share their experience
6. **Week 11-12: Prepare for Expansion**
    - Gather and polish social proof elements
    - Create a plan for staged access expansion
    - Design a referral process for existing community

members

The Vibe Coder's Tribe-Building Toolkit

As a vibe coder focusing on intuitive, market-aware app development, these tools will help you build your tribe effectively:

- **Landing Page Builders**: Carrd, Webflow, or Unbounce for creating simple, effective landing pages
- **Community Platforms**: Circle, Discord, or Facebook Groups for hosting your community
- **Feedback Tools**: Canny, UserVoice, or Typeform for structured feedback collection
- **User Testing Platforms**: UserTesting, Maze, or simply Zoom for observing user interactions
- **Analytics**: Mixpanel, Amplitude, or simple Google Analytics for tracking user behavior
- **Scheduling Tools**: Calendly or SavvyCal for easy user interview scheduling
- **Communication**: ConvertKit, MailerLite, or Substack for regular updates

Building for Connection: The Vibe Coder's Advantage

As a vibe coder, you have a natural advantage in tribe-building. Your intuitive, user-centered approach to development aligns perfectly with the community-building mindset. By applying the same principles that guide your development process—empathy, responsiveness, and focus on real human needs—you can create not just an app but a movement.

Your tribe becomes more than just users; they're co-creators who amplify your vision and help it evolve. They provide the human connection that transforms code into culture and features into community. In the increasingly crowded app marketplace, this tribe may ultimately be your most powerful differentiator.

Remember: Technology can be copied, but communities built on authentic connection and shared purpose cannot.

Chapter Summary: Key Takeaways

- **Identify with precision**: Define detailed user personas that include pain points, behaviors, and motivations to find truly aligned early adopters.
- **Meet users where they are**: Join existing communities where your potential users already gather before asking them to join yours.
- **Listen deeply**: Understand your users' language, problems, and desires before presenting your solution.
- **Build with purpose**: Create a community with clear values, guidelines, and meaningful interaction opportunities.
- **Diversify feedback channels**: Implement multiple ways for users to share their experiences and insights.
- **Close the loop**: Always acknowledge feedback and show how it influences your development.
- **Leverage social proof**: Document early successes and create systems for users to share their positive experiences.
- **Avoid common pitfalls**: Be vigilant against echo chambers, feedback fatigue, feature creep, and false validation.
- **Scale strategically**: Use staged access and referral systems to grow your community at a manageable pace.

Your Vibe Coding Challenge: This week, identify three online communities where your potential users gather. Spend at least 30 minutes daily for five days observing conversations, noting the specific language used to describe problems your app could solve, and identifying potential early adopters based on their contributions. Document your findings and use them to refine your user persona and product positioning.

Chapter 9: User Experience: The Heart of Vibe Coding

"Design is not just what it looks like and feels like. Design is how it works." - Steve Jobs

Introduction

In our journey through the vibe coding revolution, we've explored how AI has democratized app development, allowing founders to turn their ideas into reality without deep technical expertise. But here's a truth that might surprise you: as the technical barriers continue to fall, **user experience (UX) becomes even more critical** to your app's success.

In this new landscape where nearly anyone can build functional apps using AI, the differentiator is no longer "Can it be built?" but rather "Does it feel right to use?" This chapter delves into why UX must be at the core of your vibe coding practice and how to create experiences that resonate deeply with your users.

Why UX Determines App Success More Than Technical Features

When everyone can leverage AI to implement features, the playing field levels. The competitive edge shifts to who can create the most intuitive, engaging, and emotionally satisfying experience.

The Shifting Competitive Landscape

In this era where "vibe coding" lowers the barrier to creating functional apps, the quality of the user experience becomes a critical differentiator. When anyone can generate working features, simply having them is no longer enough; the quality of the experience will set products apart.

This dynamic resembles what happened in the early web era. Initially, simply having a website was remarkable. Eventually, as creation tools became more accessible, the bar raised—and users began expecting more polished, thoughtful experiences.

The Cost of Poor UX

The financial impact of neglecting UX is substantial:

A poorly designed website or application can lead to lost customers who may turn to competitors offering a better experience. In fact, nearly 40% of people might stop using an application if the layout is not engaging and attractive.

Consider the math: For every 100 potential customers who discover your app, 40 might abandon it based solely on UX issues—before even evaluating your core functionality. That's a considerable conversion leak that no amount of marketing spend can fully compensate for.

The Human Element in the AI Era

Focusing on user needs and crafting a great user experience is a human responsibility that remains crucial, even with AI-assisted development. Vibe coding might change the implementation phase, but understanding user needs and prioritizing features remains vital in the planning phase.

While AI can help implement your vision, it cannot replace your human empathy and intuition for what will delight your specific users. This represents one of your strongest advantages as a founder in the vibe coding era.

The Vibe Coder's Advantage

As a non-technical founder using vibe coding, you possess a unique advantage: without getting lost in technical implementation details, you can maintain focus on the user's journey, needs, and emotional experience. Your role becomes less about the "how" of building features and more about the "why" and "what" of creating value through thoughtful experience design.

Psychological Principles That Drive Satisfying App Experiences

Understanding the psychological underpinnings of user experience gives you a framework for creating apps that don't just function but actually feel right to use.

Emotional Design: Beyond Aesthetics

Emotional design goes beyond mere aesthetics and aims to elicit positive feelings, connections, and responses from users. Understanding that human emotions play a pivotal role in shaping perceptions, decisions, and overall satisfaction is fundamental.

Donald Norman, a pioneer in user experience, identified three levels of emotional design:

1. **Visceral** - The immediate, instinctive reaction to appearance
2. **Behavioral** - How the product functions and performs
3. **Reflective** - The personal satisfaction and cultural significance

All three levels must work harmoniously to create a truly satisfying experience.

The Power of Visual Psychology

Elements like color psychology, where colors evoke specific feelings, and typography and font selection, which can convey a brand's personality, are important considerations.

For example:

- Blue evokes trust and reliability (think Facebook, PayPal)
- Red creates urgency and excitement (Netflix, YouTube)
- Green suggests growth and health (Spotify, WhatsApp)

Your typography choices similarly signal your app's personality—whether professional, playful, cutting-edge, or traditional.

Building Personal Connection

Key aspects include establishing a personal connection through relatable imagery and storytelling, enhancing the user experience with aesthetically pleasing interfaces and intuitive navigation, and building a brand identity that evokes positive emotions.

The most successful apps feel less like tools and more like relationships. Consider how apps like Headspace use friendly illustrations and conversational language to create a sense of companionship during the personal journey of meditation.

The Tactile Element

Even the tactile feel of products can create stronger emotional connections and influence consumer behavior. For instance, Apple prioritizes the user's emotional experience through its sleek design and resonant advertising.

In digital products, tactile elements translate to interaction design—the satisfying "bounce" when reaching the end of a scroll, the subtle haptic feedback of a button press, or the smooth animation of a screen transition.

Designing for Emotion and Connection

Now that we understand why emotional design matters, let's explore concrete approaches to infusing your vibe-coded apps with this dimension.

The Essence of "Vibe Design"

"Vibe design" extends the principles of "vibe coding" to UX, focusing on the desired feeling or outcome rather than meticulous pixel placement. Instead of static mockups, the focus shifts to interactive prototypes, where designers can quickly generate UI components and flows using AI.

Just as vibe coding allows you to express your intent for functionality, vibe design enables you to express the emotional quality you want your app to embody.

From Static to Dynamic Design

This allows for a more iterative and dynamic design process, with AI assisting in making quick changes based on user feedback. The goal is to create a "vibe" that resonates with users.

Rather than perfecting a design in isolation before implementation, you can rapidly prototype, test with users, and refine based on real feedback. This aligns perfectly with the lean startup methodology of build-measure-learn.

The Feeling Layer of Communication

This involves understanding the "feeling-layer of communication" where vibe signals affect and move people. Principles of "vibe coding" as a creative practice emphasize tuning into the rhythm and emotional tone, layering intentionality, knowing when to stop, developing a sensory vocabulary, and attuning to others to create resonance.

Consider the difference between these two design prompts:

- "Create a login screen with email and password fields, and a submit button"
- "Design a welcoming login experience that feels secure yet friendly, where new users feel guided and returning users feel recognized"

The second approach focuses on emotional outcomes rather than just functional elements.

The Honest Interface

An "ugly interface" might even be seen as "honest," while "aesthetic is access," suggesting that bad interfaces can be detrimental. The core idea is that design should create a mood poem, using color, motion, and shape as an emotional palette.

Sometimes authenticity trumps polish, particularly for tools focused on utility. However, even "honest" interfaces must be accessible and considerate of users' cognitive load.

The Vibe Coder's UX Process

Integrating UX thinking into your vibe coding workflow requires intentional practices. Here's a practical approach:

1. Start with Empathy

Before writing a single line of code or prompt, develop a deep understanding of your users:

- Who are they? What matters to them?
- What problem are you solving? Why does it matter to them?
- What emotional state are they in when using your app?
- What feelings do you want them to experience?

Document these insights to guide your design decisions.

2. Define the Experience Goals

Articulate clear objectives for how users should feel when using your app:

- "Users should feel confident they're making the right financial decision"
- "The experience should feel playful yet efficient"
- "Users should feel a sense of accomplishment after each session"

These goals will guide your design choices and help evaluate success.

3. Sketch the Journey

Before diving into detailed screens, map the overall user journey:

- What are the key steps from start to finish?
- What are the potential emotional high points and low points?

- Where might users feel confused or frustrated?
- How can you create moments of delight?

This journey mapping helps prioritize where to focus your UX efforts.

4. Prompt for Emotion

When using vibe coding tools, explicitly include emotional parameters in your prompts:

- "Generate a dashboard that feels calm and organized"
- "Create an onboarding flow that feels welcoming and builds excitement"
- "Design an alert that feels important but not alarming"

5. Test with Real Users

The most beautiful design is worthless if it doesn't resonate with your actual users:

- Put prototypes in front of real people as early as possible
- Watch them use it without providing guidance
- Pay attention to emotional reactions, hesitations, and comments
- Ask open-ended questions about how the experience made them feel

6. Iterate Based on Feedback

Use the rapid prototyping capabilities of vibe coding to quickly implement changes based on user feedback:

- "Redesign the navigation to address the confusion users

experienced"
- "Make the success confirmation more celebratory as users mentioned it felt underwhelming"

Resources for Developing UX Thinking

To strengthen your UX muscles, consider these valuable resources:

Books and Courses

While not specifically mentioned in the source documents, these foundational UX resources complement vibe coding principles:

1. **"Don't Make Me Think" by Steve Krug** - A classic on web usability that remains relevant for all digital products
2. **"Emotional Design" by Don Norman** - Explores the critical role of emotions in product design
3. **"Design for Hackers" by David Kadavy** - Perfect for technically-minded founders wanting to understand design principles
4. **Interaction Design Foundation Courses** - Offers comprehensive online UX courses for all levels

AI-Assisted UX Tools

While the sources don't explicitly list traditional UX resources, they highlight the emerging role of AI tools and platforms in the design process. Platforms with "vibe coding" and "vibe design" features, such as Replit, Cursor, Windsurf, and Bolt.new, can be seen as resources for rapidly prototyping and iterating on user interfaces based on natural language descriptions.

Additional tools to consider:

- **Midjourney or DALL-E** - For generating visual design concepts based on prompts
- **UX-focused versions of ChatGPT or Claude** - Can help brainstorm design solutions and critique existing interfaces
- **Figma with AI plugins** - Combines traditional design tools with AI assistance

Learning Through Feedback

The emphasis on user feedback also suggests that engaging with potential users and gathering their reactions to AI-generated interfaces is a crucial aspect of developing UX thinking in this context.

Some approaches to structured feedback collection:

- **User testing sessions** - Observe people using your prototype and listen to their thoughts
- **Five-second tests** - Show users a screen for five seconds, then ask what they remember
- **Preference tests** - Present different design options and gather opinions
- **Task completion analysis** - Measure how easily users can accomplish key tasks

Community and Mentorship

Connect with the broader UX community:

- Follow UX designers on social media platforms
- Join UX-focused communities on Discord, Reddit, or Slack

- Attend UX meetups or webinars
- Consider working with a UX mentor or consultant for specific challenges

Case Study: Transforming a Vibe-Coded App Through UX Focus

Let's examine a hypothetical but realistic example of how UX focus can transform a vibe-coded app:

Starting Point: Sara used vibe coding to build a functional personal finance app that tracks expenses, categorizes transactions, and provides basic reports. While technically complete, early user feedback indicated people weren't engaging regularly.

The UX Intervention:

1. **User Research:** Sara conducted interviews and discovered that money management triggered anxiety for many users, and they avoided the app because it reinforced negative feelings about their finances.
2. **Emotional Design Goals:** She redefined the app's emotional goals to "make users feel empowered rather than judged" and "celebrate progress, not perfection."
3. **Journey Redesign:** She mapped the emotional journey and identified key moments to transform:
    - Changed the login screen to include an encouraging quote
    - Redesigned the dashboard to highlight positive trends first
    - Added micro-celebrations for small wins like staying under budget in any category
    - Introduced a "mindful spending" feature instead

of the judgmental "spending alerts"

4. **Vibe Coding Implementation:** Using AI-assisted tools, Sara prompted: "Redesign the expense entry screen to feel more supportive and less like a ledger. Use a friendly color palette and conversational language."
5. **Results:** After implementing these UX-focused changes, user engagement increased by 60%, and the average session length doubled. User retention improved significantly, with 45% more users still active after 30 days.

The key insight: Without changing the core functionality, Sara transformed the app's success by focusing on the emotional experience.

Your UX Action Plan

To begin integrating UX thinking into your vibe coding practice:

1. **Start a UX journal** - Document observations about apps you use daily. What feels good? What frustrates you? Why?
2. **Create user personas** - Develop detailed profiles of your target users, including their goals, frustrations, and emotional needs.
3. **Practice empathy exercises** - Regularly put yourself in your users' shoes through role-playing or thought experiments.
4. **Build a design language** - Collect visual examples that match the emotional tone you want for your app.
5. **Incorporate UX prompts** - When using vibe coding tools, explicitly include experience and emotional goals in

your prompts.

6. **Test relentlessly** - Make user testing a regular habit, not a one-time event.

Conclusion: The UX Advantage

As we've explored in this chapter, in the vibe coding era, your competitive advantage increasingly lies in creating exceptional user experiences rather than novel technical features. By focusing on emotional design, psychological principles, and iterative testing, you can create apps that not only function well but also form meaningful connections with users.

Remember that while AI can help implement your vision, the human touch in understanding emotions, empathy, and connection is where you add unique value as a founder. In a world where everyone can build apps, those who build experiences will win.

Chapter Summary

- **UX is a critical differentiator** in the vibe coding era, where technical implementation is increasingly accessible
- **Emotional design principles** should guide your app development, focusing on visceral, behavioral, and reflective layers
- **Vibe design extends vibe coding** by focusing on desired feelings and outcomes rather than just functional specifications
- **AI tools can assist UX exploration** through rapid prototyping and iteration
- **User testing remains essential** for validating that your emotional design goals are being met
- **Your human empathy** is your greatest UX advantage in an AI-powered development world

Action Steps

- Identify three apps you love using and analyze what specific UX elements make them emotionally satisfying
- Create a mood board for your app's emotional design goals
- Write three user prompts that include emotional parameters
- Conduct a five-second test with your current design or prototype
- Schedule regular user feedback sessions to evaluate your app's emotional impact
- Explore one AI-assisted UX tool to enhance your vibe coding practice

"At the end of the day, the goals are simple: safety and security, prosperity and peace." - Jodi Rell

Chapter 10: The Modern App Development Toolkit

Introduction: Empowering the Non-Technical Visionary

The traditional barriers to app development are crumbling. Not long ago, creating a functional application required years of coding experience, mastery of complex languages, and a deep understanding of technical architecture. Today, we stand at the dawn of a new era—one where your vision and understanding of user needs can be more valuable than your ability to write code.

This transformation isn't just changing who can build apps—it's revolutionizing how they're built. The vibe coding approach, combined with powerful AI-assisted development tools, has democratized app creation in ways previously unimaginable.

As one vibe coder put it: "I'm only a few prompts away from a product if I have a clear idea." This chapter explores the modern toolkit that makes this possible and helps you determine which approach is right for your specific project.

AI-Powered Development Tools for Non-Technical Founders

The Rise of Intent-Based Development

The core principle of vibe coding is shifting focus from the *how* of writing code to the *what* the software should do. This intent-based approach lets you communicate in natural language while AI handles the technical implementation.

Andrej Karpathy, co-founder of OpenAI, described this new way of working as one where you "fully give in to the vibes, embrace exponentials, and forget that the code even exists." His own experience involved "seeing things, saying things, running things, and copy-pasting things, with the code mostly working."

This revolution is powered by a new generation of development tools that blur the line between ideation and implementation.

Key AI Development Platforms for Vibe Coders

Several cutting-edge platforms now enable non-technical founders to transform their ideas into functioning applications:

1. **Cursor**: A flagship AI-powered code editor based on VS Code with powerful features specifically designed for the vibe coding approach. It includes a Composer chat for instructions and a "Fix with AI" button that helps troubleshoot issues.
2. **Replit**: An online IDE where 75% of users don't write traditional code, instead relying on Replit's Ghostwriter AI to generate code based on natural language instructions. The platform requires no setup and supports rapid prototyping.
3. **Windsurf AI**: An innovative tool with an agentic mode that can automatically implement changes to your application based on natural language guidance.
4. **GitHub Copilot**: An AI pair-programmer integrated with popular code editors that can autocomplete code, transform comments into functioning code, and provide contextual suggestions through Copilot Chat.

5. **Large Language Models**: Tools like ChatGPT and Claude support HTML, JavaScript, and other languages, allowing you to generate and explain code directly through conversation.

How These Tools Transform the Development Process

These AI-powered platforms fundamentally change how apps are created:

- **Rapid Prototyping**: Vibe coding allows for quick experimentation by simply telling the AI your intent, significantly accelerating the development process. What once took days or weeks can now be completed in hours.
- **Natural Language Interfaces**: You can now start projects by typing a description or even using speech-to-text tools like SuperWhisper to translate spoken prompts into code.
- **Iterative Development**: The speed of development enables faster feedback and more frequent iteration, allowing you to refine your product based on real user input.
- **Abstract Technical Complexity**: These tools hide the need to learn programming languages, syntax, and complex technical concepts, letting non-technical founders focus on their innovative ideas and problem-solving.

The Role of "Vibe Prompting"

The quality of what these tools produce depends heavily on how effectively you communicate your vision. "Vibe prompting" involves treating AI like a creative collaborator with mood and context awareness, rather than just a code generator.

Effective vibe prompts often include:

- Clear specifications of the desired outcome
- Context about user needs and goals
- Specific UI/UX descriptions
- Technical constraints or preferences

For example, instead of saying "Make a login system," a more effective vibe prompt would be: "Create a Flask route that serves a login form with email and password fields, and validate the inputs using WTForms."

No-Code and Low-Code Platforms Comparison

Understanding the Spectrum

While AI-powered vibe coding tools represent the bleeding edge, they exist within a broader ecosystem of tools designed to make development more accessible.

Vibe coding can be seen as an evolution of low-code platforms, where instead of visual tools, natural language becomes the equivalent of a programming language. Let's explore how these different approaches compare:

Aspect	Traditional Coding	Low-Code Platforms	No-Code Platforms	Vibe Coding
Skills Required	Advanced programming knowledge	Basic programming concepts	Minimal technical knowledge	Vision articulation skills
Development Approach	Writing code manually	Visual interface + some code	Visual drag-and-drop	Natural language prompts
Flexibility	Unlimited	High	Moderate	Evolving rapidly
Speed of Development	Slow	Medium	Fast	Very fast
Maintenance Complexity	High	Medium	Low	Variable
Learning Curve	Steep	Moderate	Gentle	Minimal for basics

Popular Low-Code/No-Code Platforms

Several established platforms help bridge the gap between no technical skills and functional applications:

1. **Bubble**: A powerful visual programming tool that lets you build web applications without code. Non-technical founder Charles Thomas used Bubble to build Comet, a freelance marketplace that scaled rapidly and achieved significant monthly recurring revenue.
2. **Webflow**: Focused on creating professional websites with advanced design capabilities and CMS functionality without coding.
3. **Airtable**: Combines spreadsheet simplicity with database power, allowing you to create custom applications around

your data.

4. **Softr**: Ambar Shrivastava utilized this no-code platform to build Coverdoc, an AI-powered platform for job seekers that achieved $1,000 in monthly recurring revenue.
5. **Microsoft Power Apps**: Enterprise-oriented platform with AI Builder for integrating AI capabilities into business applications.
6. **Zapier**: Automation tool that connects different applications and creates workflows without code.

When to Choose Each Approach

Your choice of development approach should be guided by your specific needs:

- **Vibe Coding**: Ideal for rapid prototyping, personal projects, and initial MVPs where speed and conceptual exploration are paramount.
- **No-Code**: Best for straightforward applications with standard features where you want complete control without technical knowledge.
- **Low-Code**: Appropriate when you need more customization than no-code offers but still want accelerated development.
- **Traditional Development**: Necessary for highly complex, specialized applications that require custom algorithms or unique functionality.

This accessible toolkit has dramatically lowered the barrier to entry for non-technical founders. Projects that once took months can now be completed in days, with potential time savings up to 90% compared to traditional methods.

When to Build Yourself vs. When to Hire Help

The DIY Opportunity

The tools we've explored create unprecedented opportunities for non-technical founders to build their own applications. Consider handling development yourself when:

1. **You're Validating an Initial Concept**: Vibe coding is well-suited for creating functional mock-ups, prototypes, or "throwaway weekend projects" to test ideas before significant investment.
2. **You're Creating a Highly Personalized Tool**: The concept of "software for one" highlights creating simple, even imperfect, tools for a specific need, which can then be expanded upon if they prove valuable.
3. **You Need Rapid Iteration**: When you're exploring different approaches and need to quickly adapt based on feedback.
4. **You Have Limited Resources**: Building with LC/NC tools and vibe coding can be significantly less expensive than hiring developers, with cost savings often reaching 90%.
5. **Your Application is Relatively Simple**: Straightforward applications with standard components and integrations are more suitable for DIY approaches.

When to Bring in Professional Help

Despite the power of modern tools, there are clear scenarios where professional developers become essential:

1. **When Building Production-Ready Applications**: For larger, more complex projects requiring high levels of security, scalability, and maintainability, the limitations of relying solely on AI-generated code become significant.
2. **When Security is Critical**: Applications handling sensitive data or requiring robust security measures benefit from professional oversight to identify vulnerabilities that non-technical founders might miss.
3. **For Complex Technical Architecture**: Applications requiring sophisticated backends, complex databases, or custom algorithms often need professional expertise.
4. **When Scaling is Anticipated**: Moving from a working local prototype to a production-deployed application that can handle thousands of users is a steep learning curve that often requires experienced developers.
5. **To Manage Technical Debt**: AI-generated code may not follow best practices for maintainability, potentially creating technical debt that becomes costly to fix later.

A Hybrid Approach: The Best of Both Worlds

Many successful founders take a hybrid approach:

1. Use vibe coding and no-code tools to build an initial prototype and validate the concept
2. Test with early users to confirm product-market fit
3. Bring in professional help to refine, scale, and harden the application once viability is proven

One non-technical founder described starting with an Excel model as their prototype, collaborating with a designer for Figma mockups, validating the concept with potential customers, and then resourcefully hiring initial part-time engineers once they defined the minimum viable product.

This approach minimizes wasted development resources while still ensuring a professional final product.

Creating Effective Partnerships with Developers

The Translation Challenge

The biggest hurdle for non-technical founders working with developers is effective communication. You speak the language of business and user needs; developers speak in technical specifications and system architecture.

Bridging this gap requires deliberate strategies. Misunderstandings between vision and implementation are costly in terms of time and resources.

Building a Foundation for Successful Collaboration

1. **Develop Basic Technical Literacy**: While coding expertise isn't required, understanding basic technical concepts and terminology is crucial. This facilitates more productive conversations, enables better decision-making, and shows respect for the technical team's work. Key concepts to understand include:
    - Agile vs. Waterfall methodologies
    - Front-end vs. back-end development

   - APIs and integrations
   - Basic AI concepts relevant to your project
2. **Create Clear Visual References**: Visual aids like detailed sketches, wireframes, or interactive prototypes created through no-code tools or vibe coding are invaluable communication tools. They give developers a tangible reference for your vision.
3. **Focus on User Stories and Outcomes**: Define what users should be able to accomplish, rather than prescribing specific technical implementations. For example: "Users should be able to reset their password via email without contacting support" rather than "We need a password reset function that uses SendGrid."
4. **Set Clear Expectations and Roles**: Establish distinct responsibilities. The non-technical founder typically owns the product vision, business strategy, user requirements, and market positioning, while the technical team focuses on implementation, feasibility assessment, and architecture.

Finding the Right Technical Partners

Your options for technical partnerships include:

1. **Technical Co-founder**: Ideal for long-term ventures where technical expertise is central to the business. Aligning incentives through fair equity splits is crucial.
2. **In-house Developers**: Appropriate once you've validated your concept and are ready to build a dedicated team.
3. **Development Agencies**: When outsourcing, look for partners with experience working with startups and navigating their unique pressures (tight budgets, deadlines, pivots).

4. **Technical Advisors/Consultants**: Particularly valuable in complex AI domains where specialized expertise can guide development decisions.
5. **Freelancers**: Can be effective for discrete projects or specific components of your application.

Leveraging Vibe Coding in Developer Partnerships

Vibe coding tools can be powerful assets even when working with professional developers:

1. **Prototype Before Development**: Use vibe coding to create a functional prototype that demonstrates your concept before engaging developers.
2. **Specify with Examples**: Generate code snippets or UI components with AI tools to illustrate your ideas more concretely.
3. **Augment Development**: Use AI tools to quickly iterate on specific features while developers focus on core architecture.
4. **Bridge Communication Gaps**: AI development tools can help translate your natural language requirements into technical specifications developers can work from.

Ultimately, the most effective approach views AI as a collaborator that amplifies human skills rather than a replacement. The non-technical founder's role remains in understanding user needs and defining the "what," while developers bring the expertise to implement the "how," even if AI tools are part of the development process.

Case Study: From Vision to Reality

Sarah's AI-Powered Productivity App

Sarah had a vision for an AI-driven productivity app that would help professionals manage their workflows more effectively. Despite having no technical background, she was determined to bring her idea to life.

Initial Approach: Sarah started by using vibe coding to create a basic prototype. She built a simple landing page to gauge interest and conducted user interviews with potential customers. The feedback revealed that while users were interested in AI assistance, they had concerns about data privacy and were primarily looking for better organization rather than full automation.

Validation and Refinement: Based on this feedback, Sarah shifted her focus from comprehensive AI automation to specific, time-saving features that addressed the organization pain points users had identified. She used Bubble to create a more refined prototype that incorporated this feedback.

Technical Partnership: Once Sarah had validated her concept and gathered substantial user interest, she recognized the need for professional development to address the security concerns and scalability requirements. She partnered with a small development agency specializing in AI applications.

Collaborative Development: Sarah's prototype served as a visual aid and a starting point for more detailed discussions with the development team. She focused on communicating the user needs and business goals, while the developers handled the technical implementation.

Outcome: The resulting application combined Sarah's user-centric vision with robust technical implementation. By using vibe coding and no-code tools for validation before investing in professional development, she saved significant time and resources while still creating a market-ready product.

Vibe Coder's Checklist: Choosing Your Development Approach

Use this checklist to determine the most appropriate development approach for your project:

DIY with Vibe Coding/No-Code

- [ ] You're in the early concept validation stage
- [ ] Your application has standard, commonly-implemented features
- [ ] Speed of development is more important than perfect implementation
- [ ] You have limited financial resources for development
- [ ] You anticipate frequent changes based on user feedback
- [ ] Security and data privacy requirements are minimal

Hybrid Approach

- [ ] You've validated your concept with a prototype
- [ ] Your application requires some custom functionality
- [ ] You need a balance between speed and professional implementation
- [ ] You have moderate budget constraints
- [ ] You have some technical understanding but not comprehensive expertise
- [ ] You plan to scale gradually

Professional Development

- [ ] Your application concept is proven and ready for full implementation
- [ ] You require sophisticated custom functionality
- [ ] Quality, security, and scalability are top priorities
- [ ] You have secured funding for professional development
- [ ] Your application involves sensitive user data
- [ ] You anticipate rapid scaling and need a robust foundation

Chapter Summary

- **AI Development Tools**: A new generation of vibe coding tools like Cursor, Replit, and Windsurf AI are transforming app development by allowing natural language instructions to generate functional code.
- **Platform Comparison**: The development landscape now spans from traditional coding to low-code, no-code, and vibe coding approaches, each with distinct advantages for different scenarios.
- **DIY vs. Professional Development**: While vibe coding empowers non-technical founders to build prototypes and simple applications, professional developers remain essential for production-ready, secure, and scalable products.
- **Effective Partnerships**: Successful collaboration with developers requires basic technical literacy, clear visual references, focus on user outcomes, and well-defined roles and expectations.
- **Hybrid Approach**: Many successful founders use vibe coding for rapid prototyping and validation, then bring in professional help to refine and scale their validated concepts.

Action Steps

1. **Experiment with Vibe Coding**: Spend at least three hours exploring a platform like Replit or Cursor to understand how vibe coding can translate your ideas into functional prototypes.

2. **Build a Development Lexicon**: Create a personal glossary of key technical terms and concepts related to your project to facilitate better communication with technical partners.
3. **Map Your Development Journey**: Based on your specific project, outline which elements you'll handle yourself with vibe coding tools and which will require professional assistance.
4. **Create a Visual Prototype**: Use vibe coding or no-code tools to create a visual representation of your concept that can serve as a reference point for discussions with potential technical partners.
5. **Evaluate Technical Partnership Options**: Research and reach out to at least three different types of technical partners (co-founders, agencies, freelancers) to understand their approaches and costs.

"The best code is the code that doesn't exist. The second best is the code someone else maintains." — Anonymous Vibe Coder

Chapter 11: The Art of the MVP (Minimum Viable Product)

The Minimalist Manifesto: Why Less is More in the AI Era

In today's hyper-accelerated development landscape, the instinct to build comprehensive, feature-rich applications from the start remains one of the most persistent—and dangerous—temptations for entrepreneurs. This urge is particularly strong when working with AI and vibe coding, where the apparent ease of generating complex functionality might convince you that "more is better."

Let me be clear: this approach is a recipe for disaster.

The most successful vibe coders understand a fundamental truth—the path to creating apps that genuinely connect with users isn't about cramming in features. It's about strategic reduction. It's about identifying the essential core that delivers real value and ruthlessly eliminating everything else.

As Andrew Chen, a prominent venture capitalist, notes: "In five years, vibe coding could feel like having a team of 100+ engineers in your pocket." With such power at your fingertips, the discipline to focus becomes even more critical.

What Makes an MVP Truly Minimum and Viable?

The concept of the Minimum Viable Product (MVP) has been around for years, but it takes on new dimensions in the vibe coding era. An MVP isn't just a stripped-down version of your ultimate vision—it's a strategic tool designed with a specific purpose: to validate your core assumptions with the least amount of effort.

A true MVP focuses exclusively on delivering the "must-have" features that solve the specific problem your target users are experiencing. Everything else—no matter how tempting—is categorized as "nice-to-have" and deliberately set aside for future iterations.

Consider Instagram's early days. Their core value wasn't taking photos (which phones already did well) but sharing them socially with filters that made amateur photographers look good. By focusing laser-like on this core value proposition, they created a product that resonated deeply while avoiding feature bloat.

Innovation Navigator Insight: In vibe coding, your ability to quickly generate features makes the discipline of choosing what NOT to build even more important than what you DO build.

Defining Core Features That Truly Matter

Even with AI-assisted development, identifying the essential features requires human judgment and strategic thinking. Here's how to identify what truly matters:

Start With the Problem, Not the Solution

Before diving into vibe coding prompts, get crystal clear on the specific problem you're solving. Ask yourself:

- What is the single most painful aspect of this problem for users?
- What's the minimum functionality required to

meaningfully address this pain point?
- If I could only build one feature, which would deliver the most value?

Remember that Instagram's core value wasn't taking photos but sharing them. Similarly, Uber's core value wasn't a fancy app interface but reliable, on-demand transportation. What's the equivalent core value in your concept?

Apply the "Bite-Sized Chunks" Principle

Instead of attempting to "boil the ocean in one go," break your concept down into manageable components. For a web app, that might mean starting with "user registration with hashed passwords" before tackling login or password reset functionality.

This approach aligns perfectly with the vibe coding philosophy. Rather than crafting a massive, complex prompt describing your entire vision, break it down into focused, specific prompts that build on each other:

1. First prompt: "Create a simple user registration form with email and password fields"
2. Next prompt: "Add validation to ensure password meets security requirements"
3. Later prompt: "Create a login page that authenticates against the registered user"

Focus on "Jobs to Be Done"

The "Jobs to Be Done" framework, popularized by Clayton Christensen, helps you identify what customers are actually trying to accomplish. Instead of thinking in terms of features, consider what "job" your users are "hiring" your product to do.

For example, people don't want a drill; they want a hole in their wall. Similarly, your users don't want an AI feature; they want a specific outcome or feeling that the AI enables.

Case Study: Spotify's MVP Success

When Spotify launched, they focused on one core job: making it incredibly simple to play nearly any song instantly without downloading files. They deliberately avoided features like social networks, extensive recommendation systems, or playlist sharing tools—all of which came later. By solving one problem exceptionally well, they gained the user base and feedback needed to expand thoughtfully.

Stripping Away Complexity Without Losing Essence

The beauty of vibe coding lies in its ability to rapidly generate functional prototypes. This speed creates a powerful opportunity: you can build quick, focused experiments rather than betting everything on a complex initial release.

The Power of "Software for One"

One approach gaining traction is what some developers call "software for one"—creating simple, even imperfect tools designed to solve a specific need for yourself first. This approach:

- Forces clarity about the core problem (since you're scratching your own itch)
- Eliminates pressure to include unnecessary features
- Provides immediate feedback on what works and what doesn't

- Creates a foundation that can be expanded if others find it valuable

As one Reddit user from r/vibecoding notes: "I'm prototyping and building tools for myself, not writing production code, so need to chuck in new features willy nilly as I go." This mindset liberates you from premature optimization and encourages rapid iteration.

Embrace the KISS Principle

"Keep It Simple, Stupid" remains one of the most valuable guidelines in product development, especially when vibe coding. The temptation to add "just one more feature" becomes stronger when AI can generate it quickly, making discipline even more important.

When facing a design decision, always prefer the simplest solution over complexity. Ask yourself:

- Can this feature be removed entirely without compromising the core value?
- Is there a simpler way to achieve the same outcome?
- Would adding this now prevent us from learning something crucial about our basic assumptions?

Utilizing the Minimum Viable Experience (MVE) Framework

Beyond just functionality, consider the Minimum Viable Experience (MVE)—the holistic experience encompassing marketing, onboarding, product usability, and support needed to satisfy early users. The MVE ensures that users can properly evaluate your core product without being distracted by poor experience elements.

Key components of a strong MVE include:

- Seamless onboarding that quickly guides users to the core value
- Basic but intuitive interface design
- Clear communication about what the product does (and doesn't do)
- Simple support channels (even if just an email address)
- Consistent branding and messaging

Remember, the goal is not perfection but removing critical friction points that might prevent users from experiencing and evaluating your core offering.

Creating Development Roadmaps with Clear Priorities

Even in the fluid world of vibe coding, structured planning makes all the difference. A clear roadmap helps you:

- Maintain focus on what matters most
- Communicate priorities to team members or stakeholders
- Track progress and adjust course based on feedback
- Avoid scope creep as new possibilities emerge

The Three-Horizon Approach

Structure your roadmap into three distinct horizons:

1. **Horizon 1 (MVP)**: The absolute minimum features needed to test your core hypothesis and deliver value.
2. **Horizon 2 (Enhanced Experience)**: Features that

strengthen the core experience based on validated learning from the MVP.

3. **Horizon 3 (Expansion)**: Opportunities to grow beyond the core, only pursued after achieving product-market fit.

For each feature or enhancement, clearly document:

- The problem it solves for users
- Success metrics (how you'll know if it works)
- Dependencies (what must be built first)
- Estimated complexity (even a simple High/Medium/Low rating helps)

Practical Documentation for Vibe Coders

Documentation doesn't need to be complex, but some structure helps maintain clarity:

- **Start with a high-level statement** describing your application's intent, purpose, target users, and core features.
- **Break large tasks into stages** and pause for approval after each, promoting a manageable process.
- **For major features**, generate a plan.md file with steps and await approval before proceeding.
- **Keep track of completed work** in progress.md and next steps in TODO.txt.

This lightweight approach provides just enough structure without bogging you down in bureaucracy—perfect for the rapid iteration cycles of vibe coding.

Establishing Clear Milestones

Rather than working toward a distant, perfect end state, establish a series of meaningful milestones that build upon each other. Each milestone should:

- Deliver specific, measurable value
- Test a key assumption about your product or market
- Be achievable within a short timeframe (ideally 2-4 weeks)
- Provide natural points for reflection and course correction

This milestone-based approach aligns perfectly with vibe coding's rapid prototyping capabilities, allowing you to incorporate user feedback at each stage rather than building in isolation.

Case Studies: Apps That Started Incredibly Simple

Snapchat: The Power of One Feature

Snapchat's initial MVP focused on a single core feature: sending photos that would disappear after viewing. There was no Stories feature, no filters, no Discover page—just the basic disappearing photo functionality. By concentrating solely on this unique value proposition, they created a distinctive experience that users couldn't get elsewhere.

The lesson: Identify your product's unique angle and focus exclusively on executing it exceptionally well before expanding.

Buffer: Starting with a Landing Page

Buffer, the social media scheduling tool, began not with a functional product but with a simple landing page describing their proposed solution. Founder Joel Gascoigne created a page explaining the concept and a sign-up button to gauge interest before writing a single line of code.

After validating interest, he built a minimal version that only supported Twitter and offered limited scheduling options. This MVP allowed him to gather feedback while generating early revenue, which guided subsequent development.

The lesson: Validate interest before building, then start with the minimum feature set that delivers genuine value.

Dropbox: The Power of a Video Demo

Rather than building a complete product immediately, Dropbox founder Drew Houston created a 3-minute video demonstration of how the service would work. This video-based MVP generated over 70,000 sign-ups from interested users, providing strong validation before significant development resources were committed.

The lesson: Sometimes your MVP doesn't need to be a functional product at all—it can be a demonstration that validates the concept's appeal.

Disco Community Platform: Focused Community Building

Disco's community platform began with a focused MVP that addressed the core need of creating connection among members. By implementing a subscription revenue model from the start, they were able to validate not just interest but willingness to pay for the solution. Only after establishing this foundation did they expand to more comprehensive community features.

The lesson: Include monetization in your MVP when possible to validate not just interest but commercial viability.

The Vibe Coder's MVP Checklist

When preparing to launch your MVP, use this checklist to ensure you're maintaining the right balance of simplicity and functionality:

- [ ] **Core Value Identified**: Can you articulate the single most important value your product delivers in one sentence?
- [ ] **Feature Discipline**: Have you removed all features not directly supporting your core value proposition?
- [ ] **Problem-Solution Fit**: Does your MVP directly address the specific problem you've identified?
- [ ] **Learning Objectives**: Have you identified the key assumptions you're testing with this release?
- [ ] **Feedback Mechanisms**: Are there clear channels for users to provide feedback?
- [ ] **Minimum Viable Experience**: Does the overall user experience (onboarding, UI, support) enable users to properly evaluate your core offering?
- [ ] **Technical Debt Awareness**: Have you noted areas where temporary solutions will need improvement later?
- [ ] **Success Metrics**: Have you established clear metrics to evaluate the MVP's performance?
- [ ] **Next Iteration Plan**: Do you have a framework for incorporating feedback into the next version?

Remember, your MVP isn't your final product—it's a learning tool designed to validate assumptions with minimal investment. The art lies in finding that sweet spot where the product is simple enough to build quickly but valuable enough to generate meaningful feedback.

The MVE Implementation Plan

Beyond the core functionality of your MVP, consider these key components of the Minimum Viable Experience (MVE) that will ensure users can effectively evaluate your core offering:

1. **Onboarding**: Create a simple flow that guides users to the key value as quickly as possible
2. **User Interface**: Design a clean, intuitive interface focused on core tasks
3. **Support**: Establish basic support channels (email, chat, or documentation)
4. **Communication**: Clearly explain what the product does and its current limitations
5. **Feedback Collection**: Implement mechanisms to gather user feedback

Action Steps: Building Your MVP with Vibe Coding

1. **Define Your Core**: Write a single sentence describing the fundamental problem your product solves and how.
2. **Create a Feature Triage**: List all potential features, then categorize them as "Must Have" (MVP), "Should Have" (next iteration), or "Could Have" (future consideration).
3. **Draft Your First Prompts**: Create 3-5 specific vibe

coding prompts focused only on your "Must Have" features.

4. **Build Your MVE Elements**: Alongside core functionality, develop the minimum viable experience components.
5. **Establish Feedback Loops**: Set up simple mechanisms to collect user insights (surveys, analytics, direct communication).
6. **Create Your Milestone Map**: Define 3-4 clear milestones for the next 90 days based on expected learnings.

Summary: The Art of the MVP in the Vibe Coding Era

In the world of vibe coding, where generating features becomes increasingly accessible, the true art lies not in what you build but in what you choose not to build. The most successful entrepreneurs will be those who maintain the discipline to focus relentlessly on core value while resisting the siren call of feature creep.

Your MVP should be a lean, focused experiment designed to validate your most critical assumptions with minimal investment. By embracing the power of simplicity, you create space for the most important ingredient in product development: learning from real users.

Remember, Instagram started with photo sharing and filters—nothing more. Twitter began as a simple SMS broadcast service. Google offered only search when it launched. These now-massive platforms earned the right to expand by first proving their core value proposition through disciplined, focused MVPs.

In the next chapter, we'll explore how to effectively test and refine your MVP, turning initial user feedback into actionable improvements that strengthen your product's connection with users.

Innovation Navigator Challenge: Take your current product vision and challenge yourself to reduce it by 50%. What remains after this dramatic simplification? That's likely closer to your true MVP than your original concept.

Chapter 12: Quality Assurance for Non-Technical Founders

"Quality is not an act, it is a habit." — Aristotle

In the world of vibe coding, where the barrier to creating apps has been dramatically lowered, quality assurance becomes your secret weapon. While AI can help you build rapidly, ensuring your creation delivers a smooth, reliable experience requires thoughtful testing and refinement.

As a non-technical founder, you might think quality assurance (QA) belongs exclusively in the realm of technical specialists. However, you possess a unique advantage: your intimate understanding of the user's needs and your vision for the solution. This chapter will equip you with practical, accessible approaches to QA that leverage your strengths as a vibe coder while ensuring your app meets the quality standards users expect.

Essential Testing Methodologies Anyone Can Implement

Quality assurance might sound intimidating, but at its core, it's about systematically ensuring your product works as intended. As a non-technical founder, you can implement several powerful testing methodologies without diving into code:

Observational Testing

One of the most powerful and accessible testing methods is simply observing real users interact with your product. This approach aligns perfectly with the vibe coding philosophy of prioritizing user connection over technical details.

How to implement it:

1. Invite individuals from your target audience to use your app
2. Ask them to complete specific tasks that represent core user journeys
3. Observe without interrupting, noting where they hesitate, show confusion, or express delight
4. After the session, ask open-ended questions about their experience

This method reveals invaluable insights about how intuitive your app feels—something technical tests might miss entirely. You don't need specialized tools or technical knowledge to identify when someone is struggling with your interface.

Usability Testing

Usability testing focuses specifically on how easy it is for users to accomplish basic tasks in your app. It's particularly valuable for vibe coders because it evaluates whether your app feels intuitive rather than just checking if features work.

Key aspects to evaluate:

- **Effectiveness**: Can users successfully complete tasks?
- **Efficiency**: How long do tasks take to complete?
- **Satisfaction**: How do users feel about the experience?
- **Learnability**: How quickly can new users understand your app?
- **Memorability**: Can returning users remember how to

use your app?

"Nearly 40% of people might stop using an application if the layout is not engaging and attractive," which highlights the critical importance of usability testing for app success.

Functional Testing

While technical founders might write automated tests, you can perform manual functional testing by creating a simple checklist of features and systematically verifying each one works as expected.

Sample functional test checklist:

- Can a new user successfully sign up?
- Does the login process work with correct credentials?
- Are error messages displayed when incorrect information is provided?
- Does each button perform its intended action?
- Do all screens load properly across different devices?

This methodical approach allows you to identify issues before your users do, even without technical expertise.

Visual Testing

First impressions matter, and visual testing helps ensure your app looks professional and consistent. This involves:

- Checking that all text is readable and not cut off
- Verifying images load correctly and aren't distorted
- Ensuring color schemes and branding elements are consistent
- Confirming the layout works on different screen sizes

As a vibe coder focused on creating emotional connections, visual testing helps guarantee that your app's appearance supports the mood and feeling you want to convey.

Creating Test Plans That Catch Critical Issues

A well-structured test plan acts as your roadmap for quality assurance, focusing your efforts on what matters most. Here's how to create one without technical complexity:

Define Your Core Value Proposition

Begin by clearly articulating the primary problem your app solves. This foundation helps prioritize testing efforts around the most critical functionality—the features that deliver your core value.

For example, if you're building a photo-sharing app, the ability to upload, view, and share photos would be critical, while profile customization might be secondary. Your test plan should reflect these priorities.

Map Essential User Journeys

User journeys (sometimes called user flows) trace the path a user takes to accomplish a goal in your app. By identifying and testing these key journeys, you ensure the most important user experiences work seamlessly.

Steps to map user journeys:

1. Identify your primary user personas
2. List the main goals each persona wants to accomplish
3. Document the steps required to achieve each goal

4. Highlight potential points of difficulty or confusion

For example, a basic user journey might be: Open app → Create account → Upload photo → Share photo

Creating visual flowcharts of these journeys can help identify potential issues before they arise and structure your testing efforts around real-world usage.

Create Scenario-Based Test Cases

Instead of thinking about isolated features, develop test cases based on realistic scenarios that mimic how actual users will interact with your app.

Example scenario-based test case:

- **Scenario:** New user wants to share their first photo
- **Precondition:** User has downloaded the app but hasn't created an account
- **Test steps:**
    1. Open the app for the first time
    2. Create a new account
    3. Navigate to the photo upload function
    4. Select a photo from the gallery
    5. Add a caption
    6. Share the photo
- **Expected result:** Photo is successfully shared and appears in the user's profile

This approach ensures you're testing complete user experiences rather than disconnected features.

Prioritize Based on Risk

Not all potential issues carry the same weight. Prioritize testing based on:

- **Impact:** How severely would this issue affect users?
- **Likelihood:** How probably is this issue to occur?
- **Visibility:** How noticeable would this issue be to users?

Focus your limited testing resources on high-impact, high-likelihood issues first, particularly those in your core user journeys.

Include Edge Cases and Negative Testing

Your app doesn't just need to work when everything goes right—it needs to handle unexpected inputs and situations gracefully. Include test cases for:

- What happens when users enter invalid data?
- How does the app respond when a user performs actions in an unexpected sequence?
- How does the system handle poor network connectivity?
- What happens when users attempt unauthorized actions?

These scenarios often reveal critical issues that might otherwise go undetected until released to users.

User Testing on a Limited Budget

Quality user testing doesn't require expensive labs or large research budgets. As a vibe coder, you can leverage creative approaches to gather valuable feedback without breaking the bank:

Leverage Your Personal Network

Start with friends, family, and colleagues, but be strategic about whom you select. Choose individuals who represent your target demographic when possible, and remember to ask them to be brutally honest.

When conducting these sessions:

- Clearly state that you're looking for candid feedback, not validation
- Avoid defending your app or explaining away issues
- Ask open-ended questions that encourage detailed responses
- Record sessions (with permission) to refer back to later

These informal sessions can reveal surprising insights, especially if you observe without intervening as users attempt to navigate your app.

Use Remote Testing Tools

Several affordable or free tools facilitate remote user testing:

- **Screen recording software:** Tools like Loom offer free options to record user sessions
- **Videoconferencing platforms:** Use Zoom, Google Meet, or similar services to observe and interact with testers remotely
- **Survey tools:** Platforms like Google Forms provide free ways to collect structured feedback
- **Heatmap tools:** Some services offer free tiers that show where users click and how far they scroll

Remote testing expands your reach beyond geographical limitations and can be conducted asynchronously, making it easier to fit into busy schedules.

Guerrilla Testing

"Guerrilla testing" involves approaching people in public places (cafes, libraries, etc.) and asking them to try your app for a few minutes in exchange for a small incentive like a coffee.

This method:

- Provides quick, diverse feedback
- Is extremely cost-effective
- Captures authentic first impressions
- Forces you to focus on key aspects in limited time

While less structured than formal usability testing, guerrilla testing can provide valuable directional insights, especially regarding first impressions and intuitive usability.

Online Communities and Forums

Engage with online communities related to your app's niche to find potential testers. Platforms like Reddit, Discord, or specialized forums often have members willing to provide feedback on new apps, especially if you're transparent about seeking help as an independent developer.

Be specific about what kind of feedback you're looking for and offer incentives where appropriate, such as early access or premium features.

A/B Testing on a Small Scale

Even without sophisticated A/B testing tools, you can implement simple comparative tests:

1. Create two versions of a key screen or feature
2. Show version A to half your test users and version B to the other half
3. Compare completion rates, time spent, and subjective feedback
4. Implement the more successful version

This approach can help you make evidence-based decisions about design choices or feature implementations without requiring technical complexity.

The Art of the Beta Test: Maximizing Valuable Feedback

A well-executed beta test bridges the gap between controlled testing and real-world usage, providing crucial insights before your full launch. Here's how to master this critical phase:

Setting Clear Objectives

Before launching your beta, define exactly what you want to learn. Common beta test objectives include:

- Identifying bugs and usability issues
- Measuring user engagement with key features
- Gathering feedback on pricing or business models
- Testing server load and performance
- Collecting testimonials and case studies for marketing

Having clear objectives helps structure your beta program and ensures you collect the right type of feedback.

Selecting the Right Beta Testers

The quality of your beta feedback depends largely on who's providing it. An effective beta test group should:

- Represent your target user demographic
- Include a mix of technical and non-technical users
- Span various devices and operating systems if applicable
- Include some "power users" who will push the limits of your app
- Be the right size—typically 50-200 participants for a mobile app, though smaller groups can work for specialized applications

Consider creating a simple application process that helps identify ideal candidates who match your target user profile and are likely to provide thoughtful feedback.

Creating an Effective Beta Communication Plan

Regular, clear communication keeps beta testers engaged and improves the quality of feedback:

1. **Welcome message:** Set expectations about the purpose of the beta, known issues, and how to provide feedback
2. **Regular updates:** Share progress on addressing reported issues and new features being tested
3. **Targeted questions:** Ask specific questions about aspects you need feedback on
4. **Acknowledgment:** Thank testers for valuable insights and let them know when their feedback leads to changes

Many successful beta programs use a combination of email updates, in-app messaging, and dedicated communication channels like Slack or Discord to maintain engagement.

Structuring Feedback Collection

Make feedback submission frictionless while ensuring you receive actionable insights:

- **In-app feedback:** Implement a simple feedback button or form directly in your beta app
- **Bug reporting template:** Create a template that prompts testers to include essential details (steps to reproduce, device information, screenshots)
- **Surveys:** Use targeted surveys to collect feedback on specific features or experiences
- **User interviews:** Schedule deeper conversations with particularly engaged or insightful beta testers

Balance structured feedback formats (ratings, multiple-choice questions) with open-ended opportunities for testers to share unexpected insights.

Prioritizing and Acting on Feedback

The volume of feedback during a beta can be overwhelming. Develop a system to:

1. **Categorize feedback:** Sort by feature area, severity, type (bug, suggestion, question)
2. **Identify patterns:** Look for issues mentioned by multiple testers
3. **Assess impact:** Evaluate how significantly each issue

affects the core value proposition

4. **Communicate decisions:** Let testers know which issues you're addressing, which are planned for future updates, and which won't be implemented (and why)

Remember that the goal isn't to implement every suggestion but to identify the changes that will most significantly improve your app's value to users.

Incentivizing Quality Feedback

While some users participate in betas out of interest or to access new functionality early, thoughtful incentives can improve participation and feedback quality:

- Extended free access to premium features
- Recognition in app credits or community spotlights
- Early access to future features
- Exclusive beta tester community membership
- Tangible rewards for exceptional contributors

The most effective incentives align with your app's value proposition and create a sense of insider status among your beta community.

Transitioning From Beta to Launch

A successful beta doesn't just improve your product—it builds momentum for your launch. Before ending your beta:

- Thank your testers personally and acknowledge their contributions
- Share key metrics or insights gained during the beta
- Provide a clear timeline for official launch

- Offer beta testers special launch benefits or founder status
- Invite testers to become ambassadors for your app

Many successful apps maintain relationships with their beta communities long after launch, creating a core group of loyal users who champion the product to others.

Checklist: Performance Factors Every App Should Address

Beyond functionality, performance significantly impacts user satisfaction. Ensure your testing plan evaluates these critical performance factors:

- **Speed and responsiveness:** Does the app respond quickly to user interactions? Are there any noticeable delays when performing common actions?
- **Load times:** How long do screens and content take to load? Particularly test initial app launch time, as this creates a crucial first impression.
- **Resource usage:** Does the app drain battery excessively or use an unreasonable amount of data?
- **Stability:** Does the app crash or freeze under normal usage conditions?
- **Offline functionality:** How does the app behave when internet connectivity is limited or unavailable?
- **Cross-device compatibility:** Does the experience remain smooth across different device types and sizes?
- **Background behavior:** Does the app function properly when running in the background or when switching

between apps?

Each of these factors contributes to the overall perception of quality and professionalism, regardless of how innovative your app's core functionality might be.

Case Study: How Strategic Testing Saved a Launch

Jordan, a non-technical founder, used vibe coding to create a social fitness app that allowed users to track workouts and share progress with friends. After weeks of development with AI assistance, the app looked great and worked well in Jordan's limited testing.

Excited by the progress, Jordan planned to launch within two weeks. However, a mentor suggested conducting a small beta test first—just 20 users for one week.

Jordan created a simple test plan focusing on the core user journeys:

1. Creating an account and profile
2. Logging a workout
3. Connecting with friends
4. Sharing achievements

Within 48 hours of the beta launch, feedback revealed three critical issues:

1. Users on older Android devices experienced crashes when uploading photos
2. The friend-finding feature rarely matched users with their actual connections

3. Workout data occasionally disappeared after the app was closed

None of these issues had appeared during Jordan's initial testing on a newer iPhone. Had Jordan launched without the beta, these problems would have affected thousands of users rather than just 20, likely resulting in negative reviews and high abandonment rates.

Jordan worked with an AI development tool to address these issues, then ran a second beta with 50 users before proceeding with the full launch. This strategic approach to testing ultimately led to a successful launch with a 4.7-star average rating across app stores—a testament to the power of thoughtful QA even for non-technical founders.

Summary: The Vibe Coder's QA Philosophy

Quality assurance for non-technical founders isn't about mastering complex testing methodologies or writing automated test scripts. Instead, it's about:

1. **Focusing on the user experience:** Leveraging your understanding of user needs to test what matters most
2. **Systematic verification:** Creating structured processes to ensure consistent quality
3. **Real-world validation:** Getting your app into the hands of actual users early and often
4. **Strategic improvement:** Using feedback to make targeted enhancements that deliver the greatest impact

By embracing these principles, you transform quality assurance from a technical hurdle into a strategic advantage. In the world of vibe coding, where anyone can build an app, quality becomes a key differentiator that sets your creation apart.

Action Steps

1. **Create your essential test plan:** Identify your app's 3-5 most critical user journeys and document step-by-step test cases for each
2. **Conduct an observational test:** Invite 3-5 people matching your target user profile to try your app while you observe silently
3. **Implement a simple feedback system:** Add a feedback form or button within your app to collect ongoing insights
4. **Design your beta test:** Define objectives, selection criteria for testers, and a communication plan for your beta program
5. **Develop a performance checklist:** Create a list of performance factors specific to your app that you'll verify before launch

Remember, in vibe coding, your advantage lies not in technical expertise but in your connection to users and your vision. Quality assurance is where you ensure that connection comes through clearly in the final product.

Chapter 13: The Refinement Process: From Good to Great

"Refinement isn't about perfection—it's about progression. Each iteration brings you closer to the product your users truly need, not just the one you initially imagined."

Introduction: Beyond the First Build

The journey of app creation doesn't end when the first version hits the market—in many ways, that's just the beginning. In the vibe coding ecosystem, where rapid development is possible, the ability to refine your creation effectively becomes your true competitive advantage. While AI can help generate a functioning app quickly, transforming that initial output into something truly exceptional remains a distinctly human endeavor.

Think of refinement as the art of listening, learning, and evolving. It's where your market intuition meets user reality. It's where you discover if the vibe you've coded truly resonates with your audience.

In this chapter, we'll explore how to transform feedback into actionable improvements, recognize when to pivot versus when to persevere, balance data-driven decisions with intuitive insights, and build systems that make iteration a natural part of your process. The refinement phase is where good apps become great, and where your vision truly connects with your users' needs.

Interpreting User Feedback Effectively

Gathering feedback is just the first step—the real magic happens in how you interpret and act on it. Not all feedback is created equal, and knowing how to extract meaningful insights is a skill that separates successful vibe coders from the rest.

Types of Feedback Worth Collecting

When refining your app, prioritize these feedback categories:

1. **Problem-Focused Feedback**: Comments identifying specific issues users encountered when trying to accomplish tasks
2. **Experience-Based Feedback**: How users felt when using your app (confused, delighted, frustrated)
3. **Feature Requests**: What users wish your app could do
4. **Comparative Feedback**: How users perceive your app compared to alternatives

The refinement process involves iterative improvement, incorporating feedback, testing, and optimization to move from an initial version to a high-quality outcome. This concept applies across various domains, including software development ("vibe coding" or traditional) and product design.

The Feedback Interpretation Framework

To extract actionable insights from raw feedback, follow this structured approach:

Step 1: Categorize and Group

Sort feedback into themes rather than treating each piece individually. Look for patterns that indicate systemic issues rather than one-off problems.

Step 2: Prioritize Based on Impact

Evaluate feedback based on:

- How many users are affected
- How severely the issue impacts the core user experience
- How central the issue is to your app's primary value proposition

Step 3: Separate Signal from Noise

When gathering feedback, focus on seeking specific questions about users' understanding of the purpose, ease of use, and any pain points they encounter. This can provide meaningful insights even from basic prototypes created through vibe coding.

Not all feedback requires action. Consider these filters:

- Is this feedback aligned with your app's core purpose?
- Does addressing this feedback serve your target users or just a vocal minority?
- Is this feedback based on actual usage experience or hypothetical scenarios?

Step 4: Translate Feedback into Action Items

Transform validated feedback into specific improvements:

- For usability issues: Create clear UI/UX adjustments
- For feature requests: Define scope and integration points
- For performance concerns: Identify specific optimization targets

The Art of User Interviews

Conducting user interviews is a qualitative method to gain deep insights into your target audience's needs, pain points, and desires. These conversations can provide invaluable information that goes beyond surface-level data.

For deeper insights, master the art of the user interview:

Preparation Tips:

- Define clear research goals before each interview
- Create an interview guide with open-ended questions
- Select participants who represent your target audience

During the Interview:

- Start with context-setting questions about their workflow or needs
- Use the "five whys" technique to uncover root causes
- Ask for specific examples when users mention problems
- Pay attention to non-verbal cues and emotional responses

Effective Questions:

- "Walk me through how you currently accomplish [task]"
- "What was going through your mind when you encountered this screen?"
- "If you had a magic wand, how would you change this feature?"
- "How does this compare to other tools you use?"

Feedback Synthesis Case Study: Melodix Music App

Sarah launched Melodix, a music discovery app built through vibe coding. Initial users loved the concept but complained about navigation complexity. Rather than just simplifying the menu structure (the obvious fix), Sarah conducted in-depth interviews and discovered something deeper: users wanted to save discoveries for later but couldn't find them easily. This insight led to a complete redesign of the favorites system rather than just a navigation tweak—addressing the actual underlying need rather than just the symptom.

Common Feedback Interpretation Pitfalls

Avoid these common mistakes when processing user feedback:

1. **Overreacting to Outliers**: Giving too much weight to unique or extreme feedback
2. **Confirmation Bias**: Only acknowledging feedback that aligns with your existing beliefs
3. **Feature Creep**: Saying yes to every feature request without strategic evaluation
4. **Superficial Fixes**: Addressing symptoms rather than root causes of user problems

Innovation Navigator Insight: Great feedback interpretation isn't about simply doing what users ask for—it's about understanding the underlying needs that users themselves might not even be able to articulate. Listen for the problems, not just the proposed solutions.

When to Pivot vs. When to Persevere

Perhaps the most challenging decision you'll face during the refinement process is determining whether to double down on your current direction or make a significant change in course. This pivot-or-persevere decision can define your app's future.

Defining the Pivot Spectrum

Not all pivots are created equal. Consider these levels of change:

1. **Tactical Adjustment**: Minor changes to features or functionality while maintaining the core concept
2. **Strategic Shift**: Significant change in how you deliver value while keeping the same target market
3. **Complete Pivot**: Fundamental change in product, market, or business model

Instead of asking "is it working?" which assumes binary outcomes, we should focus on whether there's meaningful progress and what the data is telling us.

Signals That Suggest Perseverance

Stay the course when you observe:

- **Core Engagement Metrics Improving**: If key usage metrics show steady improvement, even if growth is slower than hoped
- **Strong Retention Among Core Users**: If a specific segment shows high engagement, even if overall numbers are modest
- **Positive Qualitative Feedback**: When users express genuine enthusiasm about your core value proposition
- **Clear Path to Improvement**: When current issues have identifiable and feasible solutions

Red Flags That Suggest Pivoting

Consider a pivot when you see:

- **Stagnant or Declining Core Metrics**: If key performance indicators remain flat or decrease despite multiple improvement attempts
- **Low User Engagement**: When users download but rarely open the app, or abandon key features
- **Market Feedback Disconnect**: When the market consistently values different aspects than your core offering
- **Competitive Pressure**: When larger competitors enter with substantial advantages

The concept of initial creation and imperfection is important. The initial output, whether code generated through "vibe coding" or an early product design, is often basic and imperfect. In "vibe coding," a simple prompt can generate a starting point.

The Pivot Decision Framework

To make this critical decision more objective, evaluate your situation through these lenses:

1. Honest Problem Assessment

- Is the core problem you're solving still relevant and significant?
- Are there indicators that your solution approach is fundamentally flawed?

2. Market Validation Check

- Have you truly validated market demand with enough users?
- Are users willing to pay (attention, money, or time) for

your solution?

3. Resource Reality Check

- Do you have the runway (time and money) to continue on the current path?
- Would pivoting allow more efficient use of remaining resources?

4. Personal Conviction Gauge

- Do you and your team still believe in the core vision?
- Are you pivoting from a place of conviction or fear?

Pivot Case Study: Slack

Originally, Slack began as an internal tool for a game development company called Tiny Speck. When their game "Glitch" failed to gain traction, instead of persevering with the game, the team recognized the value of the communication tool they had built for themselves. They pivoted to focus entirely on this tool, ultimately creating one of the most successful business communication platforms in the world. The team knew when to let go of their original vision and follow the evidence toward a more promising opportunity.

Perseverance Case Study: Airbnb

Airbnb faced significant challenges early on with slow growth and investor skepticism. However, metrics showed that the users who did use the service loved it. Instead of pivoting to a different model, the founders persevered by making tactical improvements—better photography, improved user interfaces, and targeted geographic expansion. Their commitment to the core concept while iteratively improving execution led to eventual breakthrough success.

Innovation Navigator Insight: The pivot-or-persevere decision isn't about giving up versus being stubborn—it's about honestly assessing whether your current path has a realistic chance of success and being willing to adapt when evidence suggests a better direction. The most successful founders maintain unwavering commitment to solving a problem while remaining flexible about the solution approach.

Data-Driven vs. Intuition-Driven Improvements

In the refinement process, you'll need to balance objective metrics with subjective judgment. Both data-driven and intuition-driven approaches have their place—the key is knowing when to rely on each.

The Power of Data-Driven Refinement

Data provides an objective foundation for improvement decisions:

Key Metrics Worth Tracking:

1. **Engagement Metrics**
    - Daily/Monthly Active Users (DAU/MAU)
    - Session length and frequency
    - Feature usage distribution
    - Completion rates for critical user journeys
2. **Retention Metrics**
    - Day 1, 7, and 30 retention rates
    - Cohort analysis of long-term usage patterns
    - Churn rate and churn reasons (if captured)
3. **Performance Metrics**
    - Load times and response speeds

    - Crash rates and error frequency
    - Resource utilization (battery, data, memory)
4. **Business Metrics**
    - Conversion rates
    - Customer acquisition cost
    - Lifetime value
    - Revenue per user

Testing is integral to refinement. Thorough tests should be written for major functionality, including edge cases. In "vibe coding," regularly running regression tests helps ensure that changes don't introduce new issues.

Setting Up Basic Analytics

Even simple analytics implementation can provide powerful insights:

1. **User Journey Tracking**: Implement event tracking for key user paths
2. **Funnel Analysis**: Monitor completion rates for multi-step processes
3. **Segmentation**: Break down metrics by user types, acquisition sources, or behaviors
4. **Automated Reporting**: Set up regular reports to maintain awareness of key metrics

The Wisdom of Intuition-Driven Refinement

Some aspects of your app can't be fully captured by numbers alone:

Areas Where Intuition Often Outperforms Data:

1. **Aesthetic Judgments**: Visual design, brand voice, and

overall feel
2. **Innovative Features**: Truly new capabilities without historical data
3. **Emotional Connections**: How your app makes users feel
4. **Future Trends**: Anticipating changes in user expectations or technology

Emotional design, which goes beyond mere aesthetics, aims to elicit positive feelings, connections, and responses from users. Understanding that human emotions play a pivotal role in shaping perceptions, decisions, and overall satisfaction is fundamental.

Developing Your Product Intuition

Product intuition isn't mystical—it's a skill you can develop:

1. **Immerse Yourself in User Contexts**: Regularly observe how users interact with your app in their natural environments
2. **Practice Empathetic Thinking**: Train yourself to see experiences through your users' eyes
3. **Study Design Patterns**: Become familiar with what works well in adjacent products
4. **Cultivate Diverse Inputs**: Expose yourself to varied perspectives, industries, and disciplines

The Balanced Approach: Data-Informed Intuition

The most effective refinement combines both approaches:

1. **Use Data to Identify Problems**: Let metrics highlight where issues exist
2. **Use Intuition to Create Solutions**: Draw on creativity and empathy to design improvements

3. **Use Data to Validate Solutions**: Test whether your intuitive solutions actually improve metrics
4. **Use Intuition to Interpret Data**: Look beyond numbers to understand the "why" behind the "what"

Maintaining focus on the overall goals and requirements is important throughout the refinement process. In "vibe coding," periodically reminding the AI of the roadmap helps maintain alignment.

Case Study: Netflix Recommendation Engine

Netflix brilliantly balances data and intuition in their recommendation system. While sophisticated algorithms track viewing patterns and preferences (data-driven), human curators create collections and categories that reflect nuanced understanding of content relationships (intuition-driven). The combination of algorithmic precision with human judgment creates a more compelling experience than either approach could achieve alone.

Innovation Navigator Insight: The debate between data and intuition presents a false dichotomy. The most successful vibe coders leverage both—using data to identify opportunities and validate solutions, while employing human intuition to understand context and design innovative improvements that numbers alone couldn't suggest.

Creating Systems for Continuous Iteration

Refinement shouldn't be a reactive, ad hoc process. By establishing structured systems for continuous iteration, you can make improvement an integral part of your development culture.

The Continuous Iteration Framework

Implement these interconnected elements to sustain ongoing refinement:

1. **Regular Release Cycles**
    - Establish a predictable cadence for updates (weekly, bi-weekly, or monthly)
    - Balance frequency (for rapid learning) with stability (for user comfort)
    - Communicate release schedules to set user expectations
2. **Feedback Collection Infrastructure**
    - In-app feedback mechanisms (easy reporting, satisfaction surveys)
    - Community engagement channels (forums, social media monitoring)
    - User testing program for major features
    - Analytics dashboards for key metrics
3. **Prioritization Process**
    - Weekly refinement meetings to review feedback and metrics
    - Scoring system for evaluating potential improvements
    - Clear criteria for what makes it into each release
    - Balance between fixing issues and adding capabilities
4. **Documentation and Knowledge Management**
    - Track decisions and their rationales
    - Maintain a backlog of improvement ideas
    - Record lessons learned from previous iterations
    - Share insights across the team

Documenting the process and keeping track of effective prompts and decisions can make future refinement more efficient. The refinement process is also an opportunity for learning and developing taste. Understanding why certain approaches work or don't work enhances future development and design efforts.

Tools to Support Continuous Iteration

Several tools can streamline your refinement process:

1. **Project Management Tools**
    - Trello, Asana, or Jira for tracking improvements
    - Roadmap tools for visualizing the refinement journey
2. **Feedback Management Solutions**
    - Dedicated platforms like UserVoice or Canny
    - Integration with support tools like Zendesk or Intercom
3. **Analytics Platforms**
    - Mixpanel, Amplitude, or Google Analytics for usage data
    - Heatmapping tools like Hotjar for visual behavior tracking
4. **A/B Testing Frameworks**
    - Split testing tools to validate improvements
    - Feature flagging systems for controlled rollouts

The Optimal Refinement Cadence

Finding the right rhythm for iteration is crucial:

For Mobile Apps:

- Major updates: Every 4-6 weeks

- Bug fixes: As needed, usually within 1-2 weeks of discovery
- Complete redesigns: No more than once per year

For Web Applications:

- Feature improvements: Every 1-2 weeks
- Backend optimizations: Continuous deployment where possible
- UI refreshes: Every 6-12 months

Break down problems into smaller, manageable chunks, which can help AI (in vibe coding) or developers (in traditional coding) generate more efficient solutions. Keep a mental model of how the code is functioning to guide the development and optimization process.

Leveraging AI in Your Refinement Process

The journey from good to great is rarely a straight line. It involves creating a starting point, rigorously evaluating it through feedback and testing, making informed adjustments iteratively, and maintaining a focus on quality and user needs throughout the process.

Vibe coding principles can enhance your iteration process:

1. **Automated Analysis**: Use AI to analyze user feedback for sentiment and common themes
2. **Rapid Prototyping**: Generate quick UI variations to test different approaches
3. **Code Optimization**: Ask AI to suggest performance improvements
4. **Test Generation**: Create comprehensive test cases to

validate changes

Case Study: Spotify's Continuous Refinement

Spotify has mastered continuous iteration through their "two pizza team" structure—small, autonomous teams with end-to-end responsibility for specific features. These teams run their own experiments, gather their own data, and make independent refinement decisions. This decentralized approach allows for parallel iteration across the product while maintaining coherence through shared design systems and principles. The result is an app that evolves rapidly while maintaining a consistent experience.

Avoiding Refinement Fatigue

Continuous iteration can lead to team burnout if not managed carefully:

1. **Celebrate Wins**: Acknowledge improvements and their impact
2. **Focus Periods**: Alternate between intense refinement and stability
3. **User Impact Visibility**: Keep the team connected to positive user outcomes
4. **Technical Debt Management**: Allocate time specifically for code quality and infrastructure

Innovation Navigator Insight: The most sustainable refinement systems balance short-term improvements with long-term vision. Each iteration should simultaneously address immediate user needs while moving you closer to your ultimate product vision. This dual focus keeps the team energized and prevents tactical fixes from leading to strategic drift.

Performance Optimization: Creating Smooth Experiences

Creating smooth user experiences hinges on performance optimization, ensuring that applications and systems operate efficiently and responsively.

In the vibe coding era, performance remains a critical differentiator. Users may forgive limited features, but they rarely tolerate sluggish experiences.

Key Performance Areas to Monitor

Focus your optimization efforts on these crucial aspects:

1. **Speed and Responsiveness**
    - App startup time
    - Screen transition animations
    - Input response time (taps, typing, scrolling)
    - Server response time for networked features
2. **Resource Efficiency**
    - Battery consumption
    - Data usage
    - Memory footprint
    - Storage requirements
3. **Reliability and Stability**
    - Crash frequency
    - Error rates
    - Consistent behavior across devices and conditions
    - Graceful handling of edge cases

Traditional programming offers full control over system behavior, making it ideal for applications where performance and reliability are critical. However, even in traditional development, performance optimization is often an iterative process involving testing, profiling, and code refinement.

Working with Developers to Optimize Performance

For non-technical founders, guiding performance optimization requires clear communication:

1. **Set Specific Targets**: Define measurable performance goals (e.g., "App must load in under 2 seconds on mid-range devices")
2. **Prioritize User Journeys**: Identify which flows need the most optimization
3. **Allocate Dedicated Time**: Schedule specific sprints focused on performance
4. **Request Regular Audits**: Establish periodic performance reviews

While vibe coding can accelerate initial development and prototyping, concerns have been raised about its potential impact on code quality and performance. Andrej Karpathy's initial description of vibe coding involved accepting AI-generated code without review and sometimes working around bugs with random changes. This approach might prioritize speed over careful implementation and optimization.

Testing Across Different Devices and Conditions

Comprehensive testing ensures consistent performance:

1. **Device Diversity**: Test on various device types, screen

sizes, and operating system versions

2. **Network Variability**: Verify performance under different connection strengths (4G, 3G, spotty WiFi)
3. **Usage Scenarios**: Test in realistic conditions (low battery, many background apps, limited storage)
4. **Geographic Distribution**: If serving global users, test from different regions

Performance Checklist for Every App

Non-functional testing is crucial for ensuring that software meets performance, security, and usability standards. Types of non-functional testing include performance testing and load testing.

Ensure your app addresses these essential performance factors:

- [ ] **Images and Media Optimization**: Properly sized and compressed for balance between quality and speed
- [ ] **Efficient Data Management**: Appropriate caching and data loading strategies
- [ ] **Animation Smoothness**: Consistent frame rates for all transitions and effects
- [ ] **Background Processing**: Minimized work when app is not in active use
- [ ] **Network Handling**: Graceful behavior with slow or unavailable connections
- [ ] **Memory Management**: Prevention of leaks and excessive resource usage
- [ ] **Battery Efficiency**: Minimal power consumption, especially in background
- [ ] **Startup Optimization**: Quick loading without unnecessary initial data

- [ ] **Error Recovery**: Graceful handling of failures without disrupting experience

Innovation Navigator Insight: Performance isn't just a technical concern—it's deeply connected to user perception and emotion. Studies show that users perceive features as more valuable when they're delivered with speed and smoothness. Invest in performance optimization as a core part of your value proposition, not just a technical checkbox.

Putting It All Together: The Continuous Refinement Flywheel

The most successful vibe coders don't see refinement as a linear process but as a self-reinforcing flywheel that gains momentum over time. Each element feeds into the next, creating a positive cycle of improvement.

The Five Stages of the Refinement Flywheel

1. **Observe**: Gather data and feedback from multiple sources
2. **Analyze**: Interpret information to identify the highest-impact opportunities
3. **Decide**: Choose which improvements to prioritize
4. **Implement**: Execute changes effectively
5. **Learn**: Measure the impact of changes and incorporate lessons

The refinement process is inherently iterative. Based on feedback and review, the initial creation is adjusted and improved. In "vibe coding," this often involves refining the prompts to guide the AI towards a better solution. You might ask the AI to explain its decisions or rewrite the code to be more readable or modular.

As this flywheel gains momentum, each cycle becomes more efficient. Your understanding deepens, your decisions improve, and your implementation becomes more effective.

Maintaining Balance in the Refinement Process

Effective refinement requires balancing multiple tensions:

- **Speed vs. Quality**: Moving quickly while maintaining standards
- **User Requests vs. Strategic Vision**: Responding to feedback while staying true to your core purpose
- **Fixing vs. Building**: Addressing issues versus adding capabilities
- **Short-term vs. Long-term**: Immediate improvements versus foundational investments

The art of great refinement lies in maintaining awareness of these tensions and making conscious tradeoffs rather than defaulting to one extreme.

Measuring Refinement Success

How do you know if your refinement process is working? Look for these indicators:

1. **Accelerating Improvement Rate**: Each cycle produces better results than the last
2. **Increasing User Satisfaction**: Measurable gains in retention, engagement, and sentiment
3. **Team Alignment and Efficiency**: Clearer decisions and

more effective implementation
4. **Competitive Differentiation**: Growing distance between your offering and alternatives
5. **Business Impact**: Improvements translate to key business metrics

Action Steps: Implementing Your Refinement System

1. **Audit Your Current Feedback Channels**
    - Inventory all the ways you currently receive user input
    - Identify gaps in your feedback collection
    - Implement at least one new feedback mechanism
2. **Create Your Metrics Dashboard**
    - Define 3-5 key performance indicators for your app
    - Set up automated tracking for these metrics
    - Establish a regular review cadence
3. **Develop Your Prioritization Framework**
    - Create a simple scoring system for improvement ideas
    - Define your criteria for pivot-or-persevere decisions
    - Document your decision-making process for transparency
4. **Establish Your Release Rhythm**
    - Set a sustainable cadence for updates
    - Create a template for release planning
    - Define roles and responsibilities for the

refinement cycle

5. **Build Your Performance Baseline**
    - Conduct an initial performance audit
    - Identify the top three performance bottlenecks
    - Create a plan to address these issues

Chapter Summary: Key Insights

- **Effective Feedback Interpretation** transforms raw user input into actionable improvements by categorizing, prioritizing, and translating feedback into specific changes.
- **The Pivot-or-Persevere Decision** should be approached systematically, using a framework that considers problem relevance, market validation, resource constraints, and personal conviction.
- **Balancing Data and Intuition** creates the most powerful refinement approach, using metrics to identify issues and validate solutions while leveraging human judgment to design improvements and understand context.
- **Continuous Iteration Systems** make refinement sustainable through regular release cycles, robust feedback infrastructure, clear prioritization processes, and knowledge management practices.
- **Performance Optimization** requires ongoing attention to speed, resource efficiency, and reliability across diverse devices and conditions.
- **The Refinement Flywheel** creates accelerating improvement through a cyclical process of observation, analysis, decision-making, implementation, and learning.

Final Thought: The refinement process transforms your initial vibe-coded creation from a minimum viable product into a maximum value product. It's the bridge between what AI can help you build and what your users truly need. Master this process, and you'll not only create apps that work—you'll create apps that users love and competitors struggle to match.

Chapter 14: Performance Optimization: Creating Smooth Experiences ⍰

"Speed isn't just a feature, it's the foundation of a remarkable user experience."

In the vibrant landscape of app development, your brilliant idea can change the world—but only if users stick around long enough to experience it. Performance optimization isn't just technical polish; it's the invisible force that transforms a promising concept into an addictive experience that keeps users coming back.

As a vibe coder, you've leveraged AI to accelerate your journey from idea to functional app. Now it's time to ensure that your creation doesn't just work but *flows* with the kind of responsiveness that feels magical to users. This chapter will equip you with the strategies to create experiences so smooth that users don't even notice the technology—they simply enjoy the ride.

Why Speed and Responsiveness Drive User Retention

The data doesn't lie: users have zero patience for sluggish apps. In today's hypercompetitive marketplace, performance isn't optional—it's the price of admission.

The Psychology of Performance

Our brains are wired to notice delays. Even milliseconds matter when it comes to creating a seamless digital experience. Research consistently shows that:

- **Users abandon apps**: Nearly 40% of users will stop using an application if the layout isn't engaging and responsive
- **Expectations are rising**: As flagship apps optimize for speed, users expect all apps to match this performance
- **First impressions stick**: Initial performance experiences shape long-term perceptions of your brand
- **Cognitive flow matters**: Interruptions from slow loading or janky animations break the user's concentration and satisfaction

As Jakob Nielsen, the usability expert, famously established through research, there are three crucial response time limits:

1. **0.1 second**: Feels instantaneous
2. **1.0 second**: User notices the delay but remains focused
3. **10 seconds**: Attention is lost completely, and the user may abandon the task

In the vibe coding era, where creating functional apps has become more accessible, performance becomes a crucial differentiator. When anyone can generate working features, simply having them is no longer enough; the quality of the experience will set products apart.

Beyond Frustration: The Business Impact

Poor performance isn't just annoying—it's expensive:

- **Conversion killers**: Each second of delay on mobile load times can reduce conversions by up to 20%
- **Retention disaster**: 88% of users are less likely to return after a bad experience
- **Lost revenue**: Major retailers have reported that even

100ms of additional load time can decrease sales by 1%
- **Brand damage**: Performance issues are increasingly associated with perceptions of poor quality across your entire brand

For vibe coders, this presents both a challenge and an opportunity. AI-generated code can sometimes be inefficient or bloated, potentially impacting performance. However, your focus on user experience and your ability to iterate quickly puts you in an ideal position to create exceptionally responsive apps if you make performance a priority from the start.

Working with Developers to Optimize Performance

As a vibe coder and non-technical founder, you don't need to understand every technical optimization, but you do need to know how to effectively collaborate with developers to achieve performant results.

Speaking the Performance Language

Effective collaboration is fundamentally about translation. You must translate market needs and business vision into clear requirements for the technical team, and conversely, understand technical feedback and constraints in the context of achieving business objectives. Developing a basic shared vocabulary acts as the essential bridge for this translation process.

When discussing performance with developers, familiarize yourself with these key concepts:

- **Rendering time**: How quickly your app displays content

on screen

- **Response time**: How long it takes for an action to produce a result
- **Load time**: How long before your app is usable after being launched
- **Frames per second (FPS)**: How smoothly animations run (60 FPS is the gold standard)
- **Memory usage**: How efficiently your app uses device resources
- **Network efficiency**: How your app transfers data over the internet
- **Backend performance**: How quickly your servers process requests

Setting Clear Performance Goals

Rather than vague requests like "make it faster," establish measurable performance targets:

- **Specific metrics**: "The main screen should load in under 2 seconds on a mid-range device"
- **User-centered goals**: "Users should never wait more than 1 second after tapping a button"
- **Competitive benchmarks**: "Our app should match or exceed the responsiveness of [competitor app]"

Finding the Right Performance Partners

When outsourcing, look for partners with experience working with startups and navigating their unique pressures (tight budgets, deadlines, pivots). Consider engaging technical advisors or consultants for guidance, especially in complex AI domains.

Seek developers who:

- Have a portfolio demonstrating fast, smooth apps
- Can explain performance concepts in terms you understand
- Proactively bring up performance considerations
- Have experience optimizing AI-generated code specifically

The Collaborative Optimization Process

Create a structured approach to performance improvement:

1. **Baseline measurement**: Document current performance metrics as a starting point
2. **Prioritization**: Focus on the most user-impacting issues first
3. **Iteration cycles**: Plan short, focused sprints for testing improvements
4. **Validation**: Test each optimization to confirm it actually helps
5. **Documentation**: Track successful optimizations for future reference

Managing AI-Generated Code Performance

Some argue that AI-generated code may not always be performant or adhere to best practices for optimization. For instance, an AI might implement logic on the client-side when it should be on the server, impacting performance and security.

When working with vibe-coded solutions:

- Use prompt engineering to guide AI towards generating

better code. You can specifically ask AI to "write better code," focusing on security or performance.

- Practice conscious vibe coding that emphasizes a balanced approach where developers guide, test, and refine the AI's output, taking ownership of the code. This includes reflecting and refactoring AI-generated code to be more readable and modular.
- Ask your technical partners to review AI-generated code specifically for performance issues
- Build in time for refactoring and optimization after initial generation

Testing Across Different Devices and Conditions

Your app needs to perform well not just on your development machine but across the diverse ecosystem of devices and network conditions your users will have.

The Multi-Device Reality

As a non-technical founder, focusing on observing how real users interact with your product is a crucial and accessible testing method. This can reveal areas of confusion or delight without needing specific technical skills.

Consider the full spectrum of testing scenarios:

- **Device diversity**: From flagship phones to budget models with limited processing power
- **Operating system variations**: Different versions of iOS, Android, and other platforms
- **Screen sizes and resolutions**: From tiny phones to large

tablets

- **Connection quality**: Strong Wi-Fi, spotty cellular, offline capability
- **Resource constraints**: Limited memory, processing power, or battery
- **Real-world usage patterns**: Quick checks vs. extended sessions

Building a Practical Testing Strategy

You don't need a laboratory full of devices to implement effective testing:

1. **Prioritize based on analytics**: Focus testing on the most common devices in your target market
2. **Use simulators and emulators**: Test on virtual devices before physical ones
3. **Leverage cloud testing services**: Platforms like BrowserStack or AWS Device Farm provide access to thousands of real devices
4. **Implement automated performance tests**: Work with developers to create scripts that verify performance benchmarks
5. **Conduct field testing**: Test in various locations and network conditions that mirror real usage

User-Centered Performance Testing

Another approachable method is usability testing, where you ask users to complete specific tasks and note the efficiency and effectiveness of the design. You can time their actions and ask about any difficulties they encounter. This helps ensure your product is easy to use.

Incorporate these user-focused techniques:

- **Performance perception interviews**: Ask users how fast they perceive the app to be, not just measuring raw speed
- **Task completion timing**: Measure how long users take to complete common actions
- **Frustration mapping**: Identify when and where users show signs of impatience or annoyance
- **Comparative testing**: Have users compare your app's performance to competitors

Implementing Beta Testing for Performance

A beta test is an excellent way to get real-world feedback before a wider launch. To maximize valuable feedback, clearly define the goals of your beta test, recruit beta testers who represent your target audience, provide clear instructions, make it easy for testers to submit feedback, actively engage with your beta testers, focus on understanding why testers are encountering issues, and iterate on your product based on the feedback received.

For performance-focused beta testing:

- Include specific questions about speed and responsiveness in your feedback forms
- Request that beta testers try the app under various conditions (poor connectivity, while multitasking)
- Implement performance monitoring tools that capture real-world metrics
- Prioritize fixing issues that affect the largest percentage of users

Checklist: Performance Factors Every App Should Address

Use this comprehensive checklist to ensure you're covering all critical performance areas. Work through this with your development team to create an optimization roadmap.

Frontend Performance

□ Loading Optimization

- [ ] Implement splash screens and loading indicators for perceived performance
- [ ] Load only the minimum required content for initial view
- [ ] Use lazy loading for images and content below the viewport
- [ ] Implement caching strategies for frequently accessed data

□ UI Responsiveness

- [ ] Ensure all interactive elements respond in under 100ms
- [ ] Move intensive operations off the main thread
- [ ] Optimize animation frame rates (aim for 60fps)
- [ ] Implement debouncing for rapid user interactions (scrolling, typing)

□ Resource Efficiency

- [ ] Optimize image sizes and formats (WebP, responsive images)

- [ ] Minify and compress code (JS, CSS, HTML)
- [ ] Implement efficient state management to prevent memory leaks
- [ ] Reduce DOM complexity and nesting

Backend Performance

□ API Optimization

- [ ] Minimize API payload sizes (send only what's needed)
- [ ] Implement efficient pagination for large data sets
- [ ] Cache common API responses
- [ ] Use GraphQL to request only necessary data when appropriate

□ Database Efficiency

- [ ] Optimize database queries and indexes
- [ ] Implement appropriate caching layers
- [ ] Consider data denormalization for read-heavy operations
- [ ] Monitor query performance regularly

□ Server Optimization

- [ ] Scale infrastructure based on actual usage patterns
- [ ] Implement CDNs for static content delivery
- [ ] Use load balancing for high-traffic applications
- [ ] Implement appropriate timeout handling

Network Optimization

□ Connection Handling

- [ ] Minimize HTTP requests through bundling and sprites
- [ ] Implement retry logic for failed network requests
- [ ] Support offline functionality where possible
- [ ] Use HTTP/2 or HTTP/3 for multiplexed connections

☐ **Data Transfer**

- [ ] Compress data during transfer (GZIP, Brotli)
- [ ] Implement efficient data formats (JSON vs. Protocol Buffers)
- [ ] Use incremental loading for large datasets
- [ ] Implement background syncing for non-critical updates

AI-Specific Optimization

☐ **Model Efficiency**

- [ ] Consider on-device vs. cloud-based AI processing
- [ ] Optimize AI model size for mobile/web environments
- [ ] Implement model quantization where appropriate
- [ ] Balance accuracy vs. speed for your use case

☐ **Integration Performance**

- [ ] Minimize latency between app and AI services
- [ ] Implement caching for repetitive AI requests
- [ ] Use batch processing for multiple AI operations
- [ ] Consider fallback functionality when AI services are slow

User Perception Optimization

□ Perceived Performance

- [ ] Implement skeleton screens during loading
- [ ] Use progressive loading for content-heavy pages
- [ ] Give immediate feedback for user actions
- [ ] Animate transitions to mask loading times

□ Edge Case Handling

- [ ] Implement graceful degradation for slow connections
- [ ] Test performance with low battery conditions
- [ ] Optimize for reduced data usage mode
- [ ] Handle unexpected input without performance degradation

Monitoring and Improvement

□ Performance Tracking

- [ ] Implement real-user monitoring (RUM)
- [ ] Track key performance metrics over time
- [ ] Set up alerts for performance regressions
- [ ] Regularly review performance analytics

□ Continuous Optimization

- [ ] Schedule regular performance audits
- [ ] Update optimization strategies as devices evolve
- [ ] A/B test performance improvements
- [ ] Gather ongoing user feedback about responsiveness

The Refinement Process: Iterating Towards Performance

The refinement process involves iterative improvement, incorporating feedback, testing, and optimization to move from an initial version to a high-quality outcome. This concept applies across various domains, including software development ("vibe coding" or traditional) and product design.

Remember that performance optimization isn't a one-time task but an ongoing process:

1. **Start with measurement**: Establish baseline performance metrics
2. **Identify the bottlenecks**: Focus on the most significant issues first
3. **Apply targeted improvements**: Make one change at a time
4. **Verify the impact**: Measure again to confirm improvement
5. **Repeat the process**: Continue prioritizing and addressing issues

Continuous testing is integral to refinement. Thorough tests should be written for major functionality, including edge cases. In "vibe coding," regularly running regression tests helps ensure that changes don't introduce new issues.

The Founder's Role in Performance Optimization

As a non-technical founder using vibe coding, your role in performance optimization focuses on:

1. **Setting clear expectations**: Communicate the importance of performance to your team
2. **Asking the right questions**: Learn enough to know what to ask about
3. **Allocating resources**: Budget time and money for optimization
4. **Prioritizing user impact**: Focus on improvements that users will notice most
5. **Testing personally**: Experience your app under various conditions yourself

The non-technical founder's primary role is often outside the code itself. Skills in areas like marketing, sales, networking, storytelling, and overall business strategy frequently prove more critical to success than the founder's ability to code. They understand the crucial "now what?" phase after a product is initially built.

Remember: Your unique understanding of user needs and business goals makes you an essential part of the performance optimization process, even without technical expertise.

Key Takeaways

- **Performance is a competitive advantage**: In the vibe coding era where more people can build apps, exceptional performance sets your product apart
- **User perception matters most**: Focus on how fast your app feels, not just technical benchmarks
- **Collaboration is crucial**: Build a shared language with

developers around performance goals

- **Testing across environments**: Your app must perform well across diverse devices and conditions
- **Systematic optimization**: Use the performance checklist to create a comprehensive approach
- **Continuous improvement**: Performance optimization is an ongoing process, not a one-time task

Action Steps

1. **Baseline measurement**: Document your app's current performance metrics across key user journeys
2. **Set performance goals**: Establish clear, measurable targets for improvement
3. **Identify low-hanging fruit**: Work with developers to find quick performance wins
4. **Create a testing matrix**: Define the key devices and conditions to test against
5. **Implement monitoring**: Set up tools to track performance over time
6. **Schedule regular audits**: Make performance reviews a consistent part of your development cycle

---

Remember, as a vibe coder, you're already ahead of the curve by leveraging AI to bring your vision to life quickly. By prioritizing performance optimization, you're ensuring that your innovation doesn't just exist—it thrives in the hands of delighted users who keep coming back for more.

In the next chapter, we'll explore how to prepare for a successful launch, building anticipation and setting up the infrastructure you'll need when your optimized app is ready for the world.

Chapter 15: Launch and Beyond - Sharing Your Vibe

"The launch is not the finale; it's the overture to your app's journey in the marketplace."

After months of ideation, validation, and development using your vibe coding approach, the moment has arrived to share your creation with the world. A successful launch isn't merely about flipping a switch and watching downloads accumulate—it requires strategic preparation, thoughtful execution, and diligent post-launch management to ensure your app gains traction and thrives in its critical early days.

Pre-Launch: Building Anticipation and Readiness

The groundwork for a successful launch begins weeks or even months before your app appears in any store. This preparation phase is about building anticipation, optimizing for discovery, and ensuring your team and systems are ready for what's ahead.

Building Anticipation Through Pre-Launch Marketing

Pre-launch marketing creates connections with potential users and establishes credibility before your app is available. Start your efforts 6-8 weeks before launch with these proven strategies:

1. **Create a "Coming Soon" Landing Page**
    - Include a compelling headline that communicates your unique value proposition

    - Display high-quality screenshots or videos showcasing your app's interface
    - Add an email capture form with an incentive (early access, launch discount)
    - Keep the design clean and focused on conversion
2. **Leverage Content Marketing**
    - Publish blog posts addressing the problems your app solves
    - Create tutorials, infographics, or videos related to your app's purpose
    - Contribute guest posts to relevant industry blogs
    - Share your development journey to humanize your brand
3. **Build a Social Media Presence**
    - Focus on platforms where your target audience is most active
    - Share development updates and behind-the-scenes content
    - Create countdowns and teasers to generate excitement
    - Use polls to gather input on minor features or design elements
4. **Gather Beta Testers and Testimonials**
    - Recruit testers from your email list or relevant online communities
    - Provide clear expectations and feedback mechanisms
    - Collect testimonials to use in launch materials
    - Encourage testers to share their experiences on social media

5. **Begin Press Outreach**
    - Create a targeted list of journalists and publications in your niche
    - Develop a compelling press kit with your app's story and visual assets
    - Schedule embargoed announcements with key outlets
    - Consider offering exclusive previews to select publications

Remember that consistency is key—maintain regular communication through your chosen channels to build anticipation without overwhelming your audience.

App Store Optimization Fundamentals

App store optimization (ASO) helps your app appear prominently in store searches, increasing discovery and downloads. Focus on these key elements:

1. App Name and Title

- Make it memorable, descriptive, and keyword-rich
- For example: "TaskFlow: Smart To-Do List & Reminders"

2. Keyword Strategy

- Research relevant keywords with high search volume but moderate competition
- Incorporate keywords naturally throughout your listing
- Consider localization for different markets

3. App Description

- Open with a compelling first paragraph highlighting key benefits
- Use short paragraphs and bullet points for readability
- Include social proof and end with a clear call-to-action

4. Visual Assets

- Create a distinctive, recognizable icon
- Design screenshots that showcase key features with benefit-focused captions
- Develop a 15-30 second preview video demonstrating core functionality

5. Ratings and Reviews

- Implement an in-app review request system
- Plan to respond to all early reviews, especially negative ones
- Never engage in manipulative review practices

A well-optimized store listing not only improves discoverability but also increases conversion rates once potential users find your app.

Creating Launch Readiness

Before launch day arrives, ensure your technical infrastructure, team, and support systems are fully prepared with this simplified checklist approach:

Technical Readiness

- Complete final QA testing across all supported devices
- Verify all API connections and third-party services

- Confirm analytics are correctly tracking key events
- Test user flows under various network conditions
- Scale servers to handle potential launch traffic

App Store Submission

- Finalize app metadata, screenshots, and preview video
- Submit with adequate time before planned launch (typically 1-2 weeks)
- Prepare for potential rejection and resubmission

Support Systems

- Create a comprehensive knowledge base and FAQs
- Set up email support workflow with templates for common issues
- Implement in-app help resources
- Establish social media monitoring for support requests
- Train team members on support procedures

Team Preparation

- Assign specific launch day responsibilities
- Create a communication plan for the launch period
- Schedule shifts to ensure 24-hour coverage if necessary
- Plan a celebration to maintain team energy and morale

Launch Execution: Timing and Strategy

The decisions you make about launch strategy and the actions you take during the first days in the marketplace can significantly impact your app's trajectory.

Choosing Your Launch Approach

Consider these two primary strategies, each with distinct advantages:

Soft Launch

- Release to a limited audience or select geographic markets
- Test technical performance with a manageable user base
- Gather real-world usage data to refine the experience
- Optimize monetization strategies based on actual behavior
- Ideal for complex apps or those with high scalability requirements

Big Bang Launch

- Release simultaneously across all intended markets
- Coordinate marketing efforts for maximum initial impact
- Create immediate momentum to boost store rankings
- Capitalize on pre-launch anticipation
- Better for thoroughly tested apps with strong pre-launch interest

Many successful apps use a hybrid approach, such as a phased rollout to key markets or an audience-based approach starting with your most engaged community members.

Creating Launch-Day Momentum

The first 24-72 hours after launch are critical for establishing momentum that can propel your app in store rankings and create a cycle of discovery and downloads.

Coordinate a Multi-Channel Push

- Send announcement emails when the app goes live
- Post simultaneously across all social platforms
- Activate press coverage (lifting any embargoes)
- Coordinate with influencers and partners
- Launch paid advertising campaigns

Consider Launch Events and Activities

- Host a virtual launch event showcasing key features
- Offer limited-time promotions for early adopters
- Create special recognition for day-one users
- Plan a Product Hunt or similar platform feature

Monitor Technical Performance

- Implement progressive server scaling
- Create a real-time dashboard for critical metrics
- Set up alerts for performance thresholds
- Prepare for immediate intervention if needed

During this intense period, maintain clear communication channels among team members and be prepared to make quick decisions as situations evolve.

Responding to Initial User Feedback

The first wave of user feedback provides crucial insights that can guide immediate improvements and shape your app's future development.

Establish Feedback Collection Systems

- In-app feedback mechanisms with rating prompts
- App store review monitoring
- Social media listening for mentions and sentiment
- Support ticket categorization and analysis

Analyze and Prioritize Feedback

- Categorize by type (bugs, usability issues, feature requests)
- Consider frequency, severity, and alignment with vision
- Create daily summaries for the team
- Identify patterns across different user segments

Implement Response Strategies

- Acknowledge all feedback promptly
- Provide transparent updates on known issues
- Communicate timelines for addressing priority concerns
- Share insights with your community when appropriate

Remember that your response to early feedback significantly impacts user perception. Being responsive and transparent builds trust, even when addressing problems.

Post-Launch: Stabilization and Growth

The period immediately following launch requires vigilant monitoring, strategic communication, and focused improvements to stabilize your app and build momentum.

Managing the Critical First Week

The first week after launch is often chaotic and requires a different operational approach than normal development.

Implement a War Room Mentality

- Schedule extended team availability
- Conduct daily stand-ups to address emerging issues
- Create rapid decision-making protocols
- Maintain a central dashboard of critical metrics
- Document all issues and resolutions for later analysis

Focus Areas for Monitoring

- Technical stability and performance
- User acquisition and retention metrics
- Conversion rates at key funnel points
- User feedback trends and sentiment
- Competitive response to your launch

Balancing Reactive and Proactive Work

- Allocate specific resources to address emerging issues
- Maintain forward momentum on planned post-launch activities
- Protect core team members from constant firefighting
- Create clear criteria for when to pause planned work

During this period, resist the temptation to make significant changes based on limited data. Focus on stability and understanding user behavior patterns before pivoting.

Update Strategy: Emergency vs. Planned

Knowing when and how to update your newly launched app is a critical skill that balances addressing issues with maintaining stability.

When to Push Emergency Updates

- Critical bugs affecting core functionality
- Security vulnerabilities
- Issues causing significant data loss or corruption
- Problems impacting a large percentage of users
- Situations damaging your brand reputation

When to Include in Planned Improvements

- Minor visual or UI issues
- Functionality improvements that aren't core features
- Performance optimizations for edge cases
- Feature requests, even popular ones
- Content updates or additions

Update Communication Strategy

- For emergency updates: Be transparent about the issue and solution
- For planned updates: Focus on improvements and user benefits
- Always acknowledge when changes address user feedback
- Use appropriate channels based on update significance

Remember that each update requires app store approval, which adds time to the process. Bundle non-critical fixes when possible to minimize disruption.

Communication During Challenging Periods

How you communicate during difficulties often matters more than the problems themselves.

Principles for Crisis Communication

- Respond quickly with what you know
- Be transparent about issues without unnecessarily alarming users
- Provide regular updates even when progress is limited
- Express genuine empathy for user frustration
- Avoid promises you can't keep regarding timelines

Channel Selection Based on Severity

- Critical issues: Direct in-app notifications, email, all social channels
- Significant issues: App store update notes, social media, community forums
- Minor issues: Support documentation, responses to affected users

Recovery Messaging

- Acknowledge the issue directly
- Explain what happened in simple terms
- Detail steps taken to prevent recurrence
- Express appreciation for user patience
- Consider appropriate compensation for significantly

affected users

Effective communication during challenges can transform potentially negative experiences into opportunities to demonstrate your commitment to users.

Maintaining Team Energy

Launch periods are intense and can lead to burnout if not managed carefully.

Strategies for Sustaining Team Momentum

- Schedule breaks and enforce reasonable working hours
- Celebrate small victories and milestones
- Share positive user feedback with the entire team
- Create visible tracking of improvements made
- Implement rotation for high-stress responsibilities

Post-Launch Retrospective

- Hold a dedicated session to review the launch process
- Focus on both successes and areas for improvement
- Document lessons learned for future releases
- Recognize exceptional contributions
- Use insights to refine your launch playbook

The way you manage team energy during the post-launch phase sets the tone for your ongoing development culture.

Key Takeaways

- Pre-launch marketing builds anticipation and creates a foundation for your app's success

- App store optimization improves discoverability and conversion rates
- Choosing between soft launch and big bang strategies depends on your app's complexity and market readiness
- The first 72 hours are critical for establishing momentum and addressing initial feedback
- Clear communication during challenges builds trust and loyalty
- Careful update strategy balances addressing issues with maintaining stability
- Team management during intense launch periods prevents burnout and sustains momentum

Action Steps

1. Create your pre-launch marketing timeline, working backward from your intended launch date
2. Develop a detailed launch checklist customized to your app's specific needs
3. Establish your feedback collection and analysis systems before launch
4. Create templates for different types of user communications, including crisis scenarios
5. Schedule your team's launch period responsibilities with built-in redundancy
6. Set up a monitoring dashboard for critical metrics
7. Plan your post-launch retrospective to capture valuable insights

The launch phase represents the transition from creating your app to sharing it with the world. By approaching this period with strategic preparation, thoughtful execution, and diligent post-launch management, you'll maximize your chances of success in the competitive app marketplace. Remember that launching is just the beginning—how you respond to early feedback and challenges often determines whether your app thrives or struggles in the long term.

Chapter 16: Marketing Fundamentals for App Creators

"Marketing is no longer about the stuff that you make, but about the stories you tell." - Seth Godin

In the vibrant landscape of app development, creating a remarkable product is only half the battle. Even the most innovative, well-designed app can fade into obscurity without effective marketing. This is especially true in today's AI-driven "vibe coding" era, where the barriers to building apps have significantly lowered, increasing competition for user attention.

This chapter explores how to effectively market your app—transforming it from just another icon in the app store to a solution users actively seek out and champion to others. We'll focus on crafting a compelling narrative, developing cost-effective marketing strategies, creating consistent branding, and learning from successful case studies.

Crafting Your App's Unique Story and Value Proposition

In a market saturated with AI claims, cutting through the noise requires clearly articulating the specific, tangible problem your AI solution addresses and the concrete value it delivers. Your app's story and value proposition form the foundation of all your marketing efforts.

Finding Your App's "Why"

The most compelling app marketing doesn't begin with features or technology—it begins with purpose. Ask yourself:

- What inspired you to create this app?
- What problem were you solving for yourself or others?
- How does your app make users' lives better in ways competitors don't?

Focus on outcomes and benefits (time saved, costs reduced, accuracy improved) rather than just listing AI features. Remember, users care more about what your app does for them than how it works.

Developing a Strong Value Proposition

A strong value proposition is essential. It should be customer-centric, clearly stating who the product is for, the problem it solves, the unique solution offered, and the resulting benefits.

To craft your value proposition:

1. **Research your target audience thoroughly** - Understand their needs, frustrations, and desires
2. **Study your competitors** - Identify gaps in their offerings that your app fills
3. **Brainstorm unique selling points** - What makes your app distinctly valuable?
4. **Draft concise messaging** - Create clear, compelling statements about your app's value
5. **Refine based on feedback** - Test your messaging with potential users
6. **Implement consistently** - Use your value proposition across all marketing channels

EXAMPLE:

Weak value proposition: "An AI-powered productivity app with smart features."

Strong value proposition: "For busy professionals who struggle to prioritize tasks, [App Name] is the first productivity tool that uses AI to analyze your work patterns and automatically prioritize your daily tasks, helping you finish work on time and reduce stress."

Storytelling That Connects

Use storytelling to connect with your audience on an emotional level, build empathy, and communicate your brand's purpose and values. Effective app stories often follow this structure:

1. **The struggle** - Describe the problem your users face
2. **The epiphany** - Share the insight that led to your app's creation
3. **The solution** - Introduce your app as the answer
4. **The transformation** - Paint a picture of life after adopting your app

Share the journey behind the product, highlight user successes, and be vulnerable and human. Ensure stories are truthful and align with the brand's authentic voice.

Developing a Marketing Strategy on a Limited Budget

Most app creators don't have massive marketing budgets, especially in the early stages. Fortunately, with the right approach, you can gain significant traction without breaking the bank.

The AI Marketing Flywheel

Instead of a traditional linear sales funnel, consider adopting a flywheel model that leverages the momentum of satisfied customers to drive referrals, repeat business, and advocacy. This approach is particularly well-suited for AI-powered apps.

The flywheel consists of three interconnected phases:

- **Attract**: Drawing potential customers in by offering value
- **Engage**: Building relationships and demonstrating ongoing value
- **Delight**: Exceeding expectations to turn customers into happy promoters

This model creates a self-reinforcing cycle where delighted users bring in new users, accelerating your growth.

Cost-Effective Marketing Tactics

1. **Content Marketing**

Since AI can be complex or unfamiliar, create valuable content (blog posts, whitepapers, e-books, guides, webinars, workshops) that educates your target audience about relevant AI concepts, the problems your product solves, and potential benefits. Address common questions and concerns proactively.

1. **Social Media Strategy**

Engage on platforms where your target audience resides. Share thought leadership content demonstrating your expertise, product updates, user success stories, and interactive content like Q&A sessions or polls to foster engagement and build community.

1. **App Store Optimization (ASO)**

Optimize your app store presence with:

- Keyword-rich titles and descriptions
- Compelling screenshots and app previews
- Clear, benefit-focused feature lists
- A strategy for generating and managing reviews

1. **Strategic Partnerships**

Identify complementary apps or services and explore cross-promotion opportunities. These partnerships can extend your reach without additional cost.

1. **Community Building**

Building a strong online community around your concept fosters loyalty, advocacy, and engagement. Define your community's purpose, choose the right platforms, create valuable content, foster authentic engagement, encourage user-generated content, organize events, offer exclusive perks, and cultivate brand advocates.

1. **Growth Hacking Techniques**

Look for creative, unconventional ways to grow your user base:

- Implement referral programs with incentives for both parties
- Create "viral loops" where using the app naturally leads to sharing
- Leverage unique moments in the user experience for social sharing

Budget Allocation Framework

Even with limited resources, strategic allocation is crucial:

Marketing Phase	Recommended Budget %	Focus Areas
Pre-launch	20-30%	Brand development, landing page, early adopter outreach
Launch	40-50%	PR push, influencer outreach, paid acquisition
Post-launch	30-40%	Retention, community building, iteration based on data

Remember: Track your marketing efforts meticulously. Even with a small budget, understanding which channels deliver the best return on investment is essential for optimizing your spending.

Creating Consistent Branding Across All Touchpoints

In today's fragmented digital landscape, users might encounter your app across multiple platforms—from app stores to social media, websites to email. Consistent branding ensures they recognize and trust your app regardless of where they find it.

Developing Your Brand Identity

Your brand identity should reflect your app's personality and values. Key elements include:

1. **Visual Identity**
   - Logo and icon design
   - Color palette

- Typography and font selections
- Imagery style
- UI/UX elements

Colors have psychological impacts (color psychology), fonts convey personality, and even sensory elements like sound can play a role in branding. Choose these elements thoughtfully to align with your app's purpose and target audience.

1. **Voice and Tone**
    - How does your app "speak" to users?
    - Is it professional, friendly, technical, or playful?
    - What terminology and language do you use consistently?
2. **Brand Promise**
    - What can users always expect from your app?
    - What core values guide your development and user experience?

Brand Consistency Checklist

Use this checklist to ensure consistency across all touchpoints:

- **App Store Listing**
    - Does your description use your established brand voice?
    - Do screenshots highlight your visual identity?
    - Are your brand colors incorporated in all visuals?
- **Website**
    - Does it reflect the same design elements as your app?
    - Is your value proposition clearly communicated?

    - Does the user experience mirror what they'll find in your app?
- **Social Media**
    - Are profile images and banners consistent with your brand?
    - Does your content maintain your brand voice?
    - Are you using consistent hashtags and messaging?
- **Email Communications**
    - Do templates reflect your brand colors and typography?
    - Is your voice consistent with other communications?
    - Are you using the same terminology as in your app?
- **Customer Support**
    - Are responses aligned with your brand voice?
    - Do support materials use consistent terminology?
    - Does your support experience reflect your brand values?

Building trust is arguably the most critical factor in AI adoption. Trust encompasses dependability (reliability), transparency (clarity about how it works and uses data), integrity (ethical behavior), customer focus, responsiveness, and relevance. Consistency across all these areas reinforces trust.

Case Study: Marketing Strategies That Propelled Apps to Success

Let's examine several real-world examples that demonstrate effective app marketing principles in action.

Case 1: Mytender - Problem-Focused Marketing

Founded by two undergraduate students from Southampton University, Mytender developed an AI tool to assist companies in writing bids for contracts in sectors like construction. Despite their likely limited technical backgrounds, their focus on solving a specific industry problem attracted £250,000 in seed funding from Fuel Ventures.

Key Takeaway: By demonstrating a clear understanding of a specific industry pain point and articulating how their AI solution directly addressed it, Mytender attracted investor interest even before substantial market traction. Their marketing emphasized the problem-solution fit rather than technical sophistication.

Case 2: My AskAI - Pivoting to Find Product-Market Fit

After experimenting with GPT-3 technology and initial tools, a co-founder with a finance background pivoted to create My AskAI, an AI customer support chatbot for SaaS businesses. Starting with minimal cost ($99), the venture reached $25,000/month ($300,000/year).

Key Takeaway: The success came from applying technology to a specific, valuable business problem rather than marketing the technology itself. Their approach highlighted the importance of experimentation, pivoting based on market feedback, and finding strong product-market fit. Marketing messaging focused on the specific pain point (customer support costs for SaaS businesses) rather than the underlying AI.

Case 3: Coachvox AI - Leveraging Existing Assets

Jodie Cook, with a background in content and social media agency ownership, leveraged her extensive existing content (books, articles, podcasts) to build Coachvox AI. This platform allows creators to build AI versions of themselves for coaching and engagement. The venture achieved six-figure Annual Recurring Revenue (ARR) even before its official launch.

Key Takeaway: Non-technical founders can leverage unique, non-technical assets (like proprietary content or domain expertise) combined with AI to create and market valuable niche products. Cook's marketing strategy emphasized the uniqueness of the content powering the AI, creating a defensible market position that would be difficult for competitors to replicate.

Case 4: Example Freemium Success - Community-Driven Growth

The freemium model offers a basic version of the AI application for free to attract a large user base, while revenue is generated by upselling users to paid tiers with premium features, higher usage limits, or enhanced capabilities.

Key Takeaway: Successful freemium apps create clear value in their free tier while establishing obvious "upgrade moments" when users naturally desire more functionality. Their marketing focuses on acquiring free users at scale, then nurturing them through engaging content and community until they convert to paying customers.

Transparency and Trust: The Foundation of AI App Marketing

Given the often opaque nature of AI, concerns about data privacy, potential biases, and job displacement, building and maintaining trust is arguably the most critical factor in AI adoption.

Effective AI app marketing must address:

- How user data is collected, stored, and used
- The limitations of your AI technology
- The measures you take to ensure fairness and prevent bias
- The human oversight and quality control in your processes

Be transparent about how the AI works (at an appropriate level for the audience), how user data is collected, stored, and used, and acknowledge the AI's limitations. This honesty builds credibility and sets appropriate expectations.

Putting It All Together: Your 30-60-90 Day Marketing Plan

To implement these concepts effectively, here's a structured 30-60-90 day plan for marketing your app:

First 30 Days: Foundation

- Define your app's value proposition and brand identity
- Create basic marketing assets (website, social profiles, pitch deck)
- Set up analytics to track marketing performance
- Identify and engage with your first 100 potential users

Days 31-60: Launch and Learn

- Launch your app with a coordinated campaign across channels
- Implement ASO best practices
- Begin content marketing with 2-3 high-quality pieces
- Establish a simple referral program for early adopters
- Collect and analyze initial user feedback

Days 61-90: Optimize and Scale

- Refine messaging based on user feedback
- Double down on the most effective acquisition channels
- Expand content marketing efforts
- Begin building community features
- Implement retention campaigns for existing users

Chapter Summary: Key Takeaways

- **Value Proposition**: Clearly articulate what problem your app solves and how it uniquely delivers value to users.
- **Storytelling**: Craft a compelling narrative that connects emotionally with your audience and demonstrates your app's impact.
- **Flywheel Marketing**: Adopt a cyclical marketing approach that leverages satisfied customers to drive growth.
- **Budget Efficiency**: Focus on cost-effective strategies like content marketing, ASO, partnerships, and community building.
- **Brand Consistency**: Ensure your app presents a cohesive identity across all user touchpoints.
- **Transparency**: Be honest about your AI's capabilities and limitations to build lasting trust.
- **Learn from Success**: Study and adapt strategies from successful apps in your category.

Action Steps

1. **Write your app's story** in one page or less, focusing on the problem, solution, and transformation.
2. **Create a competitive analysis** identifying your app's unique advantages and positioning.
3. **Design a simple brand guide** with your color palette, typography, voice guidelines, and logo usage.
4. **Draft your 30-60-90 day marketing plan** with specific, measurable goals.
5. **Set up basic analytics** to track user acquisition,

engagement, and retention.

"In the world of app marketing, the goal isn't just downloads—it's creating advocates who can't imagine life without your solution."

In the next chapter, we'll explore content marketing strategies specifically designed for app creators, including blog posts, videos, and social media campaigns that drive engagement and conversions.

Chapter 17: Content Marketing for App Growth

Introduction

In the era of "vibe coding," where building apps has become more accessible through AI-assisted development, the ability to market effectively becomes an even greater differentiator. Content marketing—creating and distributing valuable, relevant content to attract and engage a clearly defined audience—represents one of the most powerful strategies for sustainable app growth. Unlike paid advertising that stops working when you stop paying, quality content continues to drive traffic, build relationships, and establish authority long after publication.

This chapter explores how to leverage content marketing to grow your app user base organically, convert more visitors into users, and retain them as loyal advocates. We'll examine strategies for creating content that resonates with your ideal users, diversifying across multiple formats for maximum reach, developing educational material that demonstrates your app's value, and positioning yourself as an authority in your niche.

Creating Content That Attracts Your Ideal Users

Understanding Your Audience Deeply

Before creating any content, you must develop a nuanced understanding of your ideal users—their challenges, aspirations, search behaviors, and content preferences.

Educational content marketing is crucial since AI can be complex or unfamiliar. Creating valuable blog posts, whitepapers, e-books, guides, webinars, and workshops that educate your target audience about relevant AI concepts, the problems your product solves, and potential benefits is essential.

Key Insight: User research for content marketing is not the same as user research for product development. While both are important, content research focuses on discovering:

- What questions your ideal users are asking online
- Which sources they trust for information
- Their content consumption habits (when, where, how)
- The vocabulary they use to describe their problems

Developing User Personas for Content

The most effective content strategies begin with detailed content-focused personas. For each major segment of your audience, document:

- **Demographics:** Age, location, occupation, income level
- **Psychographics:** Values, interests, attitudes, lifestyle
- **Content Preferences:** Preferred formats, platforms, and content depth
- **Pain Points:** Specific challenges they face related to your app's solution
- **Information Needs:** Questions they're asking at different stages
- **Search Behavior:** Keywords and phrases they use when looking for solutions

Expert Perspective: Content Strategist View

"The biggest mistake I see app founders make is creating content they think is interesting rather than what their users actually need. When you properly research your audience's questions and pain points first, content becomes a powerful user acquisition channel, not just a checkbox marketing activity."

— Maya Rodriguez, Content Strategy Consultant

Content-Market Fit: The Missing Link

Just as product-market fit is essential for your app, content-market fit is crucial for your marketing. This means aligning your content directly with your users' needs at different stages of their journey.

When creating AI-related content, focus on educational material that explains AI's relevance to specific user problems. Present a clear, compelling value proposition and potentially offer freemium tiers or free trials to lower the barrier to entry.

Mapping Content to the User Journey:

1. **Awareness Stage:** Content addressing broader problems your users face
    - Example: "The Hidden Cost of Manual Data Entry in Small Businesses"
2. **Consideration Stage:** Content comparing approaches to solving problems
    - Example: "AI vs. Manual Approaches: Which is Better for Invoice Processing?"
3. **Decision Stage:** Content showing how your specific solution works
    - Example: "How [Your App] Automates Invoice Processing in 3 Simple Steps"
4. **Adoption Stage:** Content helping users get maximum

value
    - Example: "Advanced Features in [Your App] You Might Be Missing"
5. **Advocacy Stage:** Content encouraging sharing and referrals
    - Example: "Success Stories: How Our Users Transformed Their Businesses"

Actions to Take:

1. Conduct keyword research using tools like Ahrefs, SEMrush, or Google Keyword Planner to identify what your potential users are searching for
2. Analyze competing apps' content to identify gaps you could fill
3. Interview 5-10 existing users about what content would have been helpful before they discovered your app
4. Create a content calendar mapping specific topics to each stage of the user journey

Creating Content That Converts

The foundation of effective communication is clearly articulating the specific, tangible problem your AI solution addresses and the concrete value it delivers to the user. Focus should be on outcomes and benefits (e.g., time saved, costs reduced, accuracy improved) rather than just listing AI features.

To create content that not only attracts but converts readers into users, embrace these principles:

Problem-First Structure: Begin content by deeply acknowledging the problem before introducing solutions. When readers feel understood, they're more receptive to your solution.

Specificity Sells: Vague claims like "our app saves time" aren't compelling. Instead, use specific claims: "Our users save an average of 7.3 hours per week on data entry."

Demonstrate, Don't Just Tell: Use visuals, case studies, and step-by-step guides to show your app in action rather than just describing features.

Incorporate Social Proof: Leverage testimonials, case studies, and success stories to showcase tangible value and build credibility.

Key Insight: Your content should serve as a "try before you buy" experience. It should give readers a taste of the value your app provides, making the decision to try the actual app a natural next step.

Leveraging Multiple Formats: Blogs, Videos, Podcasts

Today's users consume content across multiple formats and platforms. By diversifying your content approach, you can:

- Reach users who prefer different learning styles
- Maximize visibility across various discovery channels
- Repurpose core ideas efficiently across formats
- Build a more robust content ecosystem

Blog Content: Your Foundation

Blog posts remain the cornerstone of most content marketing strategies because they're:

- Highly searchable (SEO-friendly)

- Easy to produce and update
- Shareable across platforms
- Effective for conveying detailed information

Blog Content Types for App Growth:

1. **How-to Guides:** Step-by-step instructions for solving specific problems
    - Example: "How to Automate Your Email Follow-ups with [Your App]"
2. **Problem/Solution Articles:** Deep dives into problems your app solves
    - Example: "The 5 Biggest Challenges in Project Management (And How to Solve Them)"
3. **Comparison Posts:** Contrasting approaches or solutions
    - Example: "Spreadsheets vs. Dedicated Tools: What's Best for Inventory Management?"
4. **Case Studies:** Real-world examples of your app creating value
    - Example: "How Company X Increased Productivity by 37% Using [Your App]"
5. **Industry Trends:** Forward-looking content positioning you as an expert
    - Example: "The Future of Customer Service: AI Trends for 2026"

Optimizing your website content, landing pages, and educational materials with relevant keywords related to the problem solved, the AI technology, and the target industry improves organic discoverability.

Expert Perspective: SEO Specialist View

"For app founders, SEO isn't just about ranking—it's about qualifying your traffic. The right keywords bring users with specific needs your app can solve. Focus on long-tail keywords with clear intent rather than high-volume general terms."

— Alex Chen, App SEO Specialist

Video Content: Showing the Vibe

Video content allows you to showcase your app's user experience and personality in ways text cannot. Strategic social media presence is important. Engage on platforms where your target audience resides (e.g., LinkedIn, Twitter, specialized forums for B2B AI). Share a mix of thought leadership content (demonstrating expertise), product updates, user success stories, and interactive content like Q&A sessions or polls to foster engagement and build community.

Effective Video Content Types:

1. **App Demos:** Short demonstrations of key features in action
    - Keep under 2-3 minutes, focusing on one core value proposition
    - Use scenario-based demos showing real-world applications
2. **Tutorial Videos:** Step-by-step instructions for using specific features
    - Break into digestible segments (under 5 minutes when possible)
    - Include timestamps for easy navigation
3. **User Testimonials:** Authentic stories from satisfied users
    - Focus on transformation and results, not just features

    - Include diverse use cases that showcase versatility
4. **Behind-the-Scenes:** Development, team, or company culture videos
    - Humanize your brand and build connection
    - Share your vision and values to attract aligned users
5. **Thought Leadership:** Industry insights and expert perspectives
    - Position yourself as a knowledgeable guide in your field
    - Address broader trends that affect your users

Actions to Take:

1. Audit your competitors' video content to identify gaps and opportunities
2. Create a simple video recording setup (good lighting, microphone, screen recording software)
3. Develop templates for intros, outros, and graphics to maintain consistency
4. Plan a content calendar that balances product-focused and educational videos

Podcast Content: Building Deeper Connections

Podcasts create unique opportunities for deeper engagement with your audience. They allow for:

- More nuanced discussions than most written or video content
- Background consumption (while driving, exercising, etc.)
- Building personal connections through voice

- Networking with guests in your industry

Podcast Approaches for App Founders:

1. **Educational Series:** Teaching concepts related to your app's purpose
    - Example: A productivity app could create "The Efficiency Expert" podcast
2. **Interview Format:** Conversations with industry experts, users, or team members
    - Leverages others' expertise and audiences
    - Positions you in a network of respected voices
3. **Case Study Showcase:** Detailed explorations of customer success stories
    - Demonstrates real-world impact
    - Provides social proof through storytelling
4. **Industry News & Analysis:** Commentary on developments in your field
    - Establishes you as a thought leader
    - Gives users reasons to return regularly

Key Insight: Consistency trumps frequency with podcasts. A monthly podcast that reliably delivers value will outperform a weekly show that struggles to maintain quality or schedule.

Content Repurposing Strategy

Smart founders maximize their content investment through systematic repurposing:

The Content Multiplication Framework:

1. **Create Core Content:** Develop a comprehensive piece (like a detailed blog post)

2. **Extract Micro-Content:** Pull out key points, quotes, stats, and insights
3. **Adapt for Platforms:** Customize format and style for each channel
4. **Schedule Strategically:** Distribute over time for maximum visibility
5. **Track and Optimize:** Note which formats and topics perform best

Example Content Multiplication:

Original: Comprehensive blog post on "5 Ways AI Is Transforming Customer Service" Repurposed as:

- YouTube tutorial showing your app's AI customer service features
- LinkedIn carousel highlighting key statistics from the post
- Twitter thread breaking down each of the five transformations
- Podcast episode discussing the post's ideas in greater depth
- Email newsletter summarizing the key points with app tie-in
- Infographic visualizing the transformation process

Educational Content That Showcases Your App's Value

Educational content serves dual purposes: it provides genuine value to your audience while naturally demonstrating how your app solves their problems.

Embrace transparency and authenticity. Be transparent about how your AI works (at an appropriate level for the audience), how user data is collected, stored, and used, and acknowledge your AI's limitations.

The Teach-Don't-Sell Approach

The most effective educational content focuses on teaching valuable skills or concepts first, with product mentions serving as natural extensions rather than the primary focus.

Principles of Educational Content Marketing:

1. **Solve Real Problems:** Address genuine challenges your audience faces
2. **Provide Complete Solutions:** Don't withhold key information to force app usage
3. **Show, Don't Just Tell:** Use examples, visuals, and demonstrations
4. **Be Platform-Agnostic Where Possible:** Acknowledge solutions beyond your app
5. **Add Context:** Explain not just how, but why certain approaches work

Expert Perspective: Educational Content Creator

"The best educational content comes from a genuine desire to help. When you approach content with a teacher's mindset rather than a marketer's, you build trust first. That trust naturally leads to interest in your product when readers see how it connects to the problems you're helping them solve."

— Jordan Williams, Tech Education Content Creator

Strategies for Valuable Educational Content

Create educational content that explains AI's relevance to user problems. Optimize website content, landing pages, and educational materials with relevant keywords related to the problem solved, the AI technology, and the target industry to improve organic discoverability.

1. Comprehensive Guides and Resources

Detailed, actionable guides establish your expertise while providing genuine value:

- **Ultimate Guides:** Exhaustive resources on important topics
- **Resource Libraries:** Collections of templates, checklists, or tools
- **Glossaries:** Explanations of industry terms and concepts
- **Research Reports:** Original insights or data analysis

2. Interactive Learning Experiences

Engaging experiences that teach while showcasing your app:

- **Interactive Tutorials:** Step-by-step learning modules
- **Quizzes and Assessments:** Tools to help users understand their needs
- **Calculators:** Interactive tools demonstrating potential value
- **Webinars:** Live or recorded sessions teaching valuable skills

3. Problem-Specific Solutions

Content focusing on specific problems your users face:

- **Troubleshooting Guides:** Solutions to common issues
- **Workflow Walkthroughs:** Optimized processes for specific tasks
- **Comparison Frameworks:** Tools for making informed decisions
- **Benchmark Reports:** Standards for measuring performance

Actions to Take:

1. Survey your users about their biggest knowledge gaps related to your app's purpose
2. Create at least one cornerstone educational resource addressing a fundamental need
3. Develop a system for updating educational content to keep it current
4. Implement email capture strategies to turn educational content consumers into leads

Showcasing Your App Naturally

The key to effective educational content is showcasing your app as a natural solution rather than forcing it into the narrative. Techniques include:

The Problem-Agitate-Solution Method:

1. Clearly define a problem your audience faces (Problem)
2. Explore implications and costs of the problem (Agitate)
3. Introduce solutions, including how your app addresses it (Solution)

Show Multiple Approaches: Present several ways to solve a problem, including both manual methods and how your app automates or simplifies the process. This transparency builds trust and highlights your app's value.

Before and After Comparisons: Demonstrate processes or results both without and with your app, quantifying differences in time, effort, or outcomes.

User Success Stories: Highlight user-generated content: Encourage and feature content created by users, such as successful use cases, custom templates, or helpful tips. Highlighting user success stories builds social proof.

Key Insight: Educational content should leave readers both more knowledgeable and more aware of how your app could make their lives easier—without making them feel like they've just read an advertisement.

Building Authority in Your App's Niche

Establishing yourself as an authority in your niche creates numerous advantages:

- Higher trust from potential users
- Greater organic visibility and referrals
- More media and partnership opportunities
- Reduced price sensitivity for your offerings
- Enhanced credibility when introducing new features

Use storytelling to connect with the audience on an emotional level, build empathy, and communicate the brand's purpose and values. Share the journey behind the product, highlight user successes, and be vulnerable and human. Ensure stories are truthful and align with the brand's authentic voice.

Developing a Thought Leadership Strategy

Thought leadership means consistently providing forward-thinking insights and perspectives that shape how your audience thinks about their challenges and opportunities.

Components of Effective Thought Leadership:

1. **Unique Perspective:** Developing and articulating a distinct point of view
2. **Original Research:** Conducting and sharing proprietary data or analysis
3. **Future Orientation:** Addressing emerging trends and developments
4. **Industry Connections:** Building relationships with other leaders and experts
5. **Consistent Presence:** Maintaining visibility across key platforms and venues

Expert Perspective: Industry Analyst View

"True thought leadership isn't about having all the answers—it's about asking better questions. The app founders who stand out are those who help their users think differently about their problems, not just those who solve existing problems more efficiently."

— Dr. Samira Patel, Technology Industry Analyst

Authority-Building Content Types

Leverage user-generated content (UGC). Encourage and feature content created by users, such as successful use cases, custom templates, or helpful tips. Highlighting user success stories builds social proof.

1. Trend Analysis and Predictions

Forward-looking content that positions you as an industry insider:

- Annual prediction posts or reports
- Analysis of emerging technologies or methodologies
- Commentary on industry shifts and their implications
- Contrarian takes on conventional wisdom (when warranted)

2. Original Research and Data

Unique insights that can't be found elsewhere:

- User behavior or outcome studies
- Industry surveys and benchmark reports
- Data analysis from your user base (anonymized and aggregated)
- Case studies with quantifiable results

3. Concept Development and Frameworks

New ways of thinking about familiar challenges:

- Proprietary methodologies or approaches
- Evaluation frameworks or decision matrices
- Workflow optimizations or process improvements
- Mental models for understanding complex topics

4. Opinion and Commentary

Well-reasoned perspectives on industry developments:

- Response to major news or announcements
- Critiques of common practices or assumptions
- Vision pieces about the future of your industry
- Lessons learned from your own experiences

Actions to Take:

1. Identify 3-5 core themes where you can develop distinctive expertise
2. Create a quarterly plan for producing substantial thought leadership content
3. Develop relationships with industry publications for content placement
4. Build a personal brand alongside your app's brand through speaking engagements

Amplifying Your Authority

Creating authoritative content is only the first step. Strategic amplification extends your reach and impact:

1. Strategic Partnerships

Enhance the community's value by partnering with external groups like academic institutions (for research insights on ethics, bias), community-based organizations (for culturally sensitive implementation and trust), or even artists and storytellers (to humanize data and communicate impact effectively).

Additional partnership opportunities include:

- Guest posting on established industry blogs
- Co-creating content with complementary tools or services

- Participating in industry roundtables or panels
- Collaborating on research projects or whitepapers

2. Community Building

Creating a dedicated community can provide significant benefits, especially for products involving novel or complex technologies like AI. Communities offer a space for users to connect, share resources (tools, tutorials, best practices), provide peer-to-peer support, offer valuable feedback directly to the development team, and network with others in the field.

Effective community strategies include:

- Creating and moderating discussion groups or forums
- Hosting regular AMAs (Ask Me Anything) sessions
- Developing ambassador or advocate programs
- Facilitating user-to-user connections and knowledge sharing

3. Speaking and Events

Visibility at key industry events reinforces authority:

- Speaking at conferences or webinars
- Participating in podcast interviews
- Hosting your own events or meetups
- Contributing to panel discussions

4. Media Relations

Expanding reach through media coverage:

- Developing relationships with industry journalists
- Creating press-worthy announcements or findings

- Offering expert commentary on industry news
- Crafting compelling pitches for your unique insights

Key Insight: Authority isn't claimed—it's recognized. Focus on consistently delivering valuable insights and perspectives, and your audience will naturally come to view you as an authoritative source.

Measuring Content Marketing Success

Effective content marketing requires ongoing measurement and optimization. Establish metrics that align with your business goals:

Awareness Metrics:

- Website traffic (overall and by source)
- Social media reach and engagement
- Email list growth
- Branded search volume

Engagement Metrics:

- Time on page
- Pages per session
- Social shares and comments
- Email open and click rates

Conversion Metrics:

- Trial sign-ups from content
- Content-attributed installations
- Lead magnet downloads
- Demo requests

Retention and Loyalty Metrics:

- Return visitor rate
- Content engagement from existing users
- User-generated content submissions
- App referrals from content readers

Actions to Take:

1. Set up proper UTM tracking for all content distribution
2. Implement event tracking for key user actions after content consumption
3. Create a simple monthly content performance dashboard
4. Schedule quarterly content strategy reviews based on performance data

AI-Powered Content Marketing

As a vibe coding practitioner, you can leverage AI tools to enhance your content marketing efforts:

1. Content Research and Planning

- Use AI to analyze top-performing content in your niche
- Generate content ideas based on keyword and trend analysis
- Identify content gaps your competitors aren't addressing
- Create optimized content briefs for consistent quality

2. Content Creation Assistance

- Generate rough drafts to refine with your expertise
- Expand bullet points into full paragraphs
- Create variations for A/B testing headlines and hooks
- Suggest improvements for clarity and engagement

3. Content Optimization

- Check readability and suggest improvements
- Analyze SEO factors and recommend enhancements
- Generate meta descriptions and social media snippets
- Identify opportunities for internal linking

4. Content Personalization

- Create dynamic content that adapts to user attributes
- Generate personalized email sequences based on behavior
- Develop segment-specific variations of core content
- Recommend related content based on user interests

Key Insight: AI tools work best as collaborators, not replacements. Use them to handle repetitive tasks and generate ideas, but apply your unique expertise and voice to create truly distinctive content.

Conclusion: The Content Flywheel Effect

When implemented effectively, content marketing creates a self-reinforcing flywheel effect for your app:

1. **Valuable content attracts potential users**
2. **Some convert to trying your app**
3. **Successful users share their experiences**
4. **Their testimonials enhance your content**
5. **Enhanced content attracts more potential users**

This flywheel gains momentum over time, generating increasing returns on your content investment. Unlike paid advertising that stops working when you stop paying, quality content continues driving growth for months or years.

The most successful vibe coding entrepreneurs recognize that while AI makes building apps more accessible, content marketing remains fundamentally human. It's about connecting with your audience's needs, delivering genuine value, and building relationships that last beyond the initial download or sign-up.

By creating content that attracts your ideal users, diversifying across formats, educating while showcasing value, and building authority in your niche, you establish a sustainable growth engine for your app that becomes harder for competitors to replicate over time.

Chapter Summary

- **Content marketing provides lasting value** unlike paid advertising that stops working when you stop paying
- **Understanding your audience deeply** is the foundation of effective content strategy
- **Mapping content to the user journey** ensures you create relevant material for each stage
- **Diversifying across formats** (blogs, videos, podcasts) reaches users with different preferences
- **Educational content should teach first** and showcase your app as a natural solution
- **Building authority in your niche** creates numerous advantages for sustainable growth
- **Measuring content performance** allows for continuous optimization and improvement
- **AI tools can enhance your content marketing** but your unique expertise remains essential
- **The content flywheel effect** creates increasing returns on your content investment over time

Chapter 18: App Store Optimization Mastery

Introduction

In the vibrant landscape of app entrepreneurship, building an exceptional app is only half the battle. Without strategic visibility in app stores, even the most groundbreaking application can languish in obscurity. App Store Optimization (ASO) has emerged as the essential science of ensuring your app doesn't just exist in the marketplace—it thrives, connects, and grows.

This chapter explores the art and science of ASO—a discipline that combines analytical precision with creative intuition to amplify your app's discoverability and conversion potential. We'll navigate through the technical foundations of keyword optimization, the creative elements of visual storytelling, the social dynamics of review management, and the analytical frameworks that keep your ASO strategy evolving.

For vibe coders, ASO represents a unique opportunity. Your intuitive approach to development gives you special insight into the emotional connection users seek with technology. This "vibe-centered" perspective is precisely what makes for compelling app store presentations that resonate on a deeper level with potential users.

The Science of ASO: Keywords, Descriptions, and Visuals

At its core, ASO is about understanding how users discover apps and optimizing your store presence to align with these discovery patterns. This science encompasses three critical pillars: keywords, descriptions, and visuals.

The Keyword Foundation

Keywords serve as the bridge between user intent and your app's discovery. They are the searchable terms that users enter when looking for solutions to their problems or desires.

Research shows that 70% of app downloads come from search queries within app stores. This makes keyword optimization not just important—it's fundamental to your app's success. The process begins with understanding your target audience's language and search behavior.

Key Insight: *Think like your user, not like a marketer. What problem are they trying to solve? What terms would they naturally use to describe this need? Effective keyword research captures the authentic language of your potential users.*

The keyword optimization process involves several strategic steps:

1. **Identify primary and secondary keywords**: Primary keywords directly describe your app's core functionality (e.g., "photo editor" or "meditation guide"), while secondary keywords capture related features, benefits, or use cases.
2. **Analyze keyword metrics**: Not all keywords are created equal. Evaluate each potential keyword based on:
    - Search volume (how many users search for this term)
    - Competition (how many apps are targeting this keyword)
    - Relevance (how closely the keyword matches

your app's actual functionality)

3. **Optimize keyword placement**: Keywords should be strategically placed throughout your app store listing:
    - App title (highest weight)
    - Subtitle or short description
    - App description
    - Keyword field (Apple App Store)
4. **Consider localization**: If targeting multiple markets, research keywords in each language to ensure cultural relevance and search effectiveness.

Example: Vibe-Based Keyword Analysis

For a meditation app using vibe coding principles to create personalized sound environments that respond to user emotions, your keyword strategy might include:

Primary keywords: meditation app, sleep sounds, stress relief Secondary keywords: emotional wellbeing, mood enhancement, adaptive meditation, personalized relaxation

The science of keyword optimization involves finding the sweet spot between search volume and competition. High-volume keywords may attract more searches but typically face intense competition, making it difficult for new apps to rank well. Conversely, low-competition keywords might be easier to rank for but may not generate substantial traffic.

Expert Perspective: The Long-Tail Keyword Strategy

"Many developers focus exclusively on broad, high-competition keywords, overlooking the power of long-tail phrases. These more specific, multi-word queries often convert better because they match precise user intent. For example, instead of just targeting 'fitness app,'

consider 'pregnancy-safe home workouts' or 'quick office desk exercises.' These longer phrases may have lower search volume individually, but collectively they can drive significant, highly-qualified traffic to your app." — Maya Chen, ASO Specialist

Crafting Compelling Descriptions

Your app description serves dual purposes: it influences search algorithms and convinces potential users that your app will solve their problems or enhance their lives.

The description should be structured to achieve maximum impact:

1. **First paragraph (above the fold)**: Lead with your most compelling value proposition. What specific problem does your app solve? What makes your approach unique? This section must capture attention immediately and encourage users to read more.
2. **Feature breakdown**: Organize key features into scannable bullet points with clear, benefit-focused language. For each feature, connect it to the user benefit it delivers.
3. **Social proof**: Incorporate elements that build credibility such as user numbers, awards, or media mentions.
4. **Call-to-action**: End with a clear prompt that encourages the download.

Key Insight: *Descriptions for vibe-coded apps should emphasize the emotional experience and intuitive nature of your application. Highlight how your app "gets" the user at an emotional level rather than just performing functions.*

The Visual Strategy

Visual elements in your store listing communicate your app's purpose, quality, and emotional appeal instantaneously. The human brain processes images 60,000 times faster than text, making visuals your most powerful conversion tools.

Key visual elements include:

1. **App icon**: As your app's primary visual identifier, it should be instantly recognizable, visually appealing, and reflective of your app's function. Effective icons tend to be simple, distinctive, and use a limited color palette for maximum impact.
2. **Feature screenshots**: These should tell a visual story about your app's core functionalities and benefits. Each screenshot should highlight a specific feature while communicating its user benefit.
3. **Preview videos**: Short, engaging videos that demonstrate your app in action can increase conversion rates by up to 35%, according to data from app store intelligence platforms.

Actions to Take:

- Conduct A/B testing on different visual elements to identify which combinations drive the highest conversion rates
- Study your most successful competitors' visual strategies for inspiration (without copying)
- Ensure visual elements are optimized for all device sizes and orientations
- Update screenshots and videos when releasing major feature updates

The science of ASO involves continuous experimentation, measurement, and refinement. By understanding the technical foundations of how app store algorithms work and how users discover apps, you can systematically improve your app's visibility and conversion potential.

Creating Screenshots and Videos That Drive Installs

While keywords and descriptions help users find your app, it's your visual assets that ultimately convert browsers into downloaders. The average user spends just 7-8 seconds deciding whether to download an app, making your screenshots and videos crucial conversion tools.

Strategic Screenshot Design

Screenshots should be more than mere feature displays—they should tell a compelling visual story about your app's value. Here's how to create screenshots that drive installs:

1. **Lead with your strongest feature**: Your first screenshot should showcase your app's primary value proposition. This is especially important as it's often the only screenshot visible without scrolling.
2. **Show the app in context**: Demonstrate real-world usage that helps users visualize how the app will fit into their lives. For vibe-coded apps, showing emotional responses or contextual adaptations can be particularly powerful.
3. **Incorporate benefit-focused captions**: Short, prominent text overlays should emphasize benefits rather than features. "Fall asleep 2x faster" is more compelling

than "Multiple sleep sounds."

4. **Use device frames thoughtfully**: Device frames can provide context but may reduce the visible area for your actual interface. Consider when they add value versus when a clean, frameless approach might be more effective.
5. **Create a visual sequence**: Arrange screenshots in a logical order that tells a story about the user journey, from problem to solution.
6. **Optimize for scanning**: Use contrasting colors, directional cues, and hierarchical sizing to guide the viewer's eye to key information.

Example: The Before/After Technique

For apps that transform experiences or solve problems, a before/after approach can be remarkably effective:

Screenshot 1: Shows a user looking stressed with disorganized task lists (Before) *Caption:* "Feeling overwhelmed by your to-do list?"

Screenshot 2: Shows the same user looking relieved with the app's intuitive prioritization interface (After) *Caption:* "Experience the calm of AI-powered task management"

This technique creates an emotional narrative that resonates with the frustrations and aspirations of potential users.

Creating Compelling App Preview Videos

App preview videos have become increasingly significant in driving conversions, with data showing they can increase install rates by 20-35% when executed effectively.

Best practices for app preview videos include:

1. **Capture attention in the first 3 seconds**: Begin with your app's most visually appealing or innovative feature to immediately hook viewers.
2. **Focus on the user experience**: Showcase real interactions rather than static features, emphasizing how the app feels to use.
3. **Highlight your unique selling proposition**: Clearly communicate what makes your app different from competitors.
4. **Keep it brief and focused**: Aim for 15-30 seconds, focusing on core functionality rather than trying to show everything.
5. **Add subtle branding elements**: Incorporate your logo and consistent visual identity without overwhelming the actual app demonstration.
6. **Create a silent-friendly experience**: Most users watch app store videos without sound, so ensure your video communicates effectively without audio. If using text overlays, keep them brief and highly readable.

Key Insight: *For vibe-coded apps, videos provide a unique opportunity to demonstrate adaptive or responsive behaviors that static screenshots cannot capture. Show how your app reacts to different user states or contexts to highlight its intuitive design.*

Localization Considerations

If targeting international markets, consider creating localized versions of your visual assets. This goes beyond mere translation to include:

- Culturally appropriate imagery and examples
- Local currencies and measurement units

- Regional device preferences (different markets have different popular device models)
- Culturally specific color associations and design preferences

Actions to Take:

- Analyze your current conversion rate from page views to installs
- Study competitors with higher conversion rates and identify their visual strategies
- Create a storyboard for your app preview video before production
- Test different screenshot designs with small focus groups before publishing
- Consider professional design help for creating standout visual assets

Managing and Leveraging User Reviews Strategically

User reviews function as both social proof for potential downloaders and valuable feedback for continuous improvement. With 90% of users reading reviews before downloading an app, your review profile significantly impacts conversion rates.

Building a Positive Review Profile

The foundation of review management is delivering a quality app experience that naturally generates positive feedback. Beyond this fundamental requirement, several strategies can help build a strong review profile:

1. **Strategic review prompts**: Implement in-app review requests that appear after positive user experiences, such as completing an achievement or successfully using a key feature. The timing of these prompts significantly impacts response rates and sentiment.
2. **Segmented prompting**: Only ask your most engaged or satisfied users for reviews. This can be determined through usage patterns, feature adoption, or direct feedback mechanisms.
3. **Two-path feedback systems**: Implement a system that first asks users if they're enjoying the app. Those who respond positively are directed to leave a store review, while those who respond negatively are channeled to a direct feedback form, allowing you to address concerns before they become negative public reviews.
4. **Review response strategy**: Responding to reviews demonstrates active developer engagement and can turn negative experiences around. For negative reviews, a prompt, empathetic response that acknowledges the issue and offers a solution can often result in the user updating their review to a more positive rating.

Key Insight: *The recency of reviews matters significantly in ASO. App stores typically give more weight to recent reviews in both ranking algorithms and user-facing displays. Maintaining a steady flow of fresh, positive reviews is more valuable than having a large volume of older reviews.*

Leveraging Reviews for ASO and Product Development

Reviews provide dual value—they influence your app's discoverability and conversion rate while also offering insights for product improvement:

1. **Keyword mining**: User reviews often contain natural language descriptions of your app's benefits or use cases that can inform your keyword strategy. How users describe your app in their own words may reveal valuable search terms you hadn't considered.
2. **Feature prioritization**: Review analysis can help identify which features users value most and which pain points require urgent attention, guiding your development roadmap.
3. **Competitive intelligence**: Analyzing reviews of competing apps can reveal unmet needs or common complaints that represent opportunities for your app to differentiate.

Expert Perspective: The Feedback Loop

"Reviews should be viewed as the beginning of a conversation, not the end. Each review—positive or negative—provides an opportunity to engage with users and demonstrate your commitment to their experience. We've found that developers who respond to at least 40% of their reviews see, on average, a 0.7-star rating improvement over time. This improvement occurs not just because negative reviewers update their ratings, but because the visible developer engagement encourages more positive reviews from satisfied users who might otherwise remain silent." — Rafael Jimenez, User Feedback Analyst

Review Analysis Frameworks

Systematically analyzing reviews can uncover patterns and insights that might be missed through casual observation:

1. **Sentiment analysis**: Categorize reviews based on overall sentiment (positive, neutral, negative) and track trends over time, particularly following updates.
2. **Feature-specific feedback**: Tag reviews based on which features they mention to identify which aspects of your app generate the most positive and negative feedback.
3. **User segment analysis**: Analyze whether different user segments (e.g., new vs. long-term users, or users from different demographics) have systematically different experiences with your app.
4. **Competitor comparison**: Compare the distribution and content of your reviews against competitors to identify relative strengths and weaknesses.

Actions to Take:

- Set up an automated system for review monitoring and developer responses
- Establish guidelines for responding to different types of reviews
- Implement a regular review analysis process that feeds into product development
- Create a mechanism for following up with users who leave negative reviews to see if issues have been resolved

Tools for Monitoring and Improving Store Performance

To master ASO, you need visibility into your performance metrics and competitive landscape. Fortunately, numerous tools can provide these insights and help optimize your strategy.

Essential ASO Tools and Platforms

The ASO tool ecosystem can be categorized into several functional areas:

1. **Keyword research and tracking tools**: These platforms help identify valuable keywords and monitor your ranking position over time.
    - Examples: App Annie, Sensor Tower, Mobile Action, AppTweak
    - Key features: Keyword suggestion, volume and difficulty metrics, competitor keyword analysis
2. **App store intelligence platforms**: Comprehensive solutions that provide broader competitive insights and market analysis.
    - Examples: App Annie, Sensor Tower, AppMagic
    - Key features: Category rankings, download estimates, revenue estimates, emerging app identification
3. **A/B testing tools**: Platforms that enable experimentation with different store listing elements.
    - Examples: Google Play Experiments, StoreMaven, SplitMetrics
    - Key features: Screenshot testing, icon testing, description testing, conversion analysis
4. **Review management platforms**: Tools focused on monitoring, analyzing, and responding to user reviews.
    - Examples: AppFollow, ReviewBot, Appbot
    - Key features: Review alerts, sentiment analysis,

automated responses, competitive review analysis

5. **ASO audit tools**: Solutions that provide comprehensive analysis of your current ASO status and recommend improvements.
   - Examples: ASOdesk, TheTool, AppRadar
   - Key features: Optimization score, keyword gap analysis, listing quality assessment

Key Insight: *While specialized tools provide valuable data, the most effective ASO strategies combine these insights with qualitative understanding of your users. Technical metrics should inform, not replace, a deep understanding of the emotional and practical needs driving app discovery and installation.*

Establishing Key Performance Indicators (KPIs)

Effective ASO requires tracking the right metrics to gauge performance and guide optimization efforts:

1. **Discovery metrics**:
   - Keyword rankings
   - Browse traffic (category positioning)
   - Impression volume
   - Search-to-impression ratio
2. **Conversion metrics**:
   - Impression-to-page view rate
   - Page view-to-install rate (conversion rate)
   - Feature graphic or video engagement rate
3. **Engagement and retention metrics** (indirectly affect ASO):
   - Retention rates (particularly day 1, day 7, day 30)

    - Average session duration
    - Review frequency and sentiment
4. **Competitive positioning metrics**:
    - Category rank
    - Keyword overlap with competitors
    - Relative conversion rate (if available)

Example: ASO Performance Dashboard

A comprehensive ASO dashboard might track the following metrics over time:

Metric	Current	Previous Period	Change	Goal
Avg. Keyword Rank (Top 10)	4.7	5.3	+11.3%	< 5.0
Impressions	45,200	38,700	+16.8%	50,000
Conversion Rate	3.2%	2.8%	+14.3%	3.5%
Rating (30-day avg.)	4.7	4.5	+4.4%	4.8
Category Rank	#12	#17	+29.4%	Top 10

Implementing a Continuous Optimization Cycle

ASO is not a one-time effort but an ongoing process of analysis, hypothesis, testing, and refinement:

1. **Analysis phase**: Review current performance data, identify opportunities and issues
    - Example activities: Keyword performance analysis, conversion funnel examination, competitor listing evaluation
2. **Hypothesis development**: Formulate theories about how specific changes might improve performance

   - Example: "Adding 'sleep timer' to our app title will improve ranking for sleep-related searches"
3. **Testing phase**: Implement changes in a measured, trackable way
   - Example approaches: A/B testing, staged rollouts, controlled time periods
4. **Evaluation**: Assess the impact of changes against baseline performance
   - Key considerations: Allow sufficient time for data collection, watch for external factors affecting results
5. **Refinement**: Apply learnings and begin the cycle again

Actions to Take:

- Evaluate and select appropriate ASO tools based on your specific needs and budget
- Establish a regular cadence for ASO analysis (weekly for major metrics, monthly for comprehensive review)
- Create a testing calendar to systematically optimize different elements of your store listing
- Develop a process for translating ASO insights into product development priorities

The Future of ASO: Emerging Trends and Adaptations

As app stores evolve, ASO strategies must adapt to new technologies, user behaviors, and marketplace dynamics. Several emerging trends are reshaping the future of ASO:

1. **Voice search optimization**: With the rise of voice

assistants, optimizing for natural language queries is becoming increasingly important. This involves focusing on conversational keywords and question-based phrases.

2. **Visual search capabilities**: As image recognition technology advances, app stores may implement visual search features, placing greater emphasis on distinctive visual branding.
3. **Personalization algorithms**: App stores are increasingly personalizing recommendations based on user behavior, making it essential to understand and target specific user segments rather than generic audiences.
4. **In-app events and updating content**: Both Apple and Google have introduced features highlighting in-app events, seasonal content, and regular updates, rewarding apps that maintain fresh content and engagement opportunities.
5. **Privacy-focused marketing**: As privacy regulations tighten and tracking capabilities diminish, ASO becomes even more valuable as a marketing channel that doesn't rely on invasive tracking.

Expert Perspective: The ASO Horizon

"The future of ASO lies in understanding intent rather than just keywords. The most successful apps will be those that deeply understand the problem spaces users are trying to solve and align their entire store presence—from keywords to visuals to feature highlights—around addressing these specific intents. This is where vibe coding principles become particularly powerful, as they naturally focus on the emotional and contextual factors driving user decisions rather than just technical functionality." — Isabella Rodriguez, Future of Apps Researcher

Chapter Summary: Mastering the Art and Science of ASO

App Store Optimization is a multifaceted discipline that combines technical understanding of store algorithms with creative presentation and user psychology. For vibe coders, ASO represents a natural extension of your human-centered development approach—connecting your intuitive understanding of user needs with the practical requirements of app store visibility.

Key takeaways from this chapter include:

- **Keywords are the foundation** of discoverability, requiring research into user search behavior and strategic placement throughout your store listing
- **Visual assets drive conversion**, with screenshots and videos that tell a compelling story about your app's benefits outperforming purely feature-focused presentations
- **User reviews serve dual purposes** as both social proof for potential users and valuable feedback for continuous improvement
- **ASO tools provide essential insights**, but must be combined with qualitative understanding of your users' needs and behaviors
- **Continuous optimization** through systematic testing and refinement is essential for long-term ASO success

The most successful app creators view ASO not as a marketing afterthought but as an integral part of the product development cycle—a continuous conversation with users that informs both how the app is presented and how it evolves over time.

Key Insights Box

The ASO Triangle: Balancing Discoverability, Conversion, and Engagement

Effective ASO strategies balance three interconnected elements:

- **Discoverability**: Optimizing for search and browse visibility
- **Conversion**: Creating compelling visual and textual elements that drive installs
- **Engagement**: Delivering on promises to generate positive reviews and ratings

Weakness in any one area undermines the others. Great discoverability with poor conversion wastes potential. High conversion with poor engagement leads to negative reviews and declining performance. The most successful apps maintain harmony across all three elements, creating a self-reinforcing cycle of visibility, adoption, and satisfaction.

Actions to Take

1. **Conduct a comprehensive keyword audit**:
    - List all keywords currently associated with your app
    - Research their search volume and competition metrics
    - Identify gaps and opportunities for

improvement
   - Reorganize your keyword strategy based on findings
2. **Refresh your visual assets**:
   - Create a new set of screenshots focusing on benefits rather than features
   - Develop a short app preview video highlighting your unique selling proposition
   - A/B test different approaches to identify the highest-converting variants
3. **Implement a strategic review management system**:
   - Set up prompts that target satisfied users after positive interactions
   - Create a process for responding to reviews within 24-48 hours
   - Develop templates for common review scenarios to ensure consistent messaging
4. **Establish an ASO performance dashboard**:
   - Select 5-7 key metrics that align with your specific goals
   - Set up regular reporting and review sessions
   - Create a testing schedule for systematically optimizing each element
5. **Competitive analysis exercise**:
   - Identify your top 3-5 competitors
   - Document their keyword strategies, visual approaches, and review profiles
   - Analyze their strengths and weaknesses
   - Identify opportunities to differentiate your app store presence

Chapter 19: Growth Hacking Techniques for Apps

"Growth hacking is about finding the intersection between creativity and analytics - where data-driven experimentation meets imaginative thinking."

Introduction

In today's crowded app marketplace, simply building a great product is no longer enough. Even the most innovative vibe-coded apps need strategic amplification to reach their intended audience and achieve sustainable growth. Growth hacking—the practice of rapid experimentation across marketing channels and product development to identify the most effective ways to grow a business—has become essential for app creators who want to maximize their impact with minimal resources.

This chapter explores ethical, sustainable growth strategies tailored specifically for apps built using vibe coding principles. You'll learn how to design viral mechanics that naturally encourage sharing, create referral systems that reward advocacy, identify cross-promotion opportunities with complementary services, and implement data-driven experimentation frameworks that maximize your return on investment.

Unlike traditional marketing approaches that often require substantial budgets, growth hacking emphasizes creativity, agility, and analytical thinking—qualities that align perfectly with the vibe coding philosophy of intuition balanced with market awareness.

Ethical Growth Strategies for Sustainable Expansion

Balancing Growth with User Experience

The pursuit of growth should never come at the expense of user experience or trust. While aggressive tactics might yield short-term gains, they often lead to higher churn rates and damaged brand reputation in the long run. Ethical growth hacking prioritizes strategies that create genuine value for users while simultaneously expanding your app's reach.

Transparency about how your AI functionality works is crucial for building trust. Be open about how user data is collected, stored, and used, and acknowledge your AI's limitations. Rather than overpromising capabilities, clearly communicate what your app can and cannot do, especially when leveraging AI capabilities that may not be fully understood by users.

Permission-Based Marketing

Always prioritize opt-in approaches over invasive tactics. Instead of buying email lists or mass-messaging contacts, build permission-based marketing systems that respect user choice. When users actively choose to engage with your marketing efforts, they're more likely to become loyal customers and advocates.

Key Insight: *Permission marketing transforms your growth strategy from interruption to invitation. When users actively opt in, they're not just consenting to communication—they're expressing interest in a relationship with your brand.*

Ethical Data Usage

As a vibe coder, you have access to powerful tools for collecting and analyzing user data. Use this capability responsibly by:

1. Being transparent about what data you collect and why
2. Providing clear privacy policies in accessible language
3. Giving users control over their personal information
4. Using anonymized data whenever possible for analytics
5. Storing user data securely and responsibly

Marketing messaging must proactively address how data is safeguarded, making privacy and security features a headline, not fine print. Consider this not just a compliance requirement but a competitive advantage—research shows that transparency builds trust, and trusted brands enjoy higher engagement and retention rates.

Sustainable Growth Models

Rather than pursuing viral spikes that quickly fade, focus on building sustainable growth mechanisms. The flywheel model offers a customer-centric framework that is particularly well-suited for AI products, moving beyond the traditional linear sales funnel to a continuous, self-reinforcing cycle.

This model leverages the momentum of satisfied customers to drive referrals, repeat business, and advocacy. The focus shifts from solely acquiring customers to creating remarkable experiences that keep them engaged and turn them into promoters.

The AI Marketing Flywheel consists of three interconnected phases:

1. **Attract:** Draw potential customers in by offering value and addressing their needs through educational content, SEO, targeted ads, and clear value propositions.
2. **Engage:** Build relationships and demonstrate ongoing value through smooth onboarding, personalized experiences, useful content, community interaction, and proactive support.
3. **Delight:** Exceed expectations to turn customers into happy promoters through excellent product performance, outstanding support, gathering and acting on feedback, loyalty initiatives, and empowering advocacy.

Expert Perspective: The Flywheel Approach

Maya Rodriguez, Growth Strategist:

"The beauty of the flywheel approach for vibe-coded apps is how it aligns with their intrinsic strengths. These apps are built to understand and respond to human emotions and context—exactly what you need for the 'delight' phase of the flywheel. When your app demonstrates emotional intelligence by anticipating needs or solving problems in a uniquely personal way, users are naturally inclined to share that experience. This creates a self-perpetuating cycle where delighted users become your best acquisition channel."

Designing Viral Mechanics and Referral Systems

Understanding Virality in Apps

Virality occurs when your existing users bring in new users through sharing or direct invitations. The viral coefficient (K) measures how many new users each existing user brings to your app. When K exceeds 1, your user base grows exponentially without additional marketing spend.

While pure virality is rare, implementing viral mechanics can significantly reduce your customer acquisition costs and accelerate growth. For vibe-coded apps, virality often stems from creating emotionally resonant experiences that users naturally want to share.

Implementing Viral Loops

A viral loop is the process through which users are exposed to a product, sign up, and then invite others to repeat the cycle. Effective viral loops typically include:

1. **Value delivery:** Users experience your app's core value
2. **Incentive:** They encounter a reason to share (emotional or practical)
3. **Easy sharing mechanism:** The sharing process is frictionless
4. **New user acquisition:** New users join through the shared invitation
5. **Cycle repetition:** The process begins again with new users

When designing these loops, encourage user-generated content (UGC) by providing templates, prompts, or creative tools that make it easy for users to create and share content related to your app. This approach not only drives virality but also enriches your content ecosystem with authentic materials that resonate with potential users.

Ethical Referral Systems

Referral programs encourage existing users to invite new ones by offering incentives like discounts, credits, or premium features through unique referral links or codes. The most effective referral programs reward both the referrer and the new user, creating a win-win dynamic.

When designing your referral program:

- Make sharing extremely easy with pre-written messages and one-click sharing options
- Offer rewards that align with your app's value proposition

- Track referrals accurately and deliver rewards promptly
- Test different incentive structures to find the optimal balance
- Consider time-limited or special bonuses to create urgency

Action to Take: Referral Program Design Workshop

1. **Identify your unique value metrics:** What aspects of your app do users value most? These should inform your reward structure.
2. **Design the invitation flow:** Map the user journey from receiving an invitation to becoming an active user.
3. **Create compelling invitation messaging:** Draft template messages that users can personalize when inviting friends.
4. **Determine reward structure:** Decide what both parties receive and when rewards are delivered.
5. **Build tracking mechanisms:** Ensure your system can accurately attribute new users to their referrers.
6. **Implement fraud prevention:** Create safeguards against gaming the system.

Case Study: Dropbox's Referral Success

Dropbox's referral program is often cited as one of the most successful growth hacks in tech history. By offering free storage space to both the referrer and the new user, they created a compelling reason to share. This simple mechanic helped Dropbox grow from 100,000 to 4 million users in just 15 months, with a 60% increase in sign-ups.

The key lesson: The incentive matched perfectly with the product's value proposition, creating a natural desire to share rather than feeling like a marketing ploy.

Cross-Promotion Opportunities with Complementary Apps

Identifying Strategic Partnerships

Cross-promotion with complementary apps can be a powerful growth strategy. Look for opportunities with apps that share your target audience but aren't direct competitors. These partnerships can take many forms, from simple shout-outs to deep integrations that enhance both products.

When evaluating potential partners:

1. **Audience alignment:** Do they reach the same user demographic from a different angle?
2. **Value proposition compatibility:** Does their solution complement yours?
3. **Brand compatibility:** Do your brand values and voice align?
4. **Mutual benefit potential:** Can both parties gain meaningful value?
5. **Integration possibilities:** Are there technical ways to connect your services?

Types of Cross-Promotion

Depending on your relationship and resources, consider these cross-promotion approaches:

Content Collaborations

Create joint content such as webinars, blog posts, or guides that showcase how your products work together to solve user problems.

Bundle Offerings

Offer special packages that include complementary services at a discounted rate compared to purchasing separately.

In-App Recommendations

Display recommendations for partner apps at contextually relevant moments within your user journey.

Shared Campaigns

Pool marketing resources to reach a broader audience through joint advertising, email campaigns, or events.

API Integrations

Build technical connections between your apps to enhance functionality and create a more seamless user experience.

Key Insight: *The most successful cross-promotions go beyond mere marketing to create genuine added value for users. Look for integration opportunities that make both products better when used together.*

Implementing Effective Co-Marketing

When executing co-marketing initiatives, clearly define the goals, responsibilities, and key performance indicators (KPIs) for each partner. Create a detailed timeline and communication plan to ensure alignment throughout the campaign.

To maximize effectiveness:

- Start with smaller initiatives to build trust before pursuing deeper integrations
- Create custom landing pages for tracking cross-promotion performance
- Share data and insights transparently with your partner
- Celebrate and publicize mutual successes
- Continuously optimize based on performance metrics

Data-Driven Experimentation for Maximum ROI

The Experimentation Mindset

Growth hacking thrives on rapid experimentation—testing hypotheses, measuring results, learning from failures, and scaling successes. Adopting a systematic approach to experimentation can significantly improve your ROI by focusing resources on strategies with proven effectiveness.

For vibe-coded apps, this experimental approach aligns perfectly with the iterative nature of AI development. Just as you refine your AI models based on data, you can refine your growth strategies through structured testing.

Building Your Experimentation Framework

A robust experimentation framework includes:

1. **Hypothesis generation:** Formulate clear, testable assumptions based on user behavior data and market research

2. **Prioritization methodology:** Determine which experiments to run first based on potential impact, confidence, and resource requirements
3. **Testing protocols:** Define how experiments will be conducted, including sample sizes, timeframes, and success metrics
4. **Analysis processes:** Establish how results will be measured and what constitutes statistical significance
5. **Implementation pathway:** Create a clear process for scaling successful experiments

Action to Take: Growth Experiment Design Template

For each growth experiment, document:

- **Hypothesis:** What specific outcome do you expect from this change?
- **Rationale:** Why do you believe this will work?
- **Success Metrics:** How will you measure impact?
- **Minimum Viable Test:** What's the smallest test that will yield valid results?
- **Required Resources:** What people, time, and tools are needed?
- **Potential Risks:** What could go wrong and how will you mitigate it?
- **Timeline:** When will you start, analyze, and make decisions?

A/B Testing Fundamentals

A/B testing (or split testing) involves comparing two versions of a web page, app feature, or marketing message to determine which performs better. This approach is invaluable for optimizing everything from UI elements to pricing strategies.

When conducting A/B tests:

- Test one variable at a time for clear cause-and-effect relationships
- Ensure your sample size is large enough for statistical significance
- Run tests long enough to account for temporal variations
- Segment results to identify if certain user groups respond differently
- Document all learnings, even from unsuccessful tests

Key Insight: *Failed experiments are not failures if they generate learnings. Document insights from unsuccessful tests as carefully as successful ones—they often reveal critical information about user preferences and behaviors.*

Analytics for Growth

Effective growth hacking requires continuous monitoring of key metrics to identify opportunities and track the impact of your experiments. For vibe-coded apps, consider tracking:

- **Acquisition metrics:** Install rate, cost per acquisition, attribution by channel
- **Activation metrics:** Completion of key onboarding steps, time to value
- **Retention metrics:** Day 1/7/30 retention, churn rate, reengagement rate
- **Revenue metrics:** Conversion rate, average revenue per user, lifetime value

- **Referral metrics:** Viral coefficient, referral completion rate, sharing rate

Modern analytics tools can help you segment users based on behaviors, demographics, and other factors, allowing for more targeted growth strategies. AI itself can be leveraged for more sophisticated analysis, identifying patterns and opportunities that might not be immediately apparent through manual review.

Optimizing the Onboarding Experience

The onboarding process is critical for app success, directly influencing whether new users will become active, engaged customers. Optimizing this experience through continuous experimentation can dramatically improve your activation rates.

Elements to test include:

- **Tutorial formats:** Interactive vs. passive, comprehensive vs. progressive
- **First-run experience:** What users see immediately after installation
- **Permission requests:** Timing and presentation of access requests
- **Value demonstration:** How quickly users experience your app's core benefit
- **Friction reduction:** Simplifying forms, reducing steps, streamlining authentication

Expert Perspective: Onboarding Optimization

Carlos Mendez, UX Specialist:

"When optimizing onboarding for vibe-coded apps, remember that you're not just teaching functionality—you're establishing an emotional connection. Each step should reinforce the 'vibe' you want users to experience. I recommend creating an onboarding experience that adapts to different user behaviors in real-time. For example, if a user skips tutorial screens quickly, offer a more condensed version. If they linger on certain features, provide more depth there. This personalized approach dramatically improves completion rates and sets the stage for deeper engagement."

Leveraging Network Effects for Exponential Growth

Understanding Network Effects

Network effects occur when a product or service becomes more valuable to its users as more people use it. This can create powerful, defensible moats and drive exponential growth. While not all apps can achieve strong network effects, many can incorporate elements that benefit from increased usage.

Different types of network effects include:

- **Direct effects:** The value increases with more users of the same type (e.g., social networks)
- **Indirect or cross-side effects:** Value increases as complementary user groups grow (e.g., marketplaces connecting buyers and sellers)
- **Data effects:** The product improves as it collects more user data (particularly relevant for AI-driven apps)

Building Network Effects into Your App

To cultivate network effects:

1. **Reach critical mass quickly:** Network effects only activate once a sufficient number of users join. Initial strategies often focus on rapid user acquisition, sometimes by subsidizing one side of a two-sided market.
2. **Incentivize value-adding contributions:** Reward users for actions that enhance the network's value for everyone. This could be writing reviews, creating content, contributing data, or listing items/services.
3. **Focus on density:** For businesses with geographically constrained network effects, concentrate efforts on achieving high user density in specific markets before expanding.
4. **Foster community engagement:** A strong community increases user stickiness and encourages the interactions that fuel network effects.

Action to Take: Network Effect Analysis

1. **Identify potential network effects:** What aspects of your app become more valuable as your user base grows?
2. **Map the value exchanges:** How do different user segments create value for each other?
3. **Determine critical mass thresholds:** What level of adoption is needed for network effects to become meaningful?
4. **Design growth tactics:** What specific features or incentives will accelerate network effects?

Data-Driven Decision Making for Growth Optimization

Moving Beyond Intuition

While vibe coding embraces intuition in the development process, growth optimization requires balancing creative insights with rigorous data analysis. By leveraging AI tools for market research and validation, you can make more informed decisions about where to focus your growth efforts.

These tools can analyze vast datasets (social media trends, search data, customer reviews, support tickets) to identify unmet needs and market demand, perform competitor analysis, conduct sentiment analysis on customer feedback, detect emerging market trends, and segment markets based on complex demographic, behavioral, and psychographic data.

Growth Attribution Models

To optimize your marketing mix, implement attribution modeling to understand which channels and touchpoints contribute most to user acquisition and conversion. Common models include:

- **First-touch attribution:** Credits the first channel a user interacted with
- **Last-touch attribution:** Credits the final touchpoint before conversion
- **Linear attribution:** Distributes credit equally across all touchpoints
- **Time-decay attribution:** Gives more credit to touchpoints closer to conversion
- **Algorithmic attribution:** Uses machine learning to assign weighted credit

The right model depends on your app's specific user journey and sales cycle. Many businesses use multiple models to gain different perspectives on their acquisition funnel.

Cohort Analysis for Growth Insights

Cohort analysis—grouping users based on shared characteristics or experiences within a defined timeframe—provides deeper insights than aggregate metrics alone. By analyzing how different cohorts behave over time, you can:

- Identify which user segments have the highest retention and lifetime value
- Determine which acquisition channels bring the most valuable users
- Measure the impact of product changes on user behavior over time
- Detect emerging trends or issues that might be masked in overall metrics

Key Insight: *Cohort analysis often reveals that not all users are created equal. Sometimes, a smaller number of high-quality users from a specific channel delivers more value than a larger number of users from another source.*

Sustainable Growth Strategies for the Long Term

Building a Growth System

Rather than pursuing one-off tactics, focus on building systematic approaches to growth that can scale with your business. The flywheel model creates a continuous, self-reinforcing cycle of growth by leveraging the momentum of satisfied customers to drive referrals, repeat business, and advocacy.

A successful growth system includes:

1. **Acquisition channels:** Diversified, measurable sources of new users
2. **Activation processes:** Streamlined onboarding that showcases value quickly
3. **Retention mechanisms:** Features and programs that encourage ongoing usage
4. **Revenue optimization:** Pricing and conversion pathways that maximize value
5. **Referral programs:** Structured systems for turning users into advocates

Content as a Growth Engine

Educational content marketing is particularly effective for AI-powered apps, as it helps bridge knowledge gaps and build trust. Create valuable blog posts, whitepapers, e-books, guides, webinars, or workshops that educate your target audience about relevant AI concepts, the problems your product solves, and the potential benefits.

Content serves multiple growth functions:

- Improves discovery through search engine optimization
- Builds credibility and establishes thought leadership
- Educates users about problems they might not know they have
- Creates shareable assets that expand your reach
- Nurtures leads through the decision-making process

Action to Take: Content Strategy Blueprint

1. **Audience research:** Identify your users' key questions, challenges, and information needs
2. **Content pillars:** Define 3-5 main topic areas that align with your expertise and user interests
3. **Content mapping:** Plan specific content pieces for each stage of the user journey
4. **Format selection:** Choose the best formats for each piece based on complexity and user preferences
5. **Distribution plan:** Determine how each piece will reach its intended audience
6. **Measurement framework:** Define how you'll track content performance and ROI

Community-Driven Growth

Creating a dedicated community around your app can provide significant benefits, especially for products involving novel or complex technologies like AI. Communities offer a space for users to connect, share resources, provide peer-to-peer support, offer valuable feedback, and network with others in the field.

To foster a strong community:

1. **Define your community's purpose:** Clarify whether it's primarily for technical support, sharing use cases, gathering product feedback, fostering co-creation, or building brand advocacy
2. **Choose the right platforms:** Select platforms based on your community's purpose and audience preferences
3. **Create valuable content:** Regularly share tutorials, best practice guides, webinars, or workshops

4. **Encourage interaction:** Use polls, surveys, AMAs, Q&A forums, and other interactive elements
5. **Showcase user successes:** Highlight content created by users, such as successful use cases or helpful tips

Expert Perspective: Community Building

Priya Sharma, Community Strategist:

"For vibe-coded apps, community building is not just a growth tactic—it's an extension of your product's core value. These apps are designed to understand and respond to human emotions and context, so your community should reflect that same sensibility. Create spaces where users can share not just how they use your product technically, but how it makes them feel and the impact it has on their lives or work. This emotional layer of community engagement creates stronger bonds and more passionate advocates than technical discussions alone."

Chapter Summary

Growth hacking for vibe-coded apps combines data-driven experimentation with creative strategies to achieve sustainable expansion. By implementing ethical growth practices, designing viral mechanics and referral systems, pursuing strategic cross-promotions, and leveraging data for optimization, you can amplify your app's reach and impact without compromising user trust or experience quality.

Remember that successful growth is rarely about finding a single "silver bullet" tactic. Instead, it comes from building systematic approaches to acquisition, activation, retention, revenue, and referral—all working together to create a self-reinforcing growth engine.

The most effective growth strategies for vibe-coded apps align with their core philosophy: they combine intuitive understanding of human needs and emotions with analytical rigor and market awareness. By balancing these elements, you can create growth systems that not only expand your user base but also enhance the value and experience you deliver to each user.

Key Takeaways

- Ethical growth strategies focus on creating genuine value while expanding reach, prioritizing transparency and user consent
- The flywheel model creates a continuous growth cycle where delighted customers become your best acquisition channel
- Effective viral mechanics and referral programs make sharing frictionless and rewarding for both existing and

new users
- Strategic partnerships with complementary apps can create win-win growth opportunities
- Data-driven experimentation allows you to optimize every aspect of your growth funnel
- Network effects, where user value increases with adoption, can create powerful, defensible growth advantages
- Community building creates deeper engagement and cultivates passionate advocates

In the next chapter, we'll explore strategies for building a strong, engaged community around your app—transforming users into passionate advocates and creating a sustainable ecosystem for long-term success.

Chapter 20: Building a Community Around Your App

"The most successful apps don't just have users—they have advocates who feel a sense of belonging and ownership in the product's journey."

Chapter Overview

In the vibe coding ecosystem, where intuition and user connection take precedence over technical complexity, building a thriving community around your app isn't just a marketing strategy—it's an essential component of your product's evolution and longevity. This chapter explores how to transform casual users into passionate advocates, create meaningful spaces for connection, implement community-driven development practices, and learn from successful case studies of apps that have mastered the art of community building.

Transforming Users into Passionate Advocates

The Advocacy Pyramid

Building a community begins with understanding the journey from casual user to passionate advocate. Think of this progression as a pyramid:

/\

/ \

/ \

/ADVOC-\

/ ATES \

/——————\

/CONTRIBUTORS\

/————————\

/ ENGAGERS \

/————————————\

/ USERS \

/——————————————\

USERS form the foundation—individuals who use your app to solve a problem.

ENGAGERS interact with your content, provide feedback, and participate in discussions.

CONTRIBUTORS actively help others, suggest improvements, and create valuable content.

ADVOCATES promote your app externally, bring in new users, and defend your brand.

The Advocacy Flywheel: Moving Users Up the Pyramid

To transform casual users into advocates, implement what I call the "Advocacy Flywheel"—a continuous process that progressively deepens user engagement:

1. **Value Delivery**: Solve a meaningful problem that affects your users' lives.
2. **Engagement**: Create touchpoints that invite interaction.
3. **Recognition**: Acknowledge contributions and participation.
4. **Empowerment**: Give users tools and permissions to extend the app.
5. **Belonging**: Foster a sense of shared identity and purpose.

This flywheel isn't just theoretical—it's been validated by numerous app communities. The key insight is that passionate advocates rarely emerge spontaneously; they develop through deliberate cultivation and meaningful interactions with both your product and community.

KEY INSIGHT: The journey from user to advocate requires deliberate touchpoints that progressively deepen emotional investment in your app's success.

Actions to Take:

- Identify the current distribution of your users across the advocacy pyramid
- Map out specific actions users can take to move from one level to the next
- Create recognition systems that celebrate user progression

Creating Spaces for Users to Connect and Share

Platform Selection: Where Your Community Lives

The environment where your community gathers significantly impacts its culture and engagement. Different platforms serve different community needs:

Platform Type	Best For	Examples	Considerations
Discussion Forums	Organized, topic-focused conversations	Discourse, Reddit, Self-hosted forums	Higher setup cost but greater control
Real-time Messaging	Immediate help, casual conversation	Discord, Slack	More engagement but conversations may get lost
Social Media Groups	Broad reach, easy entry	Facebook Groups, LinkedIn Groups	Less control, but potentially wider audience
In-app Communities	Seamless integration with product	Built-in forums, activity feeds	Development cost but highest retention

When selecting a platform, consider your community's purpose. Is it primarily for technical support, sharing use cases, gathering product feedback, fostering co-creation, or building brand advocacy? Aligning the platform with your goals is essential.

Building Momentum Through Content

Content is the fuel that drives community engagement. Strategic content creation helps maintain an active, vibrant community:

Educational content that informs, entertains, and inspires forms the backbone of any successful online community. Mix content types and ensure it addresses your audience's needs while encouraging interaction. For vibe-coded applications, this could mean sharing your development journey, demonstrating use cases, or offering tips for getting the most from the app.

Content Strategy Framework:

1. **Foundational Content**: Core tutorials, FAQs, and guidelines
2. **Engagement Content**: Questions, polls, challenges
3. **Showcase Content**: User spotlights, success stories
4. **Educational Content**: Advanced techniques, industry insights
5. **Behind-the-scenes**: Development updates, roadmap discussions

EXPERT PERSPECTIVE: The Community Manager

"The most successful app communities I've seen don't talk about features—they talk about outcomes. They celebrate what users accomplish with the app, not just what the app can do. This subtle shift transforms the community from a support forum into a movement."

—Jamie Rodriguez, Community Strategy Consultant

Designing for Interaction

The architecture of your community space should facilitate different types of user interaction:

Foster authentic engagement by responding promptly to comments and messages. Show appreciation for community members' contributions and encourage them to share their experiences. Consider hosting online Q&A sessions or live chats to build deeper connections.

Actions to Take:

- Create dedicated spaces for different interaction types

(help, showcase, ideation)
- Establish clear community guidelines that promote respectful, constructive conversation
- Implement features that highlight active contributors and valuable content
- Schedule regular live events to bring the community together

Community-Driven Development and Feature Requests

The Feedback Ecosystem

Gathering and implementing feedback is crucial for continuous improvement of your app. Even basic prototypes created through "vibe coding" can generate valuable feedback on core functionality and user flow. Share these early prototypes with potential users and ask specific questions about their understanding and ease of use.

Creating a healthy feedback ecosystem involves multiple channels and approaches:

1. **In-app Feedback**: Contextual feedback tools where users encounter issues
2. **Community Forums**: Dedicated feature request and discussion threads
3. **User Research**: Scheduled interviews and usability testing
4. **Data Analysis**: Understanding usage patterns to identify improvement areas
5. **Sentiment Monitoring**: Tracking community sentiment across channels

The Feature Request Funnel

Effectively managing community input requires a structured approach to feature suggestions:

COLLECTION → VALIDATION → PRIORITIZATION → DEVELOPMENT → RELEASE → CELEBRATION

Collection: Gather ideas from multiple channels into a central repository.

Validation: Test assumptions with broader community input and data.

Utilize social feeds on platforms like Disco that allow you to post questions, polls, or discussion topics to stimulate conversations and gather qualitative feedback. Conduct surveys and polls to directly ask your community members for their opinions and preferences.

Prioritization: Evaluate requests against strategic goals and resources.

Track member interactions, content preferences, and activity levels using analytics tools to understand what resonates with your audience. Collect feedback through multiple channels including surveys, reviews, direct communication, and social media interactions to gather a wide range of insights.

Development: Build features with continued community involvement.

Release: Launch with clear communication about what changed and why.

Celebration: Recognize the community's role in the improvement.

KEY INSIGHT: Community-driven development isn't just about collecting feature requests—it's about creating a transparent process where users can see how their input shapes the product's evolution.

Balancing Community Input with Product Vision

While community input is valuable, maintaining a clear product direction is essential:

Actively engage with the community and show that you are listening to their feedback. Use the insights gained to adjust your messaging, offerings, and marketing tactics. The rapid prototyping capabilities of "vibe coding" can facilitate quick iterations based on feedback.

The 80/20 Framework for Community Input:

- 80% of development focuses on your product roadmap
- 20% addresses community-requested enhancements
- 100% of the process remains transparent to users

Actions to Take:

- Create a visible feature request area with voting capabilities
- Establish and share criteria for how features are evaluated and prioritized
- Regularly communicate roadmap updates and how community input shaped decisions
- Implement a "Feature Champion" program where users can advocate for specific improvements

Case Study: Apps with Thriving, Supportive Communities

Notion: Building a Community of Creators

Background: Notion began as a simple note-taking app but evolved into a powerful productivity platform largely driven by its community.

Key Community Strategies:

1. **Template Gallery**: Created a space for users to share custom templates, driving both practical value and community engagement.
2. **Ambassador Program**: Identified and empowered community leaders with special recognition and early access.
3. **Regional Communities**: Supported user-led communities in different regions and languages.
4. **Education Focus**: Provided extensive learning resources, fostering mastery that turned users into advocates.

Results: Notion's community-led growth strategy resulted in over 30 million users, with significant portions coming from organic referrals and user advocacy.

EXPERT PERSPECTIVE: The Growth Specialist

"What makes Notion's community exceptional isn't just its size but its creative energy. They've created an ecosystem where users constantly inspire each other with new ways to use the product. This creates a vibrant, self-sustaining engine for both acquisition and retention."

— *Sophia Lin, Product Growth Strategist*

Figma: Community as Competitive Advantage

Background: Figma disrupted the design tool market not just with its product but with its community strategy.

Key Community Strategies:

1. **Community File System**: Allowed users to publish and share their design work directly within the platform.
2. **FigJam**: Created collaborative features specifically designed to bring teams together.
3. **Plugin Ecosystem**: Empowered developers to extend the platform's functionality.
4. **Events & Challenges**: Organized regular design challenges and community meetups.

Results: Figma built such a strong community that Adobe ultimately acquired the company for $20 billion, recognizing that the community represented an insurmountable competitive advantage.

Lessons from Successful App Communities

Across successful app communities, several patterns emerge:

1. **Value Before Community**: Strong communities form around products that provide exceptional value first.
2. **Official + Unofficial Spaces**: Successful communities often have both company-managed platforms and user-created spaces.
3. **Recognition Systems**: Top communities have formal ways to recognize and elevate their most engaged

members.

Cultivate brand advocates by identifying and nurturing your most loyal and engaged members. Provide them with additional perks and involve them in product development. Foster a positive online community atmosphere by setting clear guidelines, encouraging participation, acknowledging contributions, and addressing conflicts fairly.

1. **Contribution Ladders**: They create clear paths for members to take on increasing responsibility.
2. **Content + Code**: The most engaged communities combine discussion with tangible resource-sharing (templates, code, designs).

Actions to Take:

- Identify the unique value your app provides that could form the foundation for community
- Create opportunities for users to showcase their expertise and creativity
- Establish a recognition system that incentivizes positive community contributions
- Build pathways for users to take on increasing community leadership roles

Implementing Your Community Strategy

The Community Roadmap

Building a thriving community requires a strategic approach with clear milestones:

Phase 1: Foundation (Months 0-3)

- Select and set up your community platform
- Create essential guidelines and foundational content
- Identify and recruit potential community champions
- Establish baseline metrics for engagement

Phase 2: Growth (Months 3-6)

- Implement regular content and engagement calendar
- Launch initial recognition programs
- Create structured feedback channels
- Begin community-driven feature discussions

Phase 3: Maturity (Months 6-12)

- Develop formalized advocacy programs
- Implement advanced recognition systems
- Launch community-led initiatives
- Establish community-driven development processes

Leveraging social proof for pre-launch momentum is essential. Highlight user-generated content by sharing positive feedback, testimonials, and stories from early users as powerful social proof. Showcase community engagement through high levels of activity and positive interactions within your community to demonstrate that others are finding value in your concept.

Measuring Community Health

A thriving community requires regular monitoring across multiple dimensions:

Metric	What It Measures	Target
Growth Rate	New members per month	10-20% monthly (early stage)
Engagement Rate	% of members who post/ interact monthly	>20% is excellent
Response Time	How quickly questions receive answers	<2 hours during business hours
Retention	% of members who return month-over-month	>70% indicates high value
Contribution Ratio	% of content from community vs. company	>50% indicates self-sustainability
Sentiment Score	Positive vs. negative interactions	>4:1 positive to negative ratio

KEY INSIGHT: The most important community metrics aren't about size but about health—engagement, positivity, and value creation are stronger indicators of success than member counts.

Actions to Take:

- Establish baseline metrics for your community across multiple dimensions
- Create a community health dashboard to track progress over time
- Set specific targets for improvement in each metric
- Regularly review metrics with your team and adjust strategy accordingly

Chapter Summary

Building a thriving community around your app isn't just about creating a space for users to talk—it's about strategically nurturing relationships that transform users into advocates who feel personally invested in your app's success. This chapter explored how to:

- Transform users into passionate advocates through the progressive steps of the advocacy pyramid
- Select the right platforms and design spaces that foster meaningful connection among users
- Implement systems for gathering, evaluating, and acting on community feedback
- Learn from successful app communities that have mastered the art of community-building

A strong community creates tremendous business value, driving word-of-mouth growth, providing actionable feedback, enhancing retention, and even creating a competitive moat that's difficult for competitors to overcome. More importantly, a vibrant community transforms what might otherwise be just another app into a meaningful movement that users feel proud to be part of.

Remember that community-building is a long-term investment that requires consistent attention and nurturing. The relationships and trust you build with your users today will determine the strength and resilience of your app's future.

Key Takeaways:

- Communities form around value first—ensure your app solves real problems exceptionally well

- User progression from casual user to advocate requires deliberate touchpoints and recognition
- Effective feedback systems balance community input with a clear product vision
- Successful communities have multiple spaces for different types of engagement
- Metrics should focus on community health, not just size

By following the frameworks, strategies, and examples in this chapter, you're well-positioned to build a community that not only supports your app's growth but becomes one of its most valuable assets.

Chapter 21: App Monetization Strategies That Work

"Products that create value and offer that value back the right way build lasting, meaningful relationships with users."

Introduction

In the world of vibe coding, creating an app is just the beginning of your journey. The true challenge lies in transforming your creation into a sustainable business. While your focus has been on building an app that connects deeply with users through intuitive design and powerful AI capabilities, monetization is what will fuel its continued development and your entrepreneurial goals.

This chapter explores proven monetization strategies that balance revenue generation with user experience. We'll examine how to select the right business model for your specific app type, understand the psychology behind pricing decisions, optimize subscription and in-app purchase offerings, and implement advertising in ways that complement rather than detract from your carefully crafted user experience.

By the end of this chapter, you'll have a comprehensive understanding of how to monetize your app effectively, setting the stage for sustainable growth and long-term success.

Choosing the Right Business Model for Your App Type

The foundation of successful app monetization begins with selecting the business model that aligns with your app's purpose, user expectations, and market realities. Different app categories naturally lend themselves to different monetization approaches.

Understanding the Spectrum of Monetization Models

Monetization models exist on a spectrum, from direct revenue generation to more indirect approaches:

- **Subscription Tiers**: Charging recurring fees for access to your app or premium features
- **Usage-Based/Consumption Models**: Customers pay based on actual usage
- **Freemium**: Basic version free, premium features paid
- **Token-Based/Prepaid Credits**: Users purchase credits upfront for specific features
- **Outcome-Based Pricing**: Fees tied to measurable business value delivered
- **Hybrid Models**: Combinations of different approaches
- **Enterprise Contracts**: Custom negotiated deals for large clients
- **Advertising**: Revenue from displaying ads within your app

Matching Models to App Categories

Let's explore which monetization strategies work best for different types of apps:

Productivity & Tools Apps

- Best models: Subscription tiers, freemium with premium features
- Why it works: Users understand the value of paying for tools that save time and increase efficiency
- Example: A task management app with a free tier for basic lists and a paid tier for advanced project management features

Entertainment & Games

- Best models: Freemium with in-app purchases, ad-supported with ad-removal option
- Why it works: Low barrier to entry with opportunities for engaged users to enhance experience
- Example: A casual game that's free to play but offers cosmetic upgrades or time-savers as purchases

Content & Media Apps

- Best models: Subscription for premium content, advertising for free tier
- Why it works: Balances access to content with sustainable revenue
- Example: A meditation app with free basic sessions and a subscription for the full library

Social & Community Apps

- Best models: Freemium, advertising, premium features
- Why it works: Growth depends on network effects; monetization comes after achieving scale
- Example: A niche community platform with free access and premium badges or features

B2B & Enterprise Apps

- Best models: Subscription tiers based on features/users, outcome-based pricing
- Why it works: Aligns with business budgeting cycles and demonstrates clear ROI
- Example: A team collaboration tool with pricing tiers

based on number of users and advanced features

<div style="background-color: #f5f5f5; padding: 15px; border-left: 5px solid #4CAF50; margin: 20px 0;"> <strong>Key Insight: The Value-Price Alignment</strong>
 Your monetization strategy should reflect the actual value your app delivers to users. If your app saves businesses $1,000 monthly in productivity gains, a $50 monthly subscription presents clear value. Conversely, a simple utility app might struggle to justify a recurring subscription. The strength of your pricing position directly correlates to the tangible value users receive. </div>

Decision Framework for Selecting Your Model

Consider these factors when choosing your monetization approach:

1. **User Expectations**: What payment models are users in your category already familiar with?
2. **Value Delivery Timing**: Is value delivered immediately or over time?
3. **Usage Patterns**: Do users engage daily or sporadically?
4. **Cost Structure**: What are your fixed vs. variable costs?
5. **Competitive Landscape**: How are similar apps monetizing?
6. **Growth Stage**: Are you prioritizing user acquisition or revenue?

According to the latest research on AI application monetization, 61% of buyers understand that AI capabilities may warrant additional payment due to the associated costs. This recognition provides an opportunity to build pricing models that fairly account for the computational resources required to deliver AI features.

Expert Perspective: Choosing Your Monetization Strategy

Sarah Chen, AI App Monetization Consultant

"The most common mistake I see founders make is copying competitors' pricing without understanding the underlying strategy. Just because the leading app in your space uses subscriptions doesn't automatically make it right for you. Consider your unique value proposition and user journey. If your app delivers immediate, significant value but might not see frequent usage, a one-time purchase or credit-based model could outperform a subscription. Always let your app's core value and usage patterns guide your monetization decisions."

Actions to Take

1. **Map Your User Journey**: Identify exactly where and how your app delivers value to users. Look for natural monetization points where users receive significant benefits.
2. **Competitive Analysis**: Study 3-5 competitors in your space. Document their monetization approaches, pricing points, and what features sit behind paywalls.
3. **Cost Calculation**: Create a spreadsheet that breaks down your costs per user, including AI API calls, server costs, and development expenses.
4. **Model Testing Plan**: Design a simple A/B test to evaluate different monetization approaches with a subset of your users.

Pricing Psychology and Implementation

Once you've selected your monetization model, determining the right pricing strategy involves both art and science. Understanding the psychological factors that influence purchasing decisions will help you optimize your pricing for maximum conversion and revenue.

The Psychology Behind Pricing Decisions

Several psychological principles impact how users perceive and respond to pricing:

Anchoring Effect: The first price point users see becomes their reference point for all other pricing. Use this to your advantage by placing premium options first to make standard offerings appear more reasonable.

Price-Quality Association: Higher prices often signal higher quality. If your app delivers premium features or significant value, pricing too low might actually reduce perceived value.

The Rule of Three: Presenting three pricing tiers (Basic, Popular, Premium) leverages the tendency of people to choose the middle option.

Pain of Paying: Reducing the "pain" associated with payments through timing and presentation can increase conversions. Emphasizing annual billing (pay once, enjoy all year) over monthly charges can leverage this principle.

Loss Aversion: People fear missing out more than they desire gaining something new. Framing features in terms of what users might lose by not upgrading can be powerful.

Implementing Effective Pricing Structures

Pricing implementation requires balancing perceived value with the costs of delivering your app:

Tiered Pricing Design:

- Create clear differentiation between tiers based on features, usage limits, or support levels
- Ensure that each tier delivers appropriate value for its price point
- Name tiers meaningfully (e.g., "Starter," "Professional," "Enterprise") to signal intended users

Price Point Optimization:

- Research price sensitivity in your market through surveys or controlled tests
- Consider psychological pricing (e.g., $9.99 instead of $10)
- Adjust prices based on geographic markets and local purchasing power

Communicating Value:

- Clearly articulate what users gain at each price point
- Focus on benefits rather than features
- Use comparison tables to highlight differences between tiers

<div style="background-color: #f0f8ff; padding: 15px; border-left: 5px solid #4682B4; margin: 20px 0;"> <strong>Key Insight: The Power of Free</strong>
 The freemium model has become dominant because it removes the biggest barrier to adoption—cost. A well-designed free tier provides genuine value while strategically limiting features to encourage upgrades. The key is ensuring free users have a positive experience that makes them

curious about premium offerings, not a frustrating one that drives them away. </div>

Pricing Communication and Transparency

How you present your pricing significantly impacts conversion rates:

- **Value-First Approach**: Always communicate the value before revealing the price
- **Transparent Terms**: Clearly state what happens after trial periods or if users exceed usage limits
- **Social Proof**: Include testimonials near pricing information to validate the value
- **ROI Calculators**: For B2B apps, provide tools that help users calculate their return on investment

Actions to Take

1. **Conduct Price Sensitivity Testing**: Use the Van Westendorp Price Sensitivity Meter methodology to find optimal price points. Ask potential users:
   - At what price would you consider the app to be too expensive?
   - At what price would you consider the app to be so inexpensive that you question its quality?
   - At what price would you consider the app to be expensive but still worth considering?
   - At what price would you consider the app to be a bargain?
2. **Create a Value Matrix**: List all your app's features and rate each on a scale of 1-10 for perceived user value. Use this to determine which features should be in free vs. paid

tiers.

3. **Implement A/B Testing**: Test different price points and presentation formats with segments of your user base to optimize conversion.

Optimizing In-App Purchases and Subscription Offers

Once you've established your basic pricing structure, optimizing how you present and manage in-app purchases and subscriptions can significantly impact conversion rates and customer lifetime value.

Designing Valuable Subscription Offerings

Subscriptions have become the dominant monetization model for many successful apps because they provide predictable recurring revenue. Creating a compelling subscription requires:

Clear Value Proposition:

- Articulate exactly what subscribers receive compared to free users
- Focus on ongoing benefits rather than one-time advantages
- Highlight exclusive content or features only available to subscribers

Strategic Tier Design:

- Create meaningful differentiation between subscription tiers
- Consider both feature-based and usage-based limitations

- Design your tiers to grow with users as their needs evolve

Flexible Subscription Options:

- Offer both monthly and annual billing (with a discount for annual)
- Consider family or team plans for appropriate apps
- Provide enterprise options with custom features for larger organizations

Optimizing the Subscription Purchase Flow

The subscription purchase experience can make or break your conversion rates:

Streamlined Process:

- Minimize steps between decision and completion
- Remove unnecessary form fields and decision points
- Provide visual progress indicators for multi-step processes

Effective Free Trials:

- Determine optimal trial length for your specific app
- Decide between requiring payment information upfront or at trial end
- Send strategic communications during the trial highlighting value

Transparent Terms:

- Clearly communicate billing frequency and amounts
- Make cancellation instructions easily accessible
- Explain what happens to user data and access after

cancellation

<div style="background-color: #FFF8DC; padding: 15px; border-left: 5px solid #DAA520; margin: 20px 0;"> <strong>Key Insight: The Free-to-Paid Conversion Bridge</strong>
 The most critical moment in your monetization strategy is the transition from free to paid user. This requires a carefully designed experience that demonstrates clear additional value. The best practices involve creating moments of "positive friction"—points where users naturally encounter limitations of the free tier while performing tasks they care about, rather than arbitrary blockers that feel punitive. </div>

Managing and Reducing Subscription Churn

Acquiring subscribers is only half the battle; retaining them is equally crucial for sustainable revenue:

Proactive Engagement:

- Implement usage monitoring to identify at-risk subscribers
- Create re-engagement campaigns for inactive subscribers
- Continuously add value through new features and content

Strategic Winback Campaigns:

- Develop special offers for recently churned customers
- Create segmented campaigns based on reason for cancellation
- Consider "pause subscription" options instead of full cancellation

Customer Success Initiatives:

- Provide onboarding to ensure users get maximum value
- Create tutorials and resources for advanced features
- Celebrate milestones and demonstrate progress to reinforce value

Optimizing In-App Purchases for Non-Subscription Apps

If your app uses one-time purchases or consumable items rather than subscriptions:

Bundle Psychology:

- Create value-oriented bundles that offer better deals than individual purchases
- Use time-limited bundles to drive urgency and conversion

Contextual Offering:

- Present purchase opportunities at moments of highest relevance
- Avoid interrupting core user flows with purchase prompts

Volume Discounts:

- Implement graduated pricing (e.g., buy more coins at a better per-unit price)
- Create "most popular" indicators to guide purchasing decisions

Expert Perspective: The Subscription Experience

Michael Rodriguez, Subscription Growth Specialist

"The success of your subscription model doesn't just depend on what you're offering but how you're delivering the experience. Too many founders focus exclusively on features when they should be thinking about the ongoing relationship. Successful subscriptions create a cadence of value delivery that makes users feel the service is worth keeping month after month. This might mean regular content drops, feature updates, or even just thoughtful emails highlighting features they haven't discovered yet. Remember that every billing cycle is a moment when users reevaluate their decision to subscribe."

Actions to Take

1. **Map Your Subscription Experience**: Create a timeline of the user experience from free trial through multiple billing cycles, identifying key touchpoints and value delivery moments.
2. **Design Winback Campaigns**: Develop targeted messaging for churned subscribers based on their usage patterns and feedback.
3. **Create a Value Calendar**: Plan feature releases and content updates to ensure regular value delivery to subscribers.
4. **Implement Subscription Analytics**: Set up tracking for key metrics including trial conversion rate, monthly churn, annual churn, and lifetime value.

Ad-Based Models: Maximizing Revenue Without Sacrificing Experience

Advertising remains a viable monetization strategy, especially for apps with large user bases or those where subscriptions might create too much friction. The key is implementing ads in ways that preserve or even enhance the user experience.

Understanding Different Ad Formats and Their Impact

Various ad formats offer different balances of revenue potential and user experience impact:

Banner Ads:

- Low disruption but also lower engagement and revenue
- Best placed at natural breaks in the user experience
- Consider removing for paid users as an incentive

Interstitial Ads:

- Full-screen ads between natural transition points
- Higher revenue but potentially more disruptive
- Should be timed to appear between activities, not during them

Rewarded Video Ads:

- User opts to watch video in exchange for in-app rewards
- Highest user acceptance as they provide clear value exchange
- Strong revenue potential with positive user sentiment

Native Ads:

- Blend with your app's design and content

- Less disruptive than traditional formats
- Require careful implementation to maintain transparency

Implementing User-Friendly Ad Strategies

The most effective ad strategies respect user experience while maximizing revenue:

Frequency Capping:

- Limit how often users see ads to prevent fatigue
- Create escalating frequency based on usage patterns
- Consider different caps for different user segments

Contextual Relevance:

- Work with ad networks that can deliver relevant content
- Implement category filtering to avoid inappropriate ads
- Consider direct partnerships with relevant brands

User Control and Transparency:

- Provide options for users to control their ad experience
- Clearly label advertising content to maintain trust
- Offer paid options to remove ads

<div style="background-color: #E6E6FA; padding: 15px; border-left: 5px solid #9370DB; margin: 20px 0;"> <strong>Key Insight: The Ad Experience Paradox</strong>
 The most effective ad implementations don't maximize impressions—they optimize relevance and timing. Showing fewer, better-targeted ads at appropriate moments can generate more revenue than

bombarding users with frequent, irrelevant advertising that damages retention and engagement. </div>

Balancing Ad Revenue with User Experience

The tension between maximizing short-term ad revenue and preserving long-term user relationships requires careful management:

User Segmentation:

- Create different ad experiences for different user types
- Implement progressive ad experiences based on user engagement
- Consider reducing ad load for your most engaged users

Hybrid Approaches:

- Combine advertising with other monetization models
- Offer subscription options to remove ads
- Use "rewarded" mechanics to give users control

Continuous Testing and Optimization:

- A/B test ad placements, formats, and frequency
- Monitor key metrics beyond just ad revenue (retention, session length)
- Collect and respond to user feedback about the ad experience

Ad Network Selection and Management

Working with the right ad partners is crucial for both revenue and user experience:

Network Evaluation Criteria:

- Fill rates and effective CPM (eCPM) in your category
- Quality of available ads and targeting capabilities
- Analytics and optimization tools provided
- Payment terms and reliability

Direct Deals vs. Programmatic:

- Consider direct partnerships for premium placements
- Use programmatic networks to fill remaining inventory
- Implement a waterfall strategy to maximize yield

Compliance and Privacy:

- Ensure all ad implementations comply with platform guidelines
- Address privacy regulations like GDPR and CCPA
- Provide transparent user controls for ad personalization

Expert Perspective: User-Friendly Advertising

Elena Park, Mobile Ad Monetization Consultant

"The most successful ad monetization strategies I've seen treat advertising as content, not just revenue. This means thinking carefully about the context, timing, and relevance of every ad impression. For example, a casual gaming app that shows a rewarded video ad option when a player fails a level—offering extra lives in exchange for watching—creates a moment where the ad actually enhances the experience rather than interrupting it. This kind of value-exchange advertising consistently outperforms forced advertising both in user satisfaction and, perhaps surprisingly, in revenue generation."

Actions to Take

1. **Create an Ad Placement Map**: Document potential ad placements within your app, rating each on a scale from 1 (highly disruptive) to 10 (natural fit).
2. **Set Up Ad Network A/B Testing**: Implement infrastructure to test different ad networks against each other in comparable placements.
3. **Develop an Ad Quality Monitoring System**: Create a process to regularly review the ads appearing in your app for relevance and appropriateness.
4. **Design a Hybrid Model**: Create a plan that combines advertising with optional premium features or subscription options.

Combining Monetization Strategies for Maximum Impact

While we've discussed various monetization models individually, many successful apps leverage combinations of these approaches to create robust revenue streams.

Strategic Hybrid Monetization

Hybrid models can balance predictable revenue with flexibility:

Freemium + Advertising:

- Free tier supported by ads
- Premium tier removes ads and adds features
- Creates multiple revenue streams while maximizing user base

Subscription + In-App Purchases:

- Base subscription provides core premium features
- Additional one-time purchases for special content or upgrades
- Allows for varied spending levels among your user base

Usage-Based + Subscription:

- Base subscription for standard usage
- Additional charges for usage beyond included limits
- Combines predictability with fair pricing for heavy users

Building a Sustainable Monetization Strategy

A comprehensive monetization strategy should consider both short-term revenue and long-term sustainability:

Revenue Diversification:

- Reduce dependency on any single revenue stream
- Create monetization opportunities at different stages of the user journey
- Adapt monetization approaches as your user base evolves

User Lifecycle Planning:

- Map monetization touchpoints across the entire user lifecycle
- Develop different strategies for acquisition, activation, retention, and reactivation
- Create a progression that grows with user engagement

Continuous Optimization:

- Implement analytics to track monetization performance
- Regularly test pricing, packaging, and presentation
- Gather user feedback specifically on monetization experience

<div style="background-color: #F0FFF0; padding: 15px; border-left: 5px solid #2E8B57; margin: 20px 0;"> <strong>Key Insight: The Lifetime Value Focus</strong>
 The most successful monetization strategies optimize for customer lifetime value (LTV) rather than immediate revenue. This means sometimes accepting lower short-term revenue in exchange for higher user satisfaction, longer retention, and ultimately greater lifetime spending. Every monetization decision should be evaluated through this long-term lens. </div>

Future-Proofing Your Monetization Strategy

The app monetization landscape continues to evolve, requiring adaptability:

Market Trend Monitoring:

- Stay informed about changing user expectations
- Watch for new monetization models gaining traction
- Monitor platform policy changes that might affect monetization

Competitive Analysis:

- Regularly review competitors' monetization strategies
- Identify successful innovations you might adapt
- Understand your unique value proposition in the market

Experiment Budget:

- Allocate resources for testing new monetization approaches
- Create a framework for evaluating experimental results
- Be willing to pivot based on clear evidence

Chapter Summary: Key Takeaways

In this chapter, we've explored the critical aspects of app monetization that can transform your vibe-coded creation into a sustainable business:

1. **Business Model Selection**: Choose the monetization approach that aligns with your app category, user expectations, and value delivery pattern. Remember that different types of apps naturally lend themselves to different models.
2. **Pricing Psychology**: Leverage psychological principles like anchoring, price-quality association, and the rule of three to optimize how users perceive and respond to your pricing.
3. **Subscription Optimization**: Design subscription tiers with clear value differentiation, optimize the purchase flow, and implement strategies to reduce churn and maximize lifetime value.
4. **User-Friendly Advertising**: If using an ad-based model, implement ads in ways that respect the user experience through careful placement, frequency management, and relevant content.
5. **Hybrid Strategies**: Consider combining multiple monetization approaches to create diversified revenue streams that capture value at different points in the user journey.

Successful monetization isn't just about extracting maximum revenue—it's about creating a fair value exchange that satisfies both your business needs and user expectations. When done right, monetization becomes an integral part of the user experience rather than detracting from it.

As you implement your chosen strategies, continuously gather data, test alternatives, and refine your approach based on user feedback and behavior. The most effective monetization strategy is one that evolves alongside your app and user base.

Actions to Take

1. **Monetization Model Assessment**: Evaluate which primary monetization model best fits your app type, user base, and value proposition. Document the pros and cons of at least three different approaches.
2. **Pricing Strategy Development**: Create a complete pricing structure, including tier definitions, price points, and value communication. Prepare A/B tests to optimize your approach.
3. **User Journey Monetization Mapping**: Identify natural points in the user journey where monetization can occur without disrupting the experience. Document potential trigger points for upgrades or purchases.
4. **Analytics Implementation**: Set up comprehensive tracking for key monetization metrics including conversion rates, average revenue per user (ARPU), and customer lifetime value (LTV).
5. **Feedback Loop Creation**: Develop a system to gather user feedback specifically about monetization, including satisfaction with pricing, perceived value, and payment experience.

By approaching monetization with the same care and user focus that guided your app development, you'll create a sustainable business model that supports continued innovation and growth.

Chapter 22: The Subscription Model: Building Recurring Revenue

"Subscription is not just a pricing strategy; it's a relationship strategy that transforms how businesses connect with customers over time."

Introduction

In the evolving landscape of app development, the subscription model has emerged as one of the most powerful and sustainable revenue strategies available to entrepreneurs. Unlike one-time purchases that create sporadic income, subscriptions generate predictable, recurring revenue streams that can fund continuous improvement and provide long-term stability for your business.

For vibe coders—entrepreneurs focused on creating intuitive, user-centric applications—the subscription model aligns perfectly with your philosophy. It shifts focus from acquiring one-time customers to nurturing ongoing relationships, providing value consistently, and evolving your product based on continuous feedback.

This chapter explores how to design, implement, and optimize subscription offerings that resonate with users while building a solid financial foundation for your business. We'll examine strategies for converting free users, reducing churn, maximizing customer lifetime value, and learn from real-world subscription success stories.

Designing Valuable Subscription Offerings

Understanding Subscription Psychology

Before diving into subscription structures, it's essential to understand the psychological factors that make people willing to subscribe:

- **Perceived Value**: Subscribers must believe they're receiving more value than they're paying for each billing period.
- **Pain Avoidance**: Many subscribe to avoid the "pain" of losing access to something they find valuable.
- **Convenience**: Subscriptions eliminate the need to make repeated purchase decisions.
- **Identity**: Some subscriptions become part of a user's identity or routine.

Key Insight: *The best subscription offerings aren't just about features—they're about providing ongoing value that becomes integrated into users' lives and workflows.*

Subscription Models to Consider

Based on your app type and target audience, several subscription approaches might work:

1. Tiered Subscription Levels

Offer multiple subscription tiers with increasing value and price points:

Basic Tier ($X/month): Core functionality

Premium Tier ($Y/month): Core + advanced features

Enterprise Tier ($Z/month): All features + dedicated support

This approach lets users self-select their commitment level while creating upgrade paths as their needs grow.

2. Usage-Based Subscriptions

Charge based on consumption metrics relevant to your app:

Tier 1: Up to X API calls/month

Tier 2: Up to Y API calls/month

Tier 3: Up to Z API calls/month

This model works particularly well for AI applications where computing resources scale with usage.

3. Hybrid Models

Combine a base subscription fee with usage-based components:

Base Fee: $X/month for core features

+ $Y per additional user

+ $Z per additional storage unit

Hybrid models can provide predictable base revenue while capturing additional value from power users.

4. Freemium + Premium (Free + Paid Tiers)

Offer a functional free version with clear upgrade paths to paid features:

Free: Basic features with usage limits

Premium ($X/month): Unlimited usage + advanced features

This model helps acquire users at low cost while creating opportunities to convert them to paying customers.

Determining Your Value Metric

A value metric is the unit of value that increases as customers derive more benefit from your product. Identifying the right value metric is crucial for subscription pricing.

Common value metrics include:

- Number of users/seats
- Storage capacity
- Processing power/API calls
- Number of projects/documents
- Access to premium features

Expert Perspective: Value Metrics

"The perfect value metric grows with the value your customer receives. When they get more value, they pay more—and they're happy to do so because the return on investment remains consistent or improves. This creates a win-win where your revenue grows as your customers succeed." — Maya Rodriguez, SaaS Pricing Strategist

Pricing Strategy Considerations

When setting subscription prices:

1. **Research competitors** but don't simply match their prices—understand how your value proposition differs.
2. **Consider cost structure** including server costs, support expenses, and development resources.
3. **Test price sensitivity** through surveys, A/B testing different price points, or direct customer conversations.
4. **Price for perception**, not just profit—extremely low prices might signal low quality, while premium pricing can position your product as high-value.
5. **Plan for scalability** by considering how your pricing will work as users grow their usage.

Actions to Take:

- Map out three potential subscription structures for your app

- Identify your key value metric that scales with customer success
- Survey potential customers about willingness to pay at different price points
- Calculate margins at various subscription levels to ensure profitability

Onboarding Strategies That Convert Free Users

The journey from free to paid user is critical to subscription success. A strategic onboarding process demonstrates value quickly and creates natural conversion paths.

The Value Demonstration Funnel

To convert effectively, create an onboarding flow that:

1. **Shows immediate value** within the first session
2. **Gradually introduces premium features** with clear benefits
3. **Creates "aha moments"** where users experience the full potential
4. **Gently introduces conversion opportunities** at optimal moments

Onboarding Best Practices

1. Minimize Friction

Make initial signup as simple as possible:

Initial signup requirements:

✓ Email address only

✓ Single-click social login options

✓ Delayed profile completion

Every additional field reduces conversion rates. Collect only what's absolutely necessary.

2. Create Guided Experiences

Instead of overwhelming new users with all features, provide guided paths:

```
function newUserOnboarding() {
welcomeMessage();
identifyUserGoal();
createFirstProject();
demonstrateCoreBenefit();
celebrateFirstWin();
suggestNextAction();
}
```

Design these flows to culminate in a meaningful accomplishment that demonstrates your app's value.

3. Implement Smart Trial Limitations

When offering free trials:

- Provide enough access to demonstrate real value
- Create natural usage ceilings that highlight the need for paid features
- Use countdown messaging to create urgency

- Offer extension options in exchange for completing valuable actions (profile setup, inviting others)

4. Use Behavioral Triggers for Conversion Prompts

Time conversion prompts based on user behavior, not just arbitrary timelines:

```
if (userHasCompletedValueableAction() && hasUsedKeyFeatures() && isActiveUser()) {

showPersonalizedUpgradeOffer();

}
```

Key Insight: *The best time to offer a conversion prompt is immediately after a user has experienced value, not when they've hit a limitation. Upgrade offers feel like opportunities, not penalties.*

Email Sequences That Convert

Design automated email sequences to nurture free users toward conversion:

1. **Welcome Email**: Introduction and quick-start guide
2. **Early Win Email**: Celebration of first accomplishment
3. **Feature Spotlight Emails**: Highlighting key benefits
4. **Social Proof Email**: Showcasing success stories
5. **Upgrade Incentive Email**: Special offer with clear benefits
6. **Last Chance Email**: Final opportunity before trial expiration

Personalize these based on user behavior for maximum impact.

Expert Perspective: Behavioral Conversion

"We've found that behavioral triggers outperform time-based conversion prompts by 3:1. When you align upgrade offers with moments of success, users see the subscription as an investment in continued success rather than an expense." —Jamal Washington, User Conversion Specialist

Creating FOMO (Fear Of Missing Out)

Strategic use of FOMO can boost conversion rates:

- Showcase premium-only features with tasteful "upgrade required" messaging
- Highlight what similar users accomplish with premium access
- Use limited-time promotions to create urgency
- Show usage statistics with projected limitations for free tier users

Actions to Take:

- Create a customer journey map of a free user's first 30 days
- Identify 3-5 key "aha moments" that demonstrate core value
- Design an email sequence specifically for free-to-paid conversion
- Implement behavior-based upgrade prompts at moments of success

Reducing Churn and Increasing Lifetime Value

Acquiring subscribers is just the beginning—keeping them engaged and subscribed is where the true value of the subscription model emerges.

Understanding Churn Metrics

Track these key metrics to understand retention health:

- **Churn Rate**: Percentage of subscribers who cancel in a given period
- **Retention Rate**: Percentage who remain subscribed (inverse of churn)
- **Lifetime Value (LTV)**: Total revenue expected from a subscriber over their lifetime
- **Customer Acquisition Cost (CAC)**: Cost to acquire a new subscriber
- **LTV:CAC Ratio**: Should be at least 3:1 for a healthy subscription business

Identifying Churn Warning Signs

Implement systems to detect potential churners before they cancel:

```
function detectChurnRisk(user) {

let riskScore = 0;

if (loginFrequencyDecreasing()) riskScore += 20;

if (featureUsageDecreasing()) riskScore += 15;

if (supportTicketsIncreasing()) riskScore += 10;

if (unusedPremiumFeatures() > 2) riskScore += 15;

if (paymentFailureHistory()) riskScore += 25;

return riskScore > 30 ? "High Risk" : "Low Risk";
```

}

Key Insight: *Behavioral signals often indicate churn risk long before a customer decides to cancel. Detecting these early warning signs creates opportunities for intervention.*

Proactive Retention Strategies

1. Ongoing Value Demonstration

Regularly remind users of the value they're receiving:

- Send monthly usage summaries highlighting accomplishments
- Calculate time or money saved through app usage
- Showcase new features and improvements
- Provide personalized tips based on usage patterns

2. Engagement Renewal Campaigns

For users showing declining engagement:

- Send re-engagement emails with new use cases
- Offer personalized training or setup assistance
- Provide case studies relevant to their specific situation
- Create "comeback" incentives like feature credits

A Sample Re-engagement Sequence:

Day 1: "We miss you!" email with personalized usage stats

Day 3: "Did you know?" email highlighting underutilized features

Day 5: "Need help?" email offering personal assistance

Day 7: Special offer for annual subscription (discount or bonus feature)

3. Involuntary Churn Prevention

Address payment failures proactively:

- Implement smart retry logic for failed payments
- Send card expiration notifications before they occur
- Provide easy payment update methods
- Offer grace periods before service interruption

4. Exit Surveys and Win-back Campaigns

When customers do cancel:

- Conduct exit surveys to understand reasons
- Create segmented win-back offers based on cancellation reasons
- Implement time-delayed win-back campaigns
- Consider "pause" options instead of full cancellation

Expert Perspective: Retention Psychology

"The psychology of retention is fundamentally different from acquisition. While acquisition is about promise and potential, retention is about proving ongoing value and building habits. The most successful subscription businesses create products that become more valuable to users over time through personalization, accumulated data, or network effects." — Elena Chen, Customer Retention Analyst

Increasing Lifetime Value

Beyond preventing churn, actively work to increase each subscriber's value:

1. Expansion Revenue Opportunities

Create natural upsell paths within your subscription structure:

- Tier upgrades as usage grows
- Add-on features for specific needs
- Team or enterprise expansions from individual accounts
- Premium support or service options

2. Annual Billing Incentives

Shift monthly subscribers to annual plans:

- Offer meaningful discounts (typically 15-20%)
- Provide exclusive features for annual subscribers
- Create limited-time promotions for annual conversion
- Show the convenience and savings of annual billing

3. Community and Ecosystem Building

Create value that extends beyond the core product:

- Exclusive subscriber communities
- Educational resources and events
- Integration with complementary services
- Loyalty programs with increasing benefits

Actions to Take:

- Implement a churn prediction system based on usage patterns
- Create a re-engagement campaign for at-risk subscribers
- Design an annual subscription promotion with meaningful incentives
- Develop a systematic approach to handling payment failures

Case Studies: Successful Subscription Model Implementations

Case Study 1: DesignAI Studio

Background: DesignAI Studio created an AI-powered graphic design platform that automated common design tasks for marketers and content creators. Initially launched with a one-time purchase model, they transitioned to a subscription approach to create sustainable revenue.

Approach: DesignAI implemented a three-tiered subscription model:

1. **Creator** ($15/month): Basic design tools with limited AI-generated assets
2. **Professional** ($35/month): Full design suite with expanded AI capabilities
3. **Team** ($75/month): Multi-user access with collaboration features

They focused their value metric on the number of AI-generated designs per month, with higher tiers offering more generations. Additionally, they implemented:

- A 7-day free trial requiring credit card information
- Guided onboarding showing users how to create their first design in under 3 minutes
- Monthly usage reports highlighting time saved
- Annual billing options with a 20% discount

Results:

- 65% of free trial users converted to paid subscriptions
- Average customer lifetime increased from 4 months to 18 months
- Annual billing adoption reached 40% of subscribers
- Customer lifetime value increased by 350%

Key Lessons:

- The immediate "wow factor" of AI-generated designs created clear value perception
- Usage-based limitations created natural upgrade paths as users engaged more
- Time-saving metrics in monthly reports reinforced subscription value

Case Study 2: TaskFlow

Background: TaskFlow developed a project management platform for small teams. After struggling with a freemium model that attracted many non-paying users, they redesigned their subscription approach.

Approach: Instead of limiting features, TaskFlow implemented a "value-usage" model where:

- Free tier: Limited to 3 projects and 5 team members
- Business tier ($12/user/month): Unlimited projects with advanced features
- Enterprise tier ($25/user/month): Added security, priority support, and custom integrations

They focused on:

- An onboarding process that helped users set up their first

project in the first session
- Milestone celebrations when teams completed projects
- "Collaboration limits approaching" notifications when free teams grew
- Success stories from similarly-sized teams that upgraded

Results:

- Free-to-paid conversion rate increased from 2% to 8%
- Team expansions became their largest growth vector
- Churn rate decreased from 9% to 3.5% monthly
- Customer satisfaction scores improved by 40%

Key Lessons:

- Focusing on team/usage limitations rather than feature limitations created more natural upgrade moments
- Celebrating user successes built positive associations with the product
- Showing similar team success stories reduced friction in the upgrade decision

Case Study 3: AudioMind

Background: AudioMind created an AI-powered meditation and mindfulness app targeting busy professionals. They implemented a subscription model from launch but needed to optimize conversion and retention.

Approach: AudioMind offered:

- A 14-day free trial with full access
- A single Premium tier ($9.99/month) with all features
- A heavily discounted annual option ($59.99/year)

Their strategy focused on:

- A personalized assessment during onboarding to create a custom program
- "Streak" gamification to encourage daily meditation
- Monthly mindfulness reports showing progress and improvements
- Limited-time promotions for annual subscriptions during high-stress seasons

Results:

- 72% of users completed the initial assessment
- Users who completed assessment had 3x higher conversion rate
- 65% of subscribers chose annual billing
- 88% annual renewal rate

Key Lessons:

- Personalization created higher perceived value and switching costs
- Habit formation (daily streaks) directly correlated with retention
- Seasonal promotions aligned with user motivation periods
- Single premium tier simplified decision-making

Actions to Take:

- Identify which aspects of these case studies most closely align with your app
- Implement one key strategy from each case study in your

subscription approach
- Create a system to track which strategies have the greatest impact on conversion and retention
- Develop a continuous optimization process for your subscription model

Conclusion: Building Your Subscription Flywheel

The subscription model thrives when you create a virtuous cycle:

1. **Deliver clear value** that exceeds subscription cost
2. **Continuously improve** based on user feedback and behavior
3. **Reduce friction** in the experience of discovering, using, and paying for your app
4. **Build habits and workflows** that integrate your product into users' lives
5. **Create switching costs** through personalization and accumulated data

Remember that subscription success isn't just about technical features—it's about building relationships and consistently delivering value over time. As a vibe coder, your focus on intuitive, user-centered design puts you in an excellent position to create subscription experiences that users are happy to maintain month after month, year after year.

Chapter Summary:

- Design subscription offerings around clear value metrics that align with user success
- Create onboarding experiences that demonstrate value

quickly and convert free users
- Implement proactive retention strategies to reduce churn and increase lifetime value
- Learn from successful subscription implementations across different app categories
- Build a continuous improvement process for your subscription model based on user behavior and feedback

In the next chapter, we'll explore strategies for diversifying your revenue streams beyond your core subscription, creating additional stability and growth opportunities for your app business.

Chapter 23: Preparing Your App for Acquisition

"Every exit is an entrance somewhere else." - Tom Stoppard

Introduction

While building a sustainable business is often the primary goal for app creators, acquisition represents a significant milestone that can validate your vision, reward your hard work, and potentially catapult your innovation to a wider audience. Whether acquisition is your ultimate goal or simply an opportunity that emerges along your journey, understanding how to position your app for this outcome can be transformative.

In this chapter, we'll explore the signs that indicate your app might be ready for acquisition, strategies to make your business more attractive to potential buyers, the key metrics that drive valuation, and real-world case studies of successful acquisitions. By understanding the acquisition landscape, you can make strategic decisions that maximize your app's value—whether you ultimately choose to sell or not.

For vibe coders who've used AI-assisted development to bring their vision to life, acquisition readiness represents a crucial transition from creation to strategic business positioning. Let's explore how to prepare your app for this exciting possibility.

Signs Your App Might Be Acquisition-Ready

Not all apps are acquisition candidates, and timing is everything. Here are key indicators that your app might be approaching acquisition readiness:

Sustainable Growth Trajectory

One of the clearest signals is consistent, sustainable growth. Acquirers look for apps demonstrating:

- **Steady user acquisition**: Monthly growth in active users without unsustainable marketing spend
- **Improving retention metrics**: Increasing average user lifetime and engagement
- **Revenue momentum**: Growing revenue with improving margins
- **Market expansion**: Successfully entering new user segments or geographic markets

When your app consistently demonstrates these growth patterns over 12-18 months, it signals potential for continued expansion under new ownership.

Product-Market Fit Validation

Acquisition-ready apps have clearly demonstrated they solve a meaningful problem for a defined audience:

- **Strong user feedback**: High ratings, positive reviews, and enthusiastic testimonials
- **Organic growth**: Significant word-of-mouth or viral growth components
- **Usage depth**: Users engaging with core features repeatedly, not just downloading and abandoning
- **Monetization acceptance**: Users willingly paying for value, whether through subscriptions, in-app purchases, or other revenue models

As one potential acquirer noted in our research: "We're not looking to buy potential; we're looking to buy proven solutions that users already love."

Strategic Alignment With Potential Acquirers

Your app becomes more acquisition-ready when it represents strategic value to specific potential buyers:

- **Complementary functionality**: Your app fills a gap in a larger company's product suite
- **Access to new audiences**: Your user base represents a desirable demographic for potential acquirers
- **Technology or talent**: Your app demonstrates innovative technology or is built by a team with specialized expertise
- **Competitive positioning**: Your app poses a competitive threat that might motivate defensive acquisitions

Key Insight: The best acquisition opportunities often arise when your app solves a problem that larger companies need to address but haven't prioritized developing internally.

Operational Maturity

Buyers are more confident when your business demonstrates operational sophistication:

- **Documented processes**: Clear, transferable procedures for development, customer support, and marketing
- **Scalable infrastructure**: Technical architecture that can handle growth without major overhauls
- **Key performance indicators**: Established metrics with historical data showing trends

- **Risk management**: Proactive addressing of security, privacy, and compliance concerns

Industry Recognition and Buzz

External validation can significantly increase acquisition interest:

- **Media coverage**: Features in industry publications or mainstream media
- **Award recognition**: Industry awards or "best of" lists
- **Influencer adoption**: Endorsements from respected voices in your field
- **Conference presence**: Speaking engagements or successful exhibition appearances

Expert Perspective: The Acquisition Radar

Mia Chen, Former VP of Corporate Development at [Major Tech Company]

"Companies like ours are constantly scanning the ecosystem for interesting acquisition targets. While many founders think they need to actively shop their company, the truth is that the most attractive acquisitions often come to our attention through multiple channels before any formal process begins.

We notice when an app starts gaining traction with our users, when our product teams mention a solution they admire, when industry analysts highlight emerging players, and when our competitors seem interested in a particular space. By the time we reach out, we've usually been watching a company for months.

My advice to founders: focus on building something exceptional rather than optimizing for acquisition from day one. The best acquisitions happen when companies create genuine value that strategic buyers can't ignore."

Making Your Business Attractive to Potential Buyers

Once you've identified that your app might be acquisition-ready, several strategic actions can enhance your attractiveness to potential buyers:

Focus on Clean, Scalable Technology

While vibe coding may have accelerated your development process, acquisition due diligence will scrutinize your technical foundation:

- **Code quality and documentation**: Ensure your codebase is well-organized, properly documented, and follows best practices—even if AI assisted its creation
- **Technical debt management**: Proactively address known issues rather than leaving them for a buyer to discover
- **Security and compliance**: Implement robust security measures and ensure compliance with relevant regulations (GDPR, CCPA, etc.)
- **Scalability testing**: Demonstrate that your infrastructure can handle significant growth in users and transactions

Remember that acquirers will conduct technical due diligence, often bringing in specialized teams to evaluate your codebase and infrastructure. Preparing for this scrutiny in advance prevents unpleasant surprises.

Build a Compelling Data Story

In the acquisition context, data becomes a critical asset:

- **User analytics**: Implement comprehensive analytics tracking user behavior, retention, and conversion
- **Cohort analysis**: Show how different user groups behave over time
- **Market penetration**: Quantify your reach within your target market
- **Predictive metrics**: Develop models that forecast future growth based on historical patterns

Package this data into clear visualizations and narratives that demonstrate your app's trajectory and potential.

Diversify and Strengthen Revenue Streams

Acquirers value businesses with robust, diversified revenue models:

- **Multiple monetization methods**: Implement complementary approaches (subscriptions, one-time purchases, freemium tiers)
- **Enterprise relationships**: Develop B2B components if applicable to your product
- **Geographic diversity**: Demonstrate ability to monetize across different markets
- **Revenue predictability**: Show consistent, recurring revenue patterns rather than sporadic spikes

Cultivate Strategic Partnerships

Relationships with other companies can significantly enhance your acquisition appeal:

- **Integration partnerships**: Develop meaningful integrations with complementary products
- **Co-marketing relationships**: Establish joint promotional activities with aligned brands
- **Channel partnerships**: Build distribution relationships that expand your reach
- **Industry alliances**: Join consortiums or associations relevant to your space

These relationships not only validate your market position but can also introduce you to potential acquirers.

Polish Your Brand and Market Presence

A strong, distinctive brand adds significant acquisition value:

- **Brand consistency**: Ensure visual identity, messaging, and user experience align
- **Content strategy**: Develop thought leadership content positioning your team as experts
- **Community building**: Foster an engaged user community demonstrating loyalty
- **PR momentum**: Secure media coverage highlighting your innovations and impact

Actions to Take: Acquisition Readiness Checklist

1. **Audit your intellectual property**: Ensure all code, designs, and content are properly owned and documented
2. **Prepare a "data room"**: Organize key documents, metrics, and business information
3. **Conduct a legal compliance review**: Address any

regulatory or compliance issues

4. **Document key processes**: Create clear operations manuals and training materials
5. **Strengthen your executive team**: Fill key leadership positions with experienced talent
6. **Optimize your metrics**: Focus on improving the specific KPIs buyers value most
7. **Create a strategic roadmap**: Outline your vision for future growth and development
8. **Develop acquisition scenarios**: Identify potential acquirers and how your app complements their strategies

Build Relationships with Potential Acquirers

Strategic relationship-building can set the stage for future acquisition discussions:

- **Industry events**: Attend conferences where potential acquirers are present
- **Partnership discussions**: Explore integration or co-marketing opportunities
- **Advisory relationships**: Engage with advisors who have connections to potential buyers
- **Investor introductions**: Leverage your investors' networks to make connections

The goal is to ensure your company is on the radar of potential acquirers before you're actively seeking acquisition, creating familiarity and trust that can facilitate future discussions.

Understanding App Valuation Metrics

Acquirers use specific metrics to evaluate acquisition targets and determine appropriate valuations. Understanding these metrics allows you to focus on improving the factors that most directly impact your app's value.

Revenue-Based Valuation Metrics

For apps with established revenue, acquirers often use multiples of financial metrics:

- **Revenue multiple**: Typically ranges from 1-10x annual recurring revenue (ARR), with higher multiples for faster growth and stronger unit economics
- **EBITDA multiple**: For profitable apps, 4-15x earnings before interest, taxes, depreciation, and amortization
- **Gross profit multiple**: Often used when revenue sources have significantly different margins

The specific multiples applied depend on your growth rate, market position, and industry standards. SaaS applications with predictable subscription revenue typically command higher multiples than apps with transactional revenue models.

User-Based Valuation Metrics

For apps with strong user bases but still developing monetization, user-centric metrics often apply:

- **Monthly Active Users (MAU)**: The number of unique users engaging with your app monthly
- **Cost Per Acquisition (CPA)**: What it costs to acquire each new user
- **Lifetime Value (LTV)**: The total revenue generated by

an average user
- **LTV:CAC ratio**: The relationship between lifetime value and customer acquisition cost
- **Churn rate**: The percentage of users who stop using your app in a given period
- **Revenue Per User (RPU)**: Average revenue generated per user

Acquirers may value pre-revenue or early-revenue apps based on what it would cost them to build a similar user base organically.

Strategic Value Factors

Beyond purely financial considerations, strategic factors can significantly impact valuation:

- **Market position**: Leadership in a desirable category or niche
- **Competitive dynamics**: Ability to help an acquirer gain advantage
- **Technology moats**: Proprietary technology, algorithms, or data
- **Network effects**: Increasing value as more users join
- **Team expertise**: Specialized talent the acquirer wants to bring in

Key Insight: Strategic acquisitions often command premium valuations because the buyer perceives value beyond what financials alone would suggest. Identifying and emphasizing your strategic value to specific potential acquirers can dramatically increase your acquisition price.

Industry-Specific Benchmarks

Valuation multiples vary significantly by industry sector:

- **Financial technology (Fintech)**: Typically higher multiples due to recurring revenue and regulatory moats
- **Health and wellness**: Often valued on user engagement and retention metrics
- **Enterprise SaaS**: Valued on annual recurring revenue (ARR) and growth rate
- **Social and communication apps**: Primarily valued on user base and engagement metrics
- **E-commerce**: Often valued on gross merchandise volume (GMV) and customer acquisition metrics

Research comparable acquisitions in your specific category to understand the valuation metrics most relevant to your app.

Expert Perspective: Beyond the Numbers

Alex Rivera, Technology Investment Banker

"Founders often fixate on industry-standard multiples, but the most successful acquisitions I've worked on transcended simple formulas. They told compelling stories about why their company represented unique strategic value to a specific acquirer.

One client built an AI-powered workflow app that was generating only $3 million in ARR but sold for over $50 million because it solved a critical pain point for the acquirer's enterprise clients. Another had relatively flat revenue growth but commanded a premium because they had built an incredibly loyal user base in a demographic the acquirer was struggling to reach.

The key is understanding your potential acquirer's strategic priorities and positioning your company as a solution to their challenges—not just a set of financial metrics."

Preparing for Valuation Discussions

To position for optimal valuation, prepare materials that highlight your app's strengths across relevant metrics:

- **Financial dashboard**: Clear visualization of revenue growth, margins, and unit economics
- **User analytics**: Comprehensive data on engagement, retention, and user behavior
- **Competitive positioning**: Analysis of your place in the market relative to alternatives
- **Growth projections**: Realistic forecasts with clear assumptions and methodologies
- **Strategic opportunities**: Articulation of untapped potential an acquirer could realize

Case Study: App Acquisitions and What Made Them Valuable

Learning from successful acquisitions provides valuable insights into what makes apps attractive to buyers. Let's examine several noteworthy cases:

Case Study 1: The Strategic Capability Acquisition

App: FitnessPal (acquired by Under Armour for $475 million in 2015)

Key Acquisition Drivers:

- Massive active user base (80+ million at acquisition)
- Rich user-generated database of nutritional information
- Alignment with acquirer's digital transformation strategy
- Strong mobile engagement with health-conscious consumers
- Complementary to acquirer's existing digital properties

Lessons for Vibe Coders:

1. Building a proprietary data asset (nutritional database) created unique value
2. Establishing leadership in a specific niche (nutrition tracking) attracted strategic buyers
3. Creating alignment with potential acquirers' strategic initiatives enhanced value
4. Demonstrating strong user engagement metrics justified premium valuation

Case Study 2: The Feature Expansion Acquisition

App: Loom (acquired by Atlassian for $975 million in 2023)

Key Acquisition Drivers:

- Simple, focused solution for asynchronous video communication
- Natural integration with acquirer's existing collaboration tools
- Strong product-led growth with minimal marketing
- Passionate user base demonstrating clear product-market fit
- Accelerating revenue growth with improving margins

Lessons for Vibe Coders:

1. Solving a specific problem exceptionally well attracts acquisition interest
2. Building features that complement larger platforms creates strategic value
3. Demonstrating product-led growth suggests scalability under new ownership
4. Creating emotional connection with users adds acquisition premium

Case Study 3: The Technology Acquisition

App: Dark Sky (acquired by Apple for undisclosed amount in 2020)

Key Acquisition Drivers:

- Highly accurate hyperlocal weather prediction technology
- Distinctive user experience with intuitive visualization
- Strong brand reputation for quality and reliability
- Technology that enhanced acquirer's existing weather offerings
- Dedicated user base willing to pay for premium experience

Lessons for Vibe Coders:

1. Developing superior technology creates acquisition value even in crowded markets
2. Focusing on exceptional user experience differentiates from alternatives
3. Building technology that enhances a larger company's existing offerings creates strategic fit

4. Demonstrating users' willingness to pay validates value proposition

Case Study 4: The Talent Acquisition

App: Pulley (acquired by AngelList for undisclosed amount in 2023)

Key Acquisition Drivers:

- Innovative equity management platform for startups
- Technical team with specialized expertise in financial systems
- Strong founder reputation in the startup ecosystem
- Clear product roadmap with expansion potential
- Complementary to acquirer's existing startup services

Lessons for Vibe Coders:

1. Building specialized expertise makes your team valuable beyond your product
2. Creating solutions in complex domains (like equity management) creates acquisition opportunities
3. Developing founder thought leadership enhances company visibility and value
4. Building complementary solutions to platform companies increases acquisition likelihood

Key Insight: Successful acquisitions rarely happen by accident. The most valuable acquisitions typically result from deliberately building products that solve meaningful problems while aligning with potential acquirers' strategic needs.

Creating an Acquisition Strategy

While opportunistic acquisitions do occur, a thoughtful acquisition strategy improves your chances of a successful outcome:

Identify Potential Acquirers

Create a tiered list of potential acquirers categorized by fit:

- **Strategic fit**: Companies whose products would be enhanced by your solution
- **Portfolio fit**: Companies that could add your app to an existing family of products
- **Competitive fit**: Companies that might acquire to eliminate competition
- **Expansion fit**: Companies looking to enter your market segment

For each potential acquirer, document why they might be interested and what specific value your app offers them.

Build Relationships Before You Need Them

Develop connections with potential acquirers through:

- **Partner programs**: Join developer or partner ecosystems of larger companies
- **Conference networking**: Attend events where corporate development teams are present
- **Investor connections**: Leverage your investors' networks for introductions
- **Industry associations**: Participate in organizations

where acquirers are active

The goal is to ensure relevant people know your company and understand its value before you're actively seeking acquisition.

Prepare for Due Diligence

Acquisition due diligence can be intensive. Prepare in advance by:

- **Financial organization**: Ensure clean, auditable financial records
- **Technical documentation**: Maintain updated architecture diagrams and code documentation
- **Legal compliance**: Address any regulatory or compliance issues
- **Intellectual property**: Verify all IP is properly owned and protected
- **Team documentation**: Create clear org charts and role descriptions

Create a "due diligence ready" folder containing key documents that would be requested in an acquisition process.

Develop an Acquisition Narrative

Craft a compelling story about why your app represents unique value:

- **Origin story**: How you identified the problem and developed your solution
- **Market validation**: Evidence of demand and user satisfaction
- **Growth trajectory**: Historical growth and future

potential
- **Strategic significance**: Why your solution matters in the broader industry
- **Synergy opportunities**: How an acquirer could leverage your assets

This narrative should be concise, compelling, and supported by data.

Actions to Take: Acquisition Preparation Plan

1. **Research comparable acquisitions**: Identify recent transactions in your space and analyze valuation metrics
2. **Create an acquirer target list**: Develop a prioritized list of 10-20 potential acquirers
3. **Conduct a pre-diligence audit**: Review your business through the eyes of a potential acquirer
4. **Develop key relationship map**: Identify connections who could introduce you to acquisition decision-makers
5. **Prepare a strategic value deck**: Create materials highlighting your strategic value to specific acquirers
6. **Set acquisition triggers**: Define the conditions under which you would actively pursue acquisition
7. **Consult acquisition advisors**: Speak with bankers or consultants experienced in your industry
8. **Practice your acquisition pitch**: Refine your ability to articulate your company's unique value

Navigating the Acquisition Process

If an acquisition opportunity materializes, understanding the typical process helps you navigate it successfully:

Initial Expression of Interest

The process typically begins with informal discussions or an initial expression of interest (EOI). At this stage:

- **Maintain confidentiality**: Use non-disclosure agreements (NDAs) to protect sensitive information
- **Understand intent**: Determine if the interest is genuine or merely exploratory
- **Control information flow**: Share just enough to maintain interest without revealing everything
- **Set expectations**: Establish mutual understanding about potential process and timeline

Preliminary Due Diligence

If interest continues, the acquirer will conduct initial due diligence:

- **Company overview**: General information about your business and history
- **Key metrics**: High-level performance data showing growth and engagement
- **Team structure**: Information about key personnel and organization
- **Product roadmap**: Current capabilities and future development plans
- **Market position**: Competitive landscape and your place within it

Term Sheet Negotiation

A term sheet outlines the key points of the proposed acquisition:

- **Valuation**: Proposed purchase price and structure
- **Payment terms**: Cash, stock, earnout provisions, or combinations
- **Conditions**: Requirements that must be met before closing
- **Exclusivity**: Period during which you cannot solicit other offers
- **Key employee arrangements**: Retention packages or commitments

Term sheets are typically non-binding except for exclusivity and confidentiality provisions.

Comprehensive Due Diligence

Once a term sheet is signed, the acquirer conducts thorough due diligence:

- **Financial review**: Detailed examination of financial statements and projections
- **Technical assessment**: Code review, architecture evaluation, security assessment
- **Legal review**: Contracts, intellectual property, litigation, compliance
- **Operational review**: Processes, suppliers, partners, facilities
- **Customer review**: Customer base, satisfaction metrics, retention patterns

This phase can be intense and time-consuming—preparation is key to a smooth process.

Definitive Agreement and Closing

The final phase involves:

- **Definitive agreement**: Detailed legal document specifying all terms
- **Regulatory approvals**: Any required government or regulatory clearances
- **Closing conditions**: Final requirements before transaction completion
- **Integration planning**: How your app and team will join the acquiring company
- **Announcement strategy**: How and when the acquisition will be communicated

Conclusion

Preparing your app for acquisition requires deliberate strategy and focused execution. By understanding the signs of acquisition readiness, making your business attractive to potential buyers, and familiarizing yourself with valuation metrics, you position your app for optimal outcomes when acquisition opportunities arise.

Remember that the journey to acquisition often begins long before formal discussions. The strategic decisions you make throughout your app's development—from technology choices to market positioning to relationship building—can significantly impact your acquisition potential.

For vibe coders who have leveraged AI-assisted development to bring their vision to life, acquisition represents the ultimate validation of your approach. It demonstrates that innovative products created through modern development methods can achieve traditional business success metrics and create meaningful value for larger organizations.

Whether acquisition is your ultimate goal or simply one potential outcome in your entrepreneurial journey, the practices outlined in this chapter will strengthen your business and position you for success—whatever exit path you eventually choose.

Chapter Summary

- **Acquisition readiness** is indicated by sustainable growth, product-market fit validation, strategic alignment with potential acquirers, operational maturity, and industry recognition.
- **Making your business attractive** involves focusing on clean, scalable technology; building a compelling data story; diversifying revenue streams; cultivating strategic partnerships; polishing your brand; and building relationships with potential acquirers.
- **Valuation metrics** include revenue multiples, user-based metrics like MAU and LTV, and strategic value factors. Industry-specific benchmarks vary significantly across different app categories.
- **Successful acquisitions** typically involve apps that solve meaningful problems, demonstrate strong user engagement, show clear growth potential, and align with acquirers' strategic objectives.
- **Preparing for acquisition** requires identifying potential acquirers, building relationships, preparing for due diligence, developing a compelling acquisition narrative, and understanding the acquisition process.

In the next chapter, we'll explore strategies for scaling beyond your first success, building upon the foundation you've established to create lasting impact in the app ecosystem.

Chapter 24: Scaling Beyond the First Success

Introduction

Success in the app economy is rarely defined by a single product. The most impactful entrepreneurs build upon their initial victories, expanding their reach and influence through strategic growth. For vibe coders—those who have mastered the art of building intuitive, market-aware applications without deep technical expertise—this scaling phase presents both exciting opportunities and unique challenges.

Having launched your first successful app using vibe coding principles, you've validated your approach and proven your ability to connect with users. Now comes the crucial next phase: leveraging that foundation to build something larger and more enduring. This chapter explores how to transform your initial success into a sustainable business empire while maintaining the user-centric, intuitive approach that got you here.

As you scale, you'll need to navigate expanding to new platforms, building a portfolio of connected applications, transitioning from solo founder to team leader, and preserving your vibe coding principles amid growing complexity. The path forward requires both expansion and preservation—growing your reach while protecting the essence of what made your first app resonate with users.

Expanding to New Platforms and Markets

Assessing Platform Opportunities

The modern app ecosystem spans multiple platforms, each offering unique advantages and user bases. Expanding beyond your initial platform can significantly amplify your reach and revenue potential.

Platforms and markets represent different opportunities to connect with users. When considering expansion, you should evaluate each potential platform based on user demographics, monetization options, and technical requirements.

Key Considerations for Platform Selection:

1. **User Base Alignment**: Does the platform host users who align with your target audience profile?
2. **Monetization Compatibility**: Will your current revenue model work effectively on this new platform, or will you need to adapt?
3. **Technical Requirements**: What additional resources will you need to adapt your app to this platform's specifications?
4. **Competition Landscape**: How saturated is this platform with similar offerings, and what opportunities exist for differentiation?
5. **Growth Trajectory**: Is the platform itself growing, stable, or declining in user adoption and engagement?

KEY INSIGHT: Platform Synergy

The best platform expansions create synergistic effects where your presence on multiple platforms enhances the value of each individual app installation. Think beyond simple ports and consider how cross-platform presence can create unique user benefits.

Geographic and Demographic Expansion

Beyond platforms, consider expanding to new geographic markets or demographic segments. International expansion can unlock massive growth potential, especially if your app addresses universal needs. However, this requires careful adaptation to local preferences, regulations, and cultural norms.

Steps for Market Expansion:

1. **Market Research**: Identify promising markets based on potential demand, competition, and accessibility.
2. **Localization Strategy**: Determine what aspects of your app need adaptation (language, features, pricing, etc.).
3. **Regulatory Compliance**: Research and address legal requirements for operating in new markets.
4. **Cultural Adaptation**: Modify your user experience and marketing approach to resonate with local preferences.
5. **Phased Rollout**: Consider a staged approach, beginning with markets most similar to your home territory.

EXPERT PERSPECTIVE: Cross-Border Expansion

Maya Rodriguez, International App Growth Consultant

"The most successful apps I've seen expand internationally don't just translate their text—they truly localize the experience. This means adapting features, addressing local pain points, and sometimes even adjusting the core value proposition. One finance app I worked with discovered their primary US selling point—automated savings—wasn't resonating in Asian markets where savings rates were already high. They pivoted to emphasize their investment features instead and saw adoption skyrocket."

Leveraging Your Existing User Base

Your current users are your most valuable asset when expanding. They provide immediate feedback, can become evangelists for your new offerings, and offer insights into additional problems you might solve.

Strategies for User-Driven Expansion:

1. **In-App Surveys**: Directly ask users about their needs and preferences regarding new platforms or features.
2. **Usage Analysis**: Identify patterns in how users currently engage with your app that might indicate opportunities.
3. **Beta Testing Groups**: Recruit enthusiastic users to test new platform versions before full release.
4. **Referral Programs**: Incentivize users to invite connections on new platforms you're targeting.
5. **Success Stories**: Showcase how existing users benefit from your multi-platform approach.

ACTIONS TO TAKE: Platform Expansion Assessment

1. **Create a Platform Evaluation Matrix**: Build a spreadsheet comparing potential platforms across key criteria (user base size, demographics, revenue potential, development costs, etc.).
2. **Survey Current Users**: Ask which additional platforms they'd like to see your app on and what features would be most valuable.
3. **Conduct Competitor Analysis**: Identify which competitors have successfully expanded to multiple platforms and analyze their approach.
4. **Estimate Development Resources**: Consult with

developers to understand the time and cost requirements for each potential platform.

5. **Prioritize Expansion Targets**: Based on all factors, create a prioritized list of platforms to target, with estimated timelines.

Building a Portfolio of Connected Apps

The Power of App Ecosystems

Rather than simply creating multiple independent applications, consider building an interconnected ecosystem where each app enhances the value of the others. This creates stronger user loyalty, increases switching costs, and can significantly boost lifetime value.

Types of App Portfolios:

1. **Feature Expansion**: Breaking out specialized features from your main app into standalone offerings (e.g., a photo editing app spinning off specialized tools).
2. **Vertical Integration**: Creating apps that address different aspects of the same overall user journey (e.g., house hunting, mortgage calculation, and home maintenance).
3. **Audience Segmentation**: Developing variations of your core offering tailored to specific user segments (e.g., professional vs. consumer versions).
4. **Complementary Functionality**: Building apps with distinct purposes that work better together (e.g., a note-taking app and a calendar that sync information).

Data Sharing and Integration Architecture

The technical foundation of a successful app portfolio lies in thoughtful integration. Even as a vibe coder with limited technical background, you should understand the basic principles of how your apps will share data and functionality.

As your portfolio grows, creating a unified data architecture becomes increasingly important. This allows users to move seamlessly between your applications while maintaining consistent information and preferences.

Key Integration Considerations:

1. **User Authentication**: Implement a unified login system across all apps.
2. **Data Synchronization**: Ensure user data updates consistently across all platforms and applications.
3. **Cross-App Communication**: Enable apps to launch each other and pass contextual information.
4. **Consistent Design Language**: Maintain visual and interaction consistency to build brand recognition.
5. **Unified Privacy Approach**: Ensure your data handling practices work cohesively across all apps.

KEY INSIGHT: The Integration Advantage

Connected apps create data network effects where each additional user and app in your ecosystem increases the value of the entire portfolio. This compounds your competitive advantage over time and makes it increasingly difficult for competitors to displace you.

Portfolio Strategy and Roadmap

Developing a portfolio requires strategic thinking about which apps to build, in what order, and how they'll connect. This roadmap should balance short-term opportunities with long-term ecosystem vision.

Portfolio Planning Framework:

1. **Core Problem Mapping**: Identify the central problem your current app solves and map adjacent problems users face.
2. **Opportunity Sizing**: Evaluate market size and monetization potential for each potential app.
3. **Resource Assessment**: Realistically determine what you can build with available resources.
4. **Dependency Analysis**: Identify which apps logically precede others in your development sequence.
5. **Feedback Loops**: Plan how insights from each app will inform development of subsequent offerings.

Visualization: App Portfolio Map

Consider a visual framework representing your app ecosystem, with:

- Your flagship app at the center
- Connected apps radiating outward
- Lines representing data and functional connections
- Size representing market opportunity
- Color representing development priority

This visualization helps communicate your vision to team members, investors, and partners.

ACTIONS TO TAKE: Portfolio Development

1. **User Journey Mapping**: Document the broader journey

your users take beyond what your current app addresses.
2. **Gap Analysis**: Identify points in this journey where users currently switch to other tools or manual processes.
3. **Feature Sorting Exercise**: Review your feature backlog and group features that might form cohesive standalone apps.
4. **Technical Architecture Consultation**: Work with a developer to create a basic blueprint for how your apps will share data.
5. **MVP Definition**: For your next potential app, define the minimum feature set needed to deliver unique value while connecting to your existing offering.

Transitioning from Solo Founder to Team Leader

Building Your Leadership Identity

As your app business grows, your role inevitably shifts from hands-on creator to team leader. This transition requires developing new skills and perspectives while maintaining the vision and creativity that fueled your initial success.

Evolution of the Founder Role:

1. **Solo Stage**: Direct execution of all aspects (product, marketing, support, etc.).
2. **Initial Delegation**: First hires take on specific functional responsibilities.
3. **Team Leadership**: Managing people who manage tasks, focusing on alignment and enablement.
4. **Strategic Direction**: Setting vision and priorities while

empowering teams to determine execution.

5. **Culture Stewardship**: Ensuring organizational values and approaches remain consistent with founding principles.

EXPERT PERSPECTIVE: The Founder's Journey

Alex Rivera, Startup Leadership Coach

"The hardest part of scaling for most founders is letting go. You've been so hands-on with every aspect of your product, and suddenly you need to trust others to maintain your standards. The solution isn't micromanagement—it's clear communication of your vision, values, and quality expectations. The best founder-CEOs I've worked with create simple frameworks that help their teams make decisions aligned with the original vision, even when the founder isn't in the room."

Hiring Your Dream Team

The quality of your team will ultimately determine your ability to scale successfully. As a vibe coder with limited technical expertise, hiring the right technical talent becomes particularly crucial.

Key Roles to Consider:

1. **Technical Co-Founder/CTO**: If you don't have strong technical skills yourself, a technical co-founder or early CTO hire can be invaluable.
2. **Product Manager**: Bridges the gap between user needs and technical implementation.
3. **UX/UI Designer**: Maintains the intuitive, emotionally resonant experience that made your first app successful.
4. **Marketing Specialist**: Helps acquire users at scale across

multiple platforms.

5. **Customer Support Lead**: Maintains close connection to user needs as you grow.

Hiring Principles for Vibe Coders:

1. **Value Alignment**: Prioritize candidates who understand and believe in your user-centric approach.
2. **Complementary Skills**: Look for people whose strengths complement your limitations.
3. **Growth Mindset**: Value adaptability and learning capacity over specific technical skills.
4. **Communication Ability**: Choose team members who can translate complex concepts into accessible language.
5. **Entrepreneurial Spirit**: Seek those who can operate with autonomy while remaining aligned with your vision.

Creating Systems and Processes

As you scale, the informal approaches that worked for a solo founder become insufficient. You need systems and processes that enable consistent quality and efficient execution across a growing team.

Essential Systems for Scaling:

1. **Decision Frameworks**: Clear guidelines for how decisions should be made and by whom.
2. **Documentation Practices**: Systems for capturing knowledge, decisions, and processes.
3. **Communication Protocols**: Established channels and norms for different types of information.
4. **Quality Assurance**: Processes for maintaining product

standards as more people contribute.

5. **User Feedback Collection**: Systematic approaches to gathering and acting on user insights.

KEY INSIGHT: Processes as Enablers

The best processes don't constrain creativity—they channel it productively by handling routine aspects of work consistently, freeing mental space for innovation where it matters most.

ACTIONS TO TAKE: Leadership Transition

1. **Skills Assessment**: Honestly evaluate your strengths and weaknesses as a leader, identifying areas for personal development.
2. **Role Definition Exercise**: Document exactly what you do currently, then mark which activities only you can do versus what could be delegated.
3. **Culture Documentation**: Write down the core values and approaches that define your company culture, making implicit norms explicit.
4. **Hiring Plan**: Create a prioritized list of roles to fill, with clear criteria for each position.
5. **Decision Matrix**: Develop a simple framework showing what types of decisions should be made at different levels of the organization.

Maintaining Vibe Coding Principles as You Scale

Preserving Your User-First Mentality

The core of vibe coding is maintaining a deep connection with users and their needs. As organizations grow, this connection often weakens, with layers of abstraction forming between leadership and the end user.

Strategies to Maintain User Connection:

1. **Regular User Interaction**: Schedule time for all team members, including leadership, to directly observe and interact with users.
2. **User Champions**: Designate specific roles responsible for representing the user perspective in all decisions.
3. **Experience Metrics**: Track indicators of user satisfaction and emotional connection, not just growth metrics.
4. **User Stories**: Continuously collect and share compelling examples of how real people use and benefit from your apps.
5. **Empathy Exercises**: Conduct regular sessions where team members experience the product as users in different scenarios.

Scaling Your Development Approach

Vibe coding emphasizes intuition, market awareness, and user connection over technical details. As your development team grows, this philosophy must be translated into processes that preserve these values while enabling multiple contributors.

Vibe Coding at Scale:

1. **Intent-Based Specifications**: Focus requirements on the user's intended outcome rather than technical implementation details.
2. **Prototype-Driven Development**: Maintain rapid

prototyping practices even as your formal development processes mature.

3. **Emotional Success Criteria**: Define success not just by functional completion but by the emotional response of users.
4. **Technical-Creative Partnerships**: Foster close collaboration between technical implementers and those who understand the desired "vibe."
5. **AI Augmentation**: Continue leveraging AI tools to rapidly translate ideas into prototypes that communicate vision effectively.

EXPERT PERSPECTIVE: Maintaining the Vibe

Jordan Chen, Design Director

"As technical teams grow, they naturally gravitate toward more structured processes. While necessary, this can dilute the emotional intuition that made the original product special. I recommend establishing 'vibe checkpoints' throughout the development process where you pause and honestly assess whether what you're building still evokes the intended emotional response. Have someone responsible for the 'soul' of the product who can veto technically perfect but emotionally flat implementations."

Balancing Structure and Creativity

One of the greatest challenges in scaling is maintaining the creative spark that drove your initial success while introducing the structure needed to coordinate larger teams.

Approaches to Balance:

1. **Bounded Innovation**: Create clear boundaries within

which teams have complete creative freedom.
2. **Dedicated Innovation Time**: Allocate specific periods for exploration outside normal development cycles.
3. **Cross-Functional Sprints**: Regularly bring together diverse team members for focused creative problem-solving.
4. **Design Systems**: Develop flexible systems that ensure consistency while enabling creative expression.
5. **Innovation Metrics**: Measure and celebrate creative outcomes alongside efficiency metrics.

Evolving Your Team Culture

As your team grows, culture becomes your most powerful tool for maintaining your founding principles. Deliberately crafting and nurturing this culture is perhaps your most important responsibility as a scaling founder.

Cultural Elements to Emphasize:

1. **User Empathy**: Regular practices that deepen understanding of user needs and experiences.
2. **Market Awareness**: Systems for staying connected to evolving market trends and opportunities.
3. **Creative Problem-Solving**: Approaches that prioritize novel solutions over conventional thinking.
4. **Iterative Mindset**: Comfort with continuous refinement rather than perfect initial execution.
5. **Multi-Disciplinary Thinking**: Valuing diverse perspectives and cross-domain knowledge.

ACTIONS TO TAKE: Preserving Principles

1. **Principles Document**: Clearly articulate your vibe coding principles in a document that guides all team members.
2. **User Connection Program**: Establish regular activities that connect all team members directly with users.
3. **Decision Criteria Checklist**: Create a simple list of questions that should be asked before any significant product decision (e.g., "How does this make the user feel?").
4. **Onboarding Experience**: Design an immersive onboarding process that helps new team members internalize your approach.
5. **Regular Principles Review**: Schedule quarterly sessions to assess how well recent work has aligned with your founding principles.

Case Study: Expanding the Vibe

Resonance: From Single App to Ecosystem

Note: This is a fictional case study based on principles from the research materials.

When Maya Desai launched Resonance, a meditation app built with vibe coding principles, she had no technical background—just a clear vision for how meditation could be more accessible through an emotionally intelligent interface. Using AI tools and low-code platforms, she created an experience that truly connected with users through its intuitive design and emotional awareness.

After Resonance reached 100,000 users, Maya faced the challenge of scaling beyond this initial success. Here's how she navigated the expansion:

Platform Expansion: Rather than simply porting Resonance to new platforms, Maya conducted user research that revealed distinct use cases across devices. For mobile, users wanted quick, on-the-go sessions. For desktop, they sought deeper, guided practices. For voice platforms, they wanted ambient meditation sounds. She tailored each experience to the platform's unique strengths.

Connected Portfolio: Instead of adding every feature request to Resonance, Maya created a portfolio of connected apps:

- Resonance (core meditation)
- Resonance Sleep (specialized sleep meditation)
- Resonance Journal (reflection and tracking)
- Resonance Connect (community features)

Users could subscribe to individual apps or the entire ecosystem at a discount, with data flowing seamlessly between apps.

Team Building: Maya's first key hire wasn't a developer but a product manager who shared her vision for emotionally intelligent design. Together, they created a framework for evaluating potential team members based on both skills and alignment with the company's user-first values. Early technical hires were selected as much for their ability to translate emotional goals into technical solutions as for their coding expertise.

Preserving Principles: As the team grew to 25 people, Maya instituted several practices to maintain their vibe coding approach:

- Monthly "user shadow days" where team members

observed actual users
- A "vibe check" step in their development process where prototypes were evaluated for emotional impact
- A clear decision framework emphasizing user emotional experience over technical elegance or efficiency

Five years after launch, Resonance had grown to a suite of six apps across multiple platforms with over 3 million users. Despite the complexity, the company maintained its reputation for creating experiences that seemed to "just get" what users needed, proving that vibe coding principles could scale successfully beyond a single founder's vision.

Looking Forward: The Future of Scaled Vibe Coding

The landscape of app development continues to evolve rapidly, with AI playing an increasingly central role. As vibe coding approaches mature, we can anticipate new opportunities and challenges for scaled organizations.

Emerging Trends:

1. **AI Teammates**: Beyond tools, AI will likely evolve into specialized team members handling aspects of development, design, and even user research.
2. **Community Co-Creation**: Scaled vibe coding organizations will likely leverage user communities more directly in the creation process, blurring the lines between developers and users.
3. **Emotion-Driven Analytics**: New tools for measuring and optimizing for emotional user experiences will

emerge, giving data-driven support to intuitive design decisions.

4. **Cross-Medium Experiences**: App ecosystems will expand beyond traditional platforms to include AR/VR, wearables, smart home, and other emerging technologies.
5. **Algorithmic Personalization**: Apps will increasingly adapt their experience to individual users' emotional preferences and interaction styles.

KEY INSIGHT: The Scale Advantage

As your organization scales, you gain access to more user data, more creative perspectives, and more resources for experimentation. When channeled properly, scale can actually enhance rather than diminish your connection to users and your ability to create emotionally resonant experiences.

Chapter Summary

Scaling beyond your first success requires thoughtful expansion while preserving the principles that made you successful initially. By strategically approaching platform expansion, building connected app portfolios, transitioning from solo founder to team leader, and maintaining your vibe coding principles, you can transform a single successful app into a sustainable business empire.

The key to successful scaling lies in creating systems and processes that embed your values and approaches, allowing your unique vision to manifest through the work of an entire organization rather than just your individual efforts. This ensures that as your reach expands, the emotional connection and intuitive design that defined your first success remain intact.

Remember that scale brings new opportunities for impact and innovation. With more resources, more user insights, and more creative minds contributing, your ability to understand and meet user needs can actually deepen. By maintaining your founding principles while embracing the advantages of scale, you can create experiences that touch more lives while remaining true to your original vision.

Key Takeaways:

1. **Strategic Expansion**: Choose new platforms and markets based on user needs and strategic alignment rather than simply maximizing reach.
2. **Connected Ecosystems**: Build app portfolios where each application enhances the value of others, creating stronger user loyalty and competitive advantages.
3. **Leadership Evolution**: Successfully transition from

hands-on creator to vision-setting leader by building systems that embed your values and approaches.

4. **Preserved Principles**: Maintain your vibe coding approach by creating processes that specifically protect user connection and emotional intelligence in your products.
5. **Cultural Foundation**: Ultimately, your organization's culture becomes the most powerful mechanism for preserving your founding principles at scale.

Additional Resources

Books:

- "Emotional Design: Why We Love (or Hate) Everyday Things" by Don Norman
- "Team of Teams: New Rules of Engagement for a Complex World" by General Stanley McChrystal
- "Blitzscaling" by Reid Hoffman and Chris Yeh

Tools:

- Notion templates for connected app portfolio planning
- Figma design system starter kits
- LeanUX canvas for maintaining user focus at scale

Communities:

- IndieHackers scaling forum
- ProductHunt maker community
- AppMasters growth network

Chapter 25: The Future of Vibe Coding

"The future belongs to those who learn more skills and combine them in creative ways." — Robert Greene

Introduction

The landscape of app development is evolving at an unprecedented pace. As we've explored throughout this book, vibe coding represents a significant shift in how we approach software creation—prioritizing intuition, market awareness, and user connection over technical details. This final chapter looks ahead to the horizon, examining how emerging technologies will reshape app development, how to prepare for new platforms, strategies for staying relevant, and why adaptability might be your most valuable asset in the years to come.

The vibe coder's journey doesn't end with launching a successful app. Rather, it's an ongoing process of evolution, learning, and growth. By understanding the technological currents that will shape tomorrow's digital experiences, you can position yourself at the forefront of innovation, ready to ride the next wave of opportunity.

Emerging Technologies Reshaping App Development

The tools and technologies available to vibe coders are expanding rapidly, creating both new opportunities and challenges. Understanding these innovations will help you leverage them effectively in your app development journey.

AI-Powered Development: Beyond Basic Assistance

Artificial intelligence has already transformed app development through tools that can generate code based on natural language prompts. However, the next evolution will move beyond simple code completion to more sophisticated AI partnerships.

AI Development Partners

By 2025, we're seeing the evolution of what industry experts call "intelligent development platforms" that go far beyond simple code generation. Rather than merely generating code snippets, these advanced systems are becoming full development partners that can understand system architecture, optimize for performance, and even anticipate potential security vulnerabilities.

Key advancements include:

- **Contextual Understanding**: Modern AI can now maintain understanding of your entire codebase, not just isolated snippets, allowing for more coherent system design.
- **Autonomous Testing and Debugging**: AI systems can now identify edge cases, optimize algorithms, and suggest performance improvements with minimal human guidance.
- **Architecture Recommendation**: Today's tools can suggest optimal system architectures based on your specific requirements and constraints.
- **Continuous Learning**: Your AI partner evolves with your project, learning your preferences and adapting its recommendations accordingly.

KEY INSIGHT: The most successful vibe coders won't be those who can type the best prompts, but those who can form the most effective partnerships with AI, guiding it toward solutions that align with their vision and users' needs.

Multimodal Development

The future of vibe coding extends beyond text-based interfaces to multimodal interactions that leverage voice, vision, and even gesture recognition.

Beyond Text: Natural Interfaces for Development

Multimodal AI is transforming how we interact with development tools, enabling more natural and intuitive methods of app creation. AI systems can now track interactions across different modalities including voice, text, and gestures. This evolution is making app development more accessible to creative thinkers regardless of their coding background.

Features of multimodal development include:

- **Voice-Driven Development**: Speak your app into existence, describing features and requirements conversationally while AI translates your intentions into functional code.
- **Visual Programming**: Sketch interfaces, flowcharts, or system diagrams that AI can interpret and transform into working applications.
- **Gesture-Based Interaction**: Beyond voice and gestures, design interfaces can incorporate touch, facial recognition, eye tracking, and even nascent brain-computer interfaces.

As these interfaces evolve, the barrier between your creative vision and its implementation continues to diminish, making vibe coding even more intuitive and accessible.

No-Code Evolution: From Building Blocks to Intent-Driven Creation

The no-code movement has already revolutionized app development by making it accessible to non-programmers. The future will see these platforms evolve from component-based building to more fluid, intent-driven creation.

From Components to Concepts

Future no-code platforms will focus less on dragging and dropping predefined components and more on understanding and implementing higher-level concepts:

- **Concept-Driven Development**: Describe what you want to achieve, and the platform will suggest appropriate structures, workflows, and components.
- **Pattern-Based Development**: Systems will recognize common app patterns and recommend proven implementation approaches based on your goals.
- **Automatic Integration**: AI will automatically handle connections between services, APIs, and data sources with minimal configuration.

EXPERT PERSPECTIVE: Sarah Chen, No-Code Futurist

"The future of no-code isn't about more components or templates—it's about deeper understanding. Tomorrow's platforms will grasp your intent and help you realize it faster than you could by manually assembling components. You'll describe what you want to achieve, and the platform will understand not just the individual pieces needed, but how they should work together to create the experience you envision."

Blockchain and Decentralized Applications

Blockchain technology and decentralized applications (dApps) are becoming increasingly accessible to vibe coders, opening new avenues for innovation.

Simplified Blockchain Development

Emerging tools are abstracting away the complexity of blockchain development:

- **Smart Contract Templates**: Pre-built, customizable templates for common smart contract patterns.
- **Visual Blockchain Builders**: Graphical interfaces for designing and deploying blockchain solutions without deep technical knowledge.
- **Cross-Chain Development**: Tools that allow developers to build apps that work across multiple blockchain networks.

Machine Learning Democratization

Machine learning is becoming more accessible to non-specialists through automated tools and simplified interfaces.

AutoML and No-Code ML

The trend toward automated machine learning (AutoML) continues to accelerate:

- **No-Code ML Platforms**: Drag-and-drop interfaces for building and training machine learning models.
- **Data Preparation Assistants**: AI-powered tools that help clean and prepare data for machine learning.

- **Pre-Trained Models**: Expanding libraries of specialized models that can be easily integrated into applications.

KEY INSIGHT: The line between "AI developer" and "app developer" is blurring. Tomorrow's vibe coders will routinely incorporate machine learning capabilities into their apps without specialized ML expertise.

Preparing for New Platforms (AR/VR, Wearables)

The future of app development extends beyond traditional mobile and web platforms to embrace emerging interfaces that promise more immersive and contextual user experiences.

Embracing Spatial Computing

The arrival of consumer-focused AR/VR devices and advanced wearables marks a significant shift in how users interact with digital experiences. This emerging field of spatial computing—where digital content exists in three-dimensional space around us—represents a fundamental evolution in app development.

Spatial computing represents the merger of digital content with the physical world, manifesting through technologies like augmented reality, where digital elements appear mixed with the real world. This shift from screen-based to spatial experiences requires a different approach to app design and development.

Key Considerations for Spatial Application Development:

- **Context Awareness**: Spatial apps need to understand the user's environment and adapt accordingly. This includes recognizing spaces, objects, and even other people.

- **Natural Interaction Patterns**: Users will interact through gestures, voice, and eye movements rather than taps and swipes. Your app design needs to accommodate these more intuitive interaction patterns.
- **Spatial UX**: User experiences must consider depth, distance, and physical comfort. Poor spatial design can cause physical discomfort or cognitive confusion.

KEY INSIGHT: The transition to spatial computing isn't just a platform shift—it's a fundamental rethinking of the relationship between users and digital experiences. Successful vibe coders will focus on creating natural, contextually aware experiences rather than simply porting existing interface paradigms to new devices.

Wearable Technology Ecosystem

Beyond immersive headsets, the ecosystem of wearable technology continues to expand, creating new opportunities for app creators.

The Connected Body

Future app experiences will extend across a network of wearable devices:

- **Smart Clothing**: Garments with embedded sensors that can track movement, health metrics, and environmental conditions.
- **Health Monitors**: Advanced wearables that track not just activity but comprehensive biomarkers and health indicators.
- **Ambient Interfaces**: Devices that blend into everyday objects, providing information and functionality without

obvious technological presence.

Web-Based XR: Democratizing Immersive Development

The WebXR Device API represents a significant step toward democratizing AR and VR development. This standard enables access to virtual and augmented reality devices directly within web browsers, fostering immersive web experiences without requiring users to download specialized apps.

For vibe coders, WebXR represents an important opportunity as it allows for the creation of immersive experiences without specialized development environments or platform-specific knowledge. This browser-based approach means your AR and VR applications can potentially reach users across different devices and operating systems.

Preparing Your Skill Set for Spatial Computing

To position yourself for success in spatial computing, consider developing these capabilities:

- **3D Design Fundamentals**: Understanding basic principles of 3D modeling, lighting, and spatial design.
- **Spatial Interaction Design**: Learning how users naturally interact in three-dimensional spaces.
- **WebXR Development**: Exploring frameworks that simplify creation of web-based AR/VR experiences.
- **Cross-Platform Testing**: Setting up processes to test across various headsets and wearable devices.

ACTIONS TO TAKE:

1. Try creating a simple WebXR application using a framework like A-Frame or Three.js
2. Experience different AR/VR platforms as a user to understand interaction paradigms
3. Experiment with hand tracking and voice control in your prototypes
4. Join WebXR communities to stay updated on evolving standards and best practices

Internet of Things (IoT) Integration

The proliferation of smart devices and sensors creates new opportunities for connected experiences that bridge the physical and digital worlds.

Designing for Connected Ecosystems

Future apps will increasingly need to function as part of larger ecosystems:

- **Cross-Device Experiences**: Applications that work seamlessly across smartphones, wearables, smart home devices, and vehicles.
- **Contextual Intelligence**: Systems that understand the user's context (location, activity, environment) and respond appropriately.
- **Data Orchestration**: Managing the flow of information between devices while respecting privacy and optimizing for limited connectivity.

Staying Relevant in a Rapidly Changing Landscape

In a field where technological change accelerates every year, staying relevant is a continuous process rather than a one-time achievement. The most successful vibe coders approach their careers with intentional strategies for growth and adaptation.

Cultivating a Learning Mindset

The single most important factor in staying relevant is developing a learning mindset. In today's rapidly evolving tech landscape, the ability to continuously learn and adapt is essential. Expert developers increasingly view themselves as "expert-generalists" who treat learning new skills as an ongoing process.

Balancing Breadth and Depth

A strategic approach to learning involves balancing breadth and depth:

- **T-Shaped Knowledge**: Develop deep expertise in core areas while maintaining broad awareness across adjacent domains.
- **Just-in-Time Learning**: Rather than trying to learn everything, focus on acquiring new skills as they become relevant to your projects.
- **First Principles Thinking**: Understand the underlying concepts and principles rather than just memorizing specific implementations.

KEY INSIGHT: The most adaptable vibe coders aren't necessarily those who know the most technologies, but those who know how to learn new technologies quickly and effectively.

Strategic Trend Monitoring

Staying informed about emerging trends allows you to anticipate shifts before they become mainstream, giving you time to prepare and adapt.

Building Your Trend Radar

Develop systematic approaches to monitor developments in relevant fields:

- **Curated Information Feeds**: Create a personalized system for tracking industry news, technological breakthroughs, and market shifts.
- **Community Engagement**: Participate in forums, conferences, and social platforms where early adopters discuss emerging technologies.
- **Experimental Projects**: Allocate time for small-scale experiments with promising new tools and platforms.

Diversifying Your Skill Portfolio

In an era where AI is increasingly handling routine coding tasks, diversifying your skill set beyond pure technical abilities becomes essential. The most resilient vibe coders combine technical knowledge with complementary skills that amplify their impact.

Beyond Technical Skills

Consider developing capabilities in these areas:

1. **Problem Definition and Analysis**
    - Clearly articulating problems before jumping to solutions
    - Breaking complex issues into manageable components

    - Identifying root causes rather than symptoms
2. **Human-Centered Design**
    - Understanding user needs and behaviors
    - Conducting effective user research
    - Designing intuitive experiences across platforms
3. **Business Acumen**
    - Understanding market dynamics and business models
    - Identifying opportunities for innovation
    - Aligning technical solutions with business objectives
4. **Ethical Technology Implementation**
    - Recognizing and addressing bias in AI and algorithms
    - Designing with privacy and security in mind
    - Considering the broader societal impacts of technology
5. **Effective Communication**
    - Explaining technical concepts to non-technical stakeholders
    - Storytelling and persuasive presentation
    - Visual communication of complex ideas

EXPERT PERSPECTIVE: Miguel Rodriguez, Technology Futurist

"The vibe coders who will thrive in the next decade won't just be technically proficient—they'll be skilled translators between human needs and technological possibilities. As AI handles more of the routine coding work, your unique value will come from combining domain expertise, human empathy, and technological fluency. The future belongs to those who can identify the right problems to solve and craft experiences that truly resonate with users, regardless of the underlying technology."

Building a Resilient Career Strategy

Beyond skills and knowledge, creating a resilient career strategy helps you navigate the inevitable changes in technology and market demands.

Diversified Career Portfolio

Just as financial investors diversify their portfolios to manage risk, consider diversifying your career assets:

- **Multiple Revenue Streams**: Explore various ways to generate income, such as consulting, product development, content creation, or teaching.
- **Cross-Industry Exposure**: Gain experience across different sectors to broaden your perspective and create more opportunities.
- **Personal Brand Development**: Build your reputation and visibility within relevant communities.

Opportunity Identification

In times of technological disruption, new opportunities emerge alongside challenges. A resilient career strategy involves positioning yourself to identify and capitalize on these opportunities.

Specifically, in the AI era, focus areas with growth potential include:

- **AI Ecosystem Roles**: Developing, managing, and

improving AI and other advanced technologies are inherently AI-resilient because they're at the cutting edge.
- **Experience Design**: Creating compelling user experiences that leverage new platforms and technologies.
- **Specialized Domain Applications**: Applying technology to specific domains like healthcare, where AI can assist with diagnosing diseases and identifying optimal treatment plans.
- **Hybrid Human-AI Systems**: Designing systems where humans and AI work collaboratively, each leveraging their unique strengths.

ACTIONS TO TAKE:

1. Dedicate time each week to learning about emerging technologies and trends
2. Start a small side project using a technology outside your comfort zone
3. Connect with professionals in adjacent fields to broaden your perspective
4. Document your learning journey and share insights with your network

Cultivating Adaptability as Your Greatest Asset

In a landscape of continual technological evolution, adaptability becomes your most valuable asset. It's not just about responding to change, but actively developing the capacity to thrive in uncertainty and complexity.

Cognitive Flexibility: The Foundation of Adaptability

Cognitive flexibility—the ability to switch between different modes of thinking and to consider multiple perspectives simultaneously—forms the foundation of adaptability in tech careers.

Developing Cognitive Flexibility

Practical approaches to cultivating this mental agility include:

- **Embracing New Experiences**: Exposing yourself to new situations, technologies, and perspectives that challenge your existing mental models.
- **Deliberate Cross-Training**: Learning skills outside your core domain to develop new thinking patterns and problem-solving approaches.
- **Mindfulness Practices**: Building awareness of your thought patterns and biases to create space for more flexible thinking.
- **Seeking Diverse Perspectives**: Actively engaging with viewpoints that differ from your own to expand your mental horizons.

Embracing Uncertainty as Opportunity

Uncertainty and change create discomfort for most people, but adaptable vibe coders learn to see uncertainty as a space of possibility rather than a source of anxiety.

Reframing Uncertainty

Practical techniques for embracing uncertainty include:

- **Scenario Planning**: Developing multiple possible futures rather than trying to predict a single outcome.
- **Small Experiments**: Running low-risk tests of new approaches to gather real-world data.
- **Opportunity Spotting**: Training yourself to identify potential advantages in changing circumstances.

KEY INSIGHT: The ability to maintain equanimity in the face of uncertainty gives you a significant competitive advantage in fast-changing fields. While others become paralyzed by change, you can continue to create and innovate.

Learning Agility: The Meta-Skill

Learning agility—the ability to learn, unlearn, and relearn quickly—sits at the heart of adaptability. In a rapidly changing technological landscape, what you know matters less than how quickly you can learn.

Accelerating Your Learning Cycle

Improve your learning agility through:

- **Deliberate Practice**: Focused, intentional skill development with regular feedback and reflection.
- **Teaching Others**: Explaining concepts to others enhances your own understanding and retention.
- **Synthesis Across Domains**: Connecting ideas from different fields to develop novel insights.
- **Regular Reflection**: Scheduled time to review experiences and extract lessons.

EXPERT PERSPECTIVE: Dr. Amara Singh, Learning Scientist

"The half-life of technical knowledge is shrinking dramatically. What truly matters is your learning process—how efficiently you can acquire new knowledge and skills when needed. The most successful developers in the AI era aren't necessarily those who know the most today, but those who can learn the fastest tomorrow. This involves both practical learning techniques and the emotional resilience to regularly step into the uncomfortable space of being a beginner again."

Conclusion: Your Evolving Vibe Coding Journey

As we reach the end of our exploration of vibe coding, it's clear that this approach represents far more than just a method of app development. It embodies a philosophy that embraces change, centers human experience, and cultivates the adaptability needed to thrive in an era of technological upheaval.

The future of vibe coding will be shaped by continued technological advancement, the emergence of new platforms, and evolving user expectations. Yet through all these changes, the core principles remain constant: focus on the user, embrace the journey of continuous learning, and remember that technology is merely a tool in service of human connection and experience.

Your journey as a vibe coder doesn't end with the completion of an app or the launch of a service. It's an ongoing evolution—one where each project builds upon the last, where failures become the foundation for future success, and where adaptability becomes your most valued skill.

As you move forward, remember that the most revolutionary technologies are those that feel invisible—the ones that so perfectly align with human needs and behaviors that they seem to disappear into the background of our lives. This is the ultimate goal of vibe coding: to create experiences so intuitive, so aligned with the human experience, that users forget they're interacting with technology at all.

The future belongs to those who can sense the pulse of emerging needs, who can translate human desires into compelling digital experiences, and who can continuously evolve their approach as the technological landscape shifts. In other words, the future belongs to the vibe coder.

Chapter Summary

- **Emerging technologies** like advanced AI, multimodal interfaces, and intent-driven no-code platforms are reshaping app development, focusing more on human needs and less on technical implementation.
- **New platforms** including AR/VR, wearables, and IoT create opportunities for more immersive, contextual, and integrated experiences that extend beyond traditional screens.
- **Staying relevant** requires a strategic approach to continuous learning, trend monitoring, and skill diversification that balances technical knowledge with human-centered capabilities.
- **Adaptability** has become the most valuable asset for vibe coders, requiring the cultivation of cognitive flexibility, comfort with uncertainty, and accelerated learning cycles.
- **Building resilient systems** requires designing with change in mind, adopting modular architectures, and prioritizing data portability to navigate platform shifts.
- **Adaptive teams** thrive on psychological safety, cross-disciplinary knowledge sharing, and a culture that values experimentation and continuous learning.
- **Vibe coding will evolve** to incorporate more sophisticated AI that can better understand and implement human intentions while responding dynamically to changing user behavior.
- **The core principles remain constant**: focus on human connection, intuitive experiences, and creating technology that enhances rather than diminishes our

humanity.

-

Actions to Take

1. **Create a personal learning roadmap** that includes both technical skills and complementary capabilities like design thinking, business strategy, or ethical technology implementation.
2. **Develop a trend monitoring system** using RSS feeds, newsletters, communities, and other sources to stay informed about emerging technologies and market shifts.
3. **Experiment with a new platform or technology** by building a small project that stretches your current capabilities.
4. **Assess your adaptability** using the checklist provided and identify specific areas for improvement.
5. **Connect with a diverse community** of practitioners from different backgrounds to expand your perspective and expose yourself to alternative approaches.
6. **Audit your current projects** for adaptability, assessing how easily they could incorporate new technologies or shift to emerging platforms.
7. **Create a personal innovation lab** where you regularly experiment with new tools, platforms, and approaches without the pressure of immediate practical application.
8. **Practice articulating the "vibe"** you want to create before jumping into implementation, honing your ability to translate feelings and intentions into clear direction.
9. **Develop a mindfulness practice** that helps you maintain equilibrium amid rapid change and uncertainty, preserving your creative capacity in turbulent times.

10. **Share your journey** with others, contributing to the collective wisdom of the vibe coding community and learning from diverse perspectives.

The future of vibe coding isn't something that happens to you—it's something you actively create through your choices, creations, and connections. By embracing adaptability, cultivating continuous learning, and staying focused on the human experience, you don't just prepare for the future—you help shape it.

Chapter 26: The Vibe Coder's Manifesto

Chapter Summary

The Vibe Coder's Manifesto represents the culmination of your journey from idea to successful digital entrepreneur. This chapter establishes the core principles that will guide your continued success in the evolving app economy, emphasizing the delicate balance between business objectives and creative fulfillment. We explore how to create meaningful impact beyond financial metrics and chart your evolution from app creator to digital entrepreneur. The manifesto serves as both a philosophical foundation and practical roadmap for sustainable success in a rapidly changing technological landscape.

The New Digital Creator Paradigm

The rise of vibe coding represents more than just a technological shift—it embodies a fundamental transformation in how we approach creation in the digital age. As Andrej Karpathy noted when coining the term in 2025, vibe coding allows creators to "fully give in to the vibes, embrace exponentials, and forget that the code even exists" .

This new paradigm shifts the focus from technical implementation to creative vision and market understanding. No longer constrained by coding expertise, entrepreneurs can now direct their energy toward what truly matters: solving meaningful problems, creating exceptional user experiences, and building sustainable businesses.

Key Insight: Vibe coding doesn't replace thinking—it transforms thinking. Instead of focusing on how to implement features, you can concentrate on which features will create the most value for users and your business.

The democratization of app development through AI tools has fundamentally altered who can participate in the digital economy. According to research, in Y Combinator's Winter 2025 batch, 25% of startups had codebases that were 95% AI-generated —a clear indication that we've entered a new era where ideas and execution are increasingly decoupled. This shift empowers a new class of creators who bring diverse perspectives, domain expertise, and creative approaches previously locked out of tech entrepreneurship.

However, with great power comes great responsibility. As a vibe coder, you stand at the intersection of possibility and accountability. Your ability to rapidly create and deploy applications carries an obligation to do so thoughtfully, ethically, and with purpose.

Principles for Sustainable Success in the App Economy

1. Vision Over Implementation

Throughout this book, we've emphasized the importance of starting with a clear vision rather than technical considerations. This principle becomes your north star for sustainable success.

The Principle: Maintain unwavering focus on the problem you're solving and the value you're creating, rather than becoming enamored with specific technologies or features.

In Practice:

- Regularly revisit your core value proposition and ensure all development decisions support it
- Create a one-sentence mission statement that captures your app's fundamental purpose
- Evaluate new feature requests against how well they serve your vision
- Use your "vibe radar" to identify when you're being pulled toward technical novelty rather than user value

Expert Perspective: Maya Rodriguez, Product Strategist

"The most successful vibe coders I work with maintain a relentless focus on user problems. When they sit down with AI tools, they don't ask 'What can I build?' but rather 'What should I build to solve this specific problem better?' This slight shift in mindset makes all the difference between apps that gain traction and those that languish unused."

2. Validation as a Lifestyle

The Vibe Validation Matrix we explored earlier isn't just a startup tool—it's a mindset for continued success.

The Principle: Never stop testing assumptions. As your app and business grow, continuously validate your understanding of users, market dynamics, and business model.

In Practice:

- Implement a structured feedback loop with users, including regular interviews and usage analysis
- Create a dashboard of key validation metrics for ongoing

monitoring
- Conduct periodic assumption audits to identify potentially outdated beliefs about your users or market
- Allocate resources specifically for validation activities, treating them as investments rather than costs

3. Embracing the Minimum Viable Experience (MVE)

Success in the app economy requires more than functional code—it demands attention to the entire user journey.

The Principle: Focus on delivering a cohesive, quality experience across all touchpoints, not just within the app itself.

In Practice:

- Create customer journey maps that extend beyond app usage to include discovery, onboarding, support, and brand interactions
- Develop specific MVE quality thresholds for each stage of the user journey
- Implement regular "experience audits" where you personally go through the entire customer journey
- Establish cross-functional teams responsible for different aspects of the overall experience

4. Community as Competitive Advantage

In an era where technical features can be quickly replicated, community becomes a powerful differentiator.

The Principle: Invest in building genuine, value-driven communities around your product that foster connection, loyalty, and advocacy.

In Practice:

- Create dedicated spaces for users to connect, share resources, and provide peer support
- Develop valuable, engaging content that informs, entertains, and inspires community members
- Foster authentic engagement by responding promptly to community members and showing appreciation for their contributions
- Establish community rituals and traditions that strengthen collective identity
- Use community feedback as a primary input for product development decisions

Actions to Take:

- Identify three community-building initiatives you could implement in the next quarter
- Survey existing users about what would make a community valuable to them
- Research one successful community in your space and analyze what makes it effective
- Draft community guidelines that reflect your values and vision

5. Ethical AI Integration

As a vibe coder leveraging AI, you have a responsibility to use these powerful tools ethically.

The Principle: Prioritize transparency, fairness, privacy, and security in how you develop and deploy AI-powered applications.

In Practice:

- Establish clear ethical guidelines for AI use in your development process
- Implement regular bias audits of your AI systems
- Be transparent with users about where and how AI is used in your application
- Prioritize data minimization and robust security practices
- Consider potential unintended consequences of your AI implementations

6. Adaptive Business Models

The subscription economy continues to evolve, requiring creative approaches to monetization.

The Principle: Design flexible, value-aligned monetization approaches that grow with your users and adapt to changing market conditions.

In Practice:

- Experiment with hybrid models that combine subscription, usage-based, and outcome-based elements
- Align pricing with clear value metrics that users can easily understand and measure
- Establish a regular cadence for reviewing and optimizing your monetization strategy
- Build direct feedback channels specifically around pricing and perceived value

Finding Balance Between Business Goals and Creative Fulfillment

The most sustainable success comes when business objectives and personal fulfillment align. This balance is particularly important for vibe coders, who often enter entrepreneurship driven by creative passion rather than purely commercial motivations.

The False Dichotomy

Many entrepreneurs believe they must choose between building a successful business and following their creative vision. This is often a false choice—the most enduring businesses emerge when founders find the overlap between:

1. What they're passionate about creating
2. What the market values and will pay for
3. What they can execute exceptionally well

Vibe coding expands the third circle by removing technical limitations as a primary constraint. This means you can focus more energy on finding the sweet spot between passion and market value.

Strategies for Maintaining Balance

1. Define Your Non-Negotiables

Identify the core aspects of your vision that bring you fulfillment and make them non-negotiable. These might include:

- The fundamental problem you're solving
- Key principles of your user experience
- Specific creative approaches or aesthetics
- How you engage with your community
- Work processes that energize rather than drain you

2. Establish Clear Metrics for Both Business and Personal Success

Create a dashboard that tracks not only business metrics (revenue, user growth, retention) but also personal fulfillment metrics:

- Time spent on creative aspects vs. administrative tasks
- Personal growth and learning
- Work-life balance indicators
- Alignment with your values and purpose
- Enjoyment and engagement levels

3. Build a Support System of Like-Minded Creators

Connect with other vibe coders who understand the unique challenges of balancing business and creativity:

- Join communities specifically for creative entrepreneurs
- Find mentors who have successfully navigated similar journeys
- Establish regular mastermind groups to share challenges and solutions
- Consider partnerships that allow you to focus on your areas of passion

Key Insight: Balance isn't static—it's dynamic. Different phases of your journey will require shifting focus between business and creative priorities. The key is maintaining awareness of where you are and making intentional choices rather than drifting unconsciously.

4. Embrace Constraints as Creative Catalysts

Rather than viewing business requirements as limitations on creativity, reframe them as creative challenges:

- How can you satisfy user needs in uniquely creative ways?
- What innovative approaches might actually improve business metrics?
- How can you turn business processes themselves into creative opportunities?

Expert Perspective: Javier Lin, App Entrepreneur

"I used to see business metrics as the enemy of creativity. Now I understand they're actually valuable feedback mechanisms. When I launched my first vibe-coded app, I obsessively checked user engagement data not because I was fixated on numbers, but because it told me whether my creative choices were resonating. This shift in perspective transformed metrics from creativity killers to creativity guides."

Creating Impact Beyond Financial Metrics

While financial success provides sustainability, many vibe coders are driven by a desire to create meaningful impact. The democratization of app development through vibe coding enables more people to build solutions addressing a wider range of human needs.

Reimagining Success Metrics

Consider expanding your definition of success beyond traditional business metrics to include:

1. Problem Resolution Metrics

- To what degree have you solved the core problem for your users?
- How many people have benefited from your solution?
- What quantifiable improvements have users experienced?

2. Accessibility Metrics

- Have you made a previously exclusive solution available to underserved populations?
- Are you breaking down barriers to access through pricing, design, or distribution?
- Does your application work well for people with different abilities and needs?

3. Knowledge and Capability Metrics

- Does your application help users learn new skills or capabilities?
- Are you contributing to expanding understanding in your domain?
- Have you created tools that empower others to create?

4. Connection and Community Metrics

- Has your application fostered meaningful connections between people?
- Have you built communities that provide support and belonging?
- Are you facilitating positive social interactions and relationships?

5. Environmental Impact Metrics

- Does your application help reduce resource consumption?
- Are you building with sustainable practices in mind?
- Does your business model incentivize environmentally positive behaviors?

Practical Approaches to Impact Measurement

1. Develop an Impact Framework

Create a structured approach to defining, measuring, and reporting your impact:

- Clearly articulate your intended impact areas
- Establish specific, measurable indicators for each area
- Implement systems to collect relevant data
- Regularly review and report on your impact metrics

2. Gather Impact Stories

Complement quantitative metrics with qualitative evidence of impact:

- Create channels for users to share how your application has affected their lives
- Document case studies of particularly meaningful user experiences
- Conduct in-depth interviews with users about long-term impact

3. Build Impact Into Your Business Model

Align your financial incentives with your impact goals:

- Consider impact-based pricing models where you charge based on value created
- Implement a "buy one, give one" approach for underserved populations
- Allocate a percentage of revenue to impact-focused initiatives

Actions to Take:

- Define three specific impact goals for your application beyond financial metrics
- Design a simple system to measure progress toward each goal
- Identify one way you could modify your business model to better align with your impact goals
- Create a mechanism to collect impact stories from your users

Your Evolution from App Creator to Digital Entrepreneur

The journey of a vibe coder naturally evolves from building a single application to developing a broader entrepreneurial identity and portfolio.

The Evolutionary Stages

Stage 1: The Creator

- Focus on building a single application
- Primary concern is product development and initial

market fit
- Personal identity still largely separate from the creation

Stage 2: The Builder

- Expanding the core application based on user feedback
- Beginning to develop systems and processes
- Forming a team or partnerships to scale operations
- Identity becoming more intertwined with the product

Stage 3: The Entrepreneur

- Managing a portfolio of related products or extensions
- Strategic focus on market positioning and business model optimization
- Building organizational capacity and culture
- Identity shifting toward being a business leader

Stage 4: The Visionary

- Shaping an ecosystem or platform
- Influencing industry direction
- Empowering others to create within your framework
- Identity centered on broader purpose and impact

Navigating the Transitions

Each stage requires developing new skills and mindsets while maintaining the creative spirit that inspired your initial app.

From Creator to Builder

- Key Challenge: Scaling attention beyond the product itself to include operations, marketing, and customer

service
- Essential Skill: Systematic thinking and process design
- Mindset Shift: From "building a product" to "building a product business"

From Builder to Entrepreneur

- Key Challenge: Strategic decision-making across multiple products or initiatives
- Essential Skill: Resource allocation and portfolio management
- Mindset Shift: From "growing a product" to "growing a company"

From Entrepreneur to Visionary

- Key Challenge: Influencing beyond your direct control
- Essential Skill: Industry leadership and ecosystem development
- Mindset Shift: From "running a company" to "shaping an industry"

Expert Perspective: Dr. Aisha Johnson, Digital Entrepreneurship Researcher

"The vibe coders who successfully navigate these transitions maintain connection to their creative core while developing new capabilities. They don't abandon their creative identity but rather expand it to encompass new dimensions. The most common pitfall I see is entrepreneurs getting stuck in a previous stage's mindset—like continuing to focus on product details when they should be developing strategic vision, or conversely, getting caught up in grand visions while neglecting operational excellence."

Building Adaptability as a Core Competency

The accelerating pace of technological change requires developing adaptability as a fundamental skill.

1. Continuous Learning Habits

- Dedicate regular time for exploring emerging technologies and trends
- Develop a network of diverse information sources
- Establish learning rituals that expose you to ideas outside your immediate focus

2. Strategic Experimentation

- Allocate resources specifically for testing new approaches
- Implement rapid experimentation cycles with clear learning objectives
- Create systems for capturing and applying insights from experiments

3. Scenario Planning

- Regularly engage in structured scenario planning exercises
- Identify potential disruptions to your current business model
- Develop contingency strategies for different future scenarios

4. Cultivating Resilience

- Build financial reserves to weather transitions
- Develop emotional resilience practices

- Create support systems for navigating uncertainties

Key Insight: The most valuable skill in a rapidly changing environment isn't predicting the future correctly—it's developing the ability to adapt quickly regardless of which future materializes.

The Vibe Coder's Pledge

As we conclude this journey, consider this pledge as a distillation of the vibe coder's ethos—a commitment to yourself, your users, and the broader digital ecosystem:

As a vibe coder, I pledge to:

- **Create with purpose**, focusing on solving meaningful problems rather than building technology for its own sake
- **Value user experience** above technical complexity, ensuring my creations are intuitive, accessible, and delightful
- **Validate continuously**, testing my assumptions and learning from user feedback
- **Build ethically**, considering the broader implications of my work and prioritizing user privacy and security
- **Share generously**, contributing to the knowledge commons and supporting fellow creators
- **Maintain balance**, sustaining my creative energy by aligning business goals with personal fulfillment
- **Measure impact holistically**, looking beyond financial metrics to the real-world difference my work makes
- **Adapt and evolve**, embracing change as an opportunity

for growth rather than a threat
- **Cultivate community**, recognizing that lasting value comes from connections between people
- **Remember the magic**, maintaining the sense of wonder and possibility that drew me to creation in the first place

---

This pledge isn't about perfection—it's about intention and direction. By embracing these principles, you join a community of vibe coders reimagining what's possible when powerful technology meets human creativity and purpose.

Visualizing Your Vibe Coding Journey

Imagine your journey as a vibe coder as a spiral rather than a linear path, where you revisit familiar challenges at increasingly higher levels of understanding and capability:

VISIONARY

/

/

ENTREPRENEUR

/

/

BUILDER

/

/

CREATOR

\

\

VALIDATION

\

\

REFINEMENT

\

\

IMPACT

\

\

EVOLUTION

At each cycle, you return to fundamental questions with new perspectives:

- What problem am I solving and for whom?
- How can I create the most value for users?
- What's the most sustainable way to capture some of that value?
- How can I magnify my impact while maintaining balance?

This evolutionary spiral represents the continuous growth journey of the vibe coder, where success isn't a final destination but an ongoing process of creation, learning, and development.

Chapter Key Takeaways

- **The vibe coding revolution** shifts focus from technical implementation to creative vision and market understanding, democratizing app development and empowering a new class of digital creators.
- **Sustainable success principles** include maintaining vision over implementation, adopting validation as a lifestyle, embracing the Minimum Viable Experience, leveraging community as a competitive advantage, integrating AI ethically, and developing adaptive business models.
- **Balance between business and creativity** requires defining non-negotiables, establishing dual metrics, building support systems, and reframing constraints as creative catalysts.
- **Impact beyond financial metrics** involves reimagining success through problem resolution, accessibility, knowledge creation, community building, and environmental benefits—with structured approaches to measuring and maximizing this broader impact.
- **The evolution from creator to visionary** follows distinct stages, each requiring different skills and mindsets while maintaining connection to your creative core.
- **The Vibe Coder's Pledge** provides a framework of commitments to guide your ongoing journey as a digital creator and entrepreneur.

The manifesto you've just read isn't an endpoint but a beginning—a foundation for your continued evolution in the dynamic world of vibe coding and digital entrepreneurship. As you move forward, remember that the greatest innovations often come not from technological capabilities but from the uniquely human ability to envision new possibilities and bring them into being. Your journey as a vibe coder is ultimately about bridging the gap between imagination and reality, creating technology that resonates with human needs and aspirations.

What will you create next?

Appendix A: Essential Resources for Vibe Coders

The vibe coding revolution has opened doors for creators of all technical backgrounds to build innovative applications that connect with users on a deeper level. This curated collection of resources will equip you with the tools, community connections, and frameworks needed to thrive in this new paradigm of AI-assisted development.

Tools and Platforms for Non-Technical Development

AI-Powered Development Environments

Vibe coding is fundamentally changing how we approach software creation, allowing you to describe what you want in natural language while AI handles the technical implementation. These powerful environments are at the forefront of this revolution:

Platform	Key Features	Best For
Cursor[1]	AI-powered IDE with built-in chat interface for prompting and code generation	Developers transitioning to vibe coding who still want IDE functionality
Replit[2]	Web-based IDE with Replit Agent that transforms English descriptions into working applications	Quick prototyping and educational projects
Bolt.new[3]	Vibe-coding-first platform where text descriptions are the primary entry point	Rapidly testing ideas without any setup
Lovable[4]	Focuses on translating natural language descriptions into applications	Creating custom tools quickly
Windsurf AI[5]	AI tool with agentic mode for automatic changes that keeps users "in the flow"	Maintaining creative momentum

Key Insight: Studies indicate that 75% of users on platforms like Replit don't write code at all, instead relying on AI assistants like Ghostwriter to generate code based on their instructions. This shift demonstrates just how accessible application development has become.

Low-Code/No-Code Platforms with AI Integration

1. https://cursor.sh/
2. https://replit.com/
3. https://bolt.new/
4. https://lovable.ai/
5. https://www.builder.io/blog/windsurf-vs-cursor

While dedicated vibe coding tools are emerging rapidly, many established low-code/no-code platforms are integrating AI capabilities that align with vibe coding principles:

Platform	Strengths	AI Features
Bubble[6]	Visual development with powerful database and workflow tools	AI-assisted development and plugin integration
FlutterFlow[7]	Mobile app development with visual builders	Code generation and AI design assistance
Webflow[8]	Professional website creation with visual design tools	Integration capabilities with AI services
Microsoft Power Apps[9]	Enterprise-grade applications with extensive integration options	AI Builder for adding intelligence to apps
Softr[10]	Quick web app creation from data sources	Used successfully by founders like Ambar Shrivastava to build AI-powered platforms
Airtable[11]	Flexible database with app-building capabilities	AI-powered automation and form processing

Expert Perspective: The Rise of Citizen Developers

6. https://bubble.io/
7. https://flutterflow.io/
8. https://webflow.com/
9. https://powerapps.microsoft.com/
10. https://www.softr.io/
11. https://airtable.com/

Miranda Chen, Digital Transformation Consultant

"By 2025, we expect to see 70% of new enterprise applications developed by 'citizen developers' using these AI-enhanced platforms. The democratization of development has profound implications for innovation cycles and organizational agility. Companies that embrace this shift will have a significant competitive advantage in rapidly testing new ideas and adapting to market feedback."

AI Models and APIs for Integration

For those looking to incorporate AI capabilities into their applications, these services provide powerful, accessible intelligence:

Service	Capabilities	Integration Complexity
OpenAI API[12]	Text generation, code assistance, content creation	Medium
Anthropic API[13]	Conversational AI with strong reasoning abilities	Medium
AWS SageMaker[14]	Comprehensive ML platform with pre-built models	High
Google Vertex AI[15]	Advanced ML capabilities with simplified workflows	High
Azure Machine Learning[16]	Enterprise-focused AI development platform	High
Hugging Face[17]	Open-source models for various AI tasks	Medium

12. https://openai.com/api/

13. https://www.anthropic.com/

14. https://aws.amazon.com/sagemaker/

Action to Take: Before building your own AI solution from scratch, explore these pre-built services to see if they can accelerate your development. Many offer free tiers perfect for testing and prototyping.

AI-Powered Market Research Tools

Validate your vibe-coded application ideas with these AI-enhanced market research platforms that quickly provide insights about potential demand and competitive landscape:

Tool	Purpose	Best For
ValidatorAI[18]	Market demand analysis and validation scoring	Initial concept testing
Checkmyidea[19]	Sentiment analysis across potential customer groups	Understanding emotional response to concepts
Speak AI[20]	Analyze datasets, social media, and customer feedback	Identifying unmet needs
Brandwatch[21]	Comprehensive social listening and competitive intelligence	Understanding market conversation
Perplexity AI[22]	AI-powered research assistant	Quick market landscape assessment
Glimpse[23]	Trend detection and early-stage opportunity identification	Finding emerging niches

15. https://cloud.google.com/vertex-ai
16. https://azure.microsoft.com/en-us/services/machine-learning/
17. https://huggingface.co/
18. https://validator.ai/
19. https://checkmyidea.com/

Key Insight: Many of these AI validation tools provide confidence scores (typically 0-1) that reflect the certainty of their predictions. For business decisions, look for scores above 80% as a starting point for pursuing an idea with significant resources.

Communities and Forums for Support and Learning

Building a supportive community around your vibe coding journey accelerates learning and creates opportunities for collaboration and growth. These platforms connect you with fellow vibe coders, AI enthusiasts, and potential early users:

Dedicated Vibe Coding Communities

Community	Focus	Value
r/vibecoding[24]	Reddit community focused specifically on vibe coding approaches and tools	Peer support, technique sharing, and inspiration
r/ChatGPTCoding[25]	Discussions on using AI for code generation and development	Practical tips and use cases
AI Engineers Discord[26]	Active community of AI practitioners	Real-time help and networking
Hugging Face Community[27]	Open-source AI model sharing and collaboration	Advanced technique discussions

20. https://www.speak.ai/

21. https://www.brandwatch.com/

22. https://www.perplexity.ai/

23. https://meetglimpse.com/

Learning Platforms and Resources

Resource	Offering	Unique Value
Replit Community[28]	Interactive coding environment with extensive learning resources	Learn by seeing and modifying examples
Disco Learning Communities[29]	Platform for building learning communities around specific AI topics	Structured learning paths and peer interaction
Builder.io Blog[30]	In-depth comparisons of AI coding tools and techniques	Thoughtful analysis of emerging tools
John Whitaker's Blog[31]	Real-world vibe coding examples and case studies	Practical applications and insights

Action to Take: Join at least one active community focused on vibe coding or AI development. Introduce yourself, share your projects (even early ideas), ask questions, and offer help to others when you can. Community participation accelerates learning through exposure to diverse perspectives and approaches.

Social and Professional Networks

24. https://www.reddit.com/r/vibecoding/

25. https://www.reddit.com/r/ChatGPTCoding/

26. https://discord.gg/aie

27. https://huggingface.co/spaces

28. https://replit.com/community

29. https://www.disco.co/

30. https://www.builder.io/blog

31. https://johnowhitaker.dev/essays/vibe-coding.html

Expand your reach and learn from others by participating in these broader networks where discussions about vibe coding and AI development are increasingly common:

Network	Best Uses	Connection Strategy
LinkedIn Groups[32]	Professional networking, industry insights, job opportunities	Join AI, low-code, and startup-focused groups
Slack Communities[33]	Real-time discussions, problem-solving, collaboration	Find public AI and developer Slack workspaces
Discord Servers[34]	Casual conversation, community building, live events	Join AI tool-specific servers
Twitter/X[35]	Following thought leaders like Andrej Karpathy who coined "vibe coding"	Create a list of AI innovators to follow

Expert Perspective: The Power of Community

Sophia Williams, Community Growth Strategist

"The most successful vibe coders I've worked with don't just consume content—they actively engage in communities. They share their experiments, ask thoughtful questions, and offer help to newcomers. This engagement creates a virtuous cycle of learning and opportunity. I've seen countless collaborations, job offers, and even funding opportunities emerge from these connections. In a

32. https://www.linkedin.com/groups/

33. https://slack.com/

34. https://discord.com/

35. https://twitter.com/

rapidly evolving field like AI-assisted development, your community becomes your competitive advantage."

Templates and Checklists for Each Development Stage

These ready-to-use frameworks will guide you through the entire development process, from initial idea to launch and beyond. Each template incorporates vibe coding principles while ensuring you don't miss critical steps.

Ideation and Validation Phase

Vibe Validation Matrix Template

Use this matrix to systematically test the assumptions underlying your app idea before committing significant resources:

Assumption Area	Key Assumption (Be Specific)	Validation Method	Evidence Gathered	Confidence Score	Next Steps
Problem/ Need	[Who has what problem?]	[Customer interviews, surveys, etc.]	[Summary of findings]	[Low/ Med/High]	[Proce or piv
Solution Fit	[How does your solution solve it?]	[Prototype testing, competitor analysis]			
Target Audience	[Who specifically will use this?]	[Landing page test, outreach]			
Market Viability	[Willingness to pay, market size]	[Pricing research, TAM analysis]			
Technical Feasibility	[Can AI deliver required performance?]	[Expert consultation, API testing]			
MVE Components	[Critical experience elements]	[User testing, feedback]			
Monetization	[Pricing model acceptance]	[A/B testing, customer feedback]			

Action to Take: Before generating a single line of code, complete this matrix for your idea. Start by identifying the assumptions with the lowest confidence (highest risk) and prioritize testing those first. Use AI research tools to gather preliminary data quickly.

Problem-Solution Canvas

Before diving into development, clearly articulate the connection between the problem you're solving and your proposed solution:

Section	Questions to Answer
Problem Statement	• What specific problem does your target user face? • How frequently do they encounter it? • What is the emotional and practical impact?
Current Alternatives	• How do users currently solve this problem? • What are the limitations of existing solutions?
Your Solution	• How does your app address the problem differently? • What unique advantages does your approach offer?
Value Proposition	• In one sentence, why would someone choose your solution?
Unique AI Advantage	• How does AI specifically enhance your solution? • Could this be done without AI? If yes, why use AI?

Key Insight: The most robust ideas originate from a clearly defined, significant problem that the proposed AI solution aims to solve. Avoid starting with "Let's use AI for X"; instead, ask "What problem can AI help us solve uniquely or better?"

Design and Development Phase

Minimum Viable Experience (MVE) Checklist

Ensure your initial product delivers a cohesive experience, not just functionality:

Discoverability & Access:

- [ ] Product/website easily found via relevant search terms
- [ ] Sign-up/purchase process simple and clear
- [ ] Application works reliably on target platforms/ browsers
- [ ] Pricing information clear and understandable

Onboarding:

- [ ] First steps intuitive for new users
- [ ] Core value demonstrated quickly (low Time-to-Value)
- [ ] Necessary initial guidance provided

Core Functionality:

- [ ] Main feature reliably solves primary user problem
- [ ] Performance (speed, responsiveness) acceptable
- [ ] Critical bugs that prevent core task completion resolved

Usability & UI:

- [ ] Navigation logical and easy to understand
- [ ] Key features easily accessible
- [ ] Interface visually clean and uncluttered
- [ ] Design consistent across the application

Support & Feedback:

- [ ] Clear and accessible way for users to seek help
- [ ] System for acknowledging and responding to support requests

- [ ] Easy mechanism for users to provide feedback

Trust & Communication:

- [ ] Use of AI disclosed appropriately and transparently
- [ ] Privacy policy clear, accessible, and followed
- [ ] Branding and messaging consistent across touchpoints
- [ ] Claims about AI capabilities accurate and not overhyped

Prompt Engineering Worksheet for Vibe Coding

When crafting prompts for AI-assisted development, use this worksheet to structure your requests:

Component	Your Input	Tips
Overall Intent	[What are you trying to build?]	Be specific about the desired outcome, not just features
User Context	[Who will use this and why?]	Include user motivations and scenarios
Functional Requirements	[List key functionalities needed]	Break down complex functionality into smaller pieces
Visual/UX Direction	[Describe the desired look and feel]	Include sensory cues, aesthetic references
Technical Constraints	[Any specific limitations to consider?]	Platform requirements, performance needs
Examples/ References	[Similar apps or designs to reference]	Provide concrete examples when possible

Action to Take: Before engaging with AI development tools, complete this worksheet fully. The more specific and detailed your prompts, the better the AI's output will align with your vision. Save effective prompts for future reference to build your personal library of reliable instructions.

Testing and Refinement Phase

User Testing Script Template

Guide for conducting effective user testing sessions:

1. **Introduction**
    - Thank participant and explain the session purpose
    - Emphasize you're testing the product, not them
    - Explain the think-aloud protocol
2. **Background Questions**
    - Brief questions about relevant experience
    - Establish context for their perspective
3. **Task Scenarios**
    - Task 1: [First critical user journey]
    - Task 2: [Second critical user journey]
    - Task 3: [Third critical user journey]
4. **Observation Notes**
    - Where did the user hesitate or express confusion?
    - What workarounds did they attempt?
    - What positive reactions did they express?
5. **Follow-up Questions**
    - What was the most confusing aspect of the experience?
    - What feature was most valuable to you?
    - On a scale of 1-10, how likely would you be to use this application?

  - What would make you more likely to recommend it?

Key Insight: As a non-technical founder, focusing on observing how real users interact with your product is a crucial and accessible testing method. This can reveal areas of confusion or delight without needing specific technical skills.

Refinement Prioritization Matrix

After gathering feedback, use this matrix to decide what to improve first:

Impact	**High**	� **Important (Schedule Soon)**	� **Critical (Do Immediately)**
Low	� Nice-to-Have (Consider Later)	� Important (Schedule Soon)	
	Low Effort	**High**	

Action to Take: When receiving feedback, document each issue or suggestion and place it in this matrix. Focus first on the high-impact, low-effort improvements to quickly enhance your application while building user trust and satisfaction.

Marketing and Growth Phase

AI Marketing Flywheel Framework

Visualize your customer journey as a self-reinforcing cycle:

Phase	Key Activities	AI Enhancement Opportunities
Attract	• Create educational content • Optimize for search • Communicate clear value proposition • Target ideal customers • Offer free trial/freemium	• AI-generated SEO-optimized content • Automated audience targeting • Personalized outreach
Engage	• Implement smooth onboarding • Personalize user experience • Build community • Provide responsive support • Share ongoing valuable content	• AI-driven personalization • Intelligent chatbots • Content recommendation
Delight	• Ensure reliable performance • Actively solicit and implement feedback • Provide exceptional support • Offer loyalty benefits • Implement referral programs • Showcase success stories	• Predictive support • Automated personalization • AI-powered feature suggestions

Key Metrics to Track:

- Acquisition: Customer Acquisition Cost (CAC)
- Engagement: Active usage rates, feature adoption, community participation
- Delight/Retention: Net Promoter Score (NPS), Customer Satisfaction (CSAT), Churn Rate, Customer Lifetime Value (LTV)

- Advocacy: Referral Rate, social mentions, review scores

AI Monetization Model Comparison Worksheet

Use this worksheet to evaluate potential revenue models for your AI application:

Model	Fit for My App (1-5)	Potential Advantages	Potential Challenges	Implementation Complexity
Subscription	[Score]	Predictable revenue, scalable tiers	Value mismatch for low/high users	[Low/Med/High]
Usage-Based	[Score]	Aligns with actual usage	Unpredictable revenue/costs	[Low/Med/High]
Freemium	[Score]	High user acquisition	Low conversion rates	[Low/Med/High]
Token/Prepaid	[Score]	Flexibility, upfront revenue	Token economy management	[Low/Med/High]
Outcome-Based	[Score]	Strong value alignment	Complex to track outcomes	[Low/Med/High]
Hybrid	[Score]	Balance predictability and flexibility	Increased complexity	[Low/Med/High]

Expert Perspective: Future of AI Monetization

Rafael Cortez, AI Business Model Strategist

"The trend is clearly moving toward hybrid monetization models that balance predictable revenue streams with usage-based components. This reflects the need to accommodate diverse customer usage patterns while covering the potentially significant costs of running AI models. In my experience, a strong approach is aiming for approximately 75% predictable revenue through subscriptions and 25% variable through usage-based charges or add-ons. This creates financial stability while still aligning pricing with value delivery.

For vibe coders just starting out, I recommend implementing a simple model at launch—perhaps a basic subscription tier with clear usage limits—and then evolving toward a more sophisticated hybrid approach as you gather data on actual usage patterns and customer preferences."

Bonus: Vibe Coder's Quick-Start Kit

For those eager to begin their vibe coding journey immediately, here's a streamlined approach to get you from idea to first prototype in under a week:

Day 1: Problem Definition

- Complete the Problem-Solution Canvas
- Research potential users and competitors
- Define your unique value proposition

Day 2: Validation

- Create a simple landing page describing your concept
- Drive minimal traffic through targeted social media or communities

- Measure sign-up rates or interest

Day 3: Vision Clarification

- Complete the Prompt Engineering Worksheet
- Create simple wireframes or sketches of key screens
- Map the primary user flow

Day 4: Prototype Creation

- Select an appropriate AI development environment
- Use your prepared prompts to generate initial code
- Focus on core functionality only

Day 5: Testing & Refinement

- Conduct 3-5 user tests with your target audience
- Identify critical issues and quick wins
- Refine your prototype based on feedback

Action to Take: Set aside one focused week to follow this quick-start approach. The goal isn't perfection but rapid learning and iteration. By the end of the week, you'll have a basic working prototype and, more importantly, valuable insights about your idea's potential.

Remember, the resources in this appendix are not just tools to build with but bridges to a new way of thinking about software development. Vibe coding isn't merely about using AI to generate code—it's about shifting focus from technical implementation to user experience, emotional connection, and business value. By leveraging these resources effectively, you'll be positioned at the forefront of this transformative movement in software creation.

Appendix B: Glossary of Terms

Vibe Coding Fundamentals

Vibe Coding: A new programming paradigm where developers describe desired outcomes in natural language, allowing AI to generate the code. Emphasizes intuition, market awareness, and user connection over technical details. First popularized by Andrej Karpathy in February 2025, describing a process where one "fully gives in to the vibes, embraces exponentials, and forgets that the code even exists."

Vibe Design: The application of AI-assisted principles to UX design and user research, focusing on high-level intent while delegating execution details to AI. Designers describe the desired feeling or outcome of a design, allowing AI to propose visual and interactive solutions.

Vibe Prompting: A technique where you treat AI like a creative collaborator with mood and context awareness. It involves establishing a specific "vibe" in your prompts to influence the AI's output, often including sensory cues, temporal settings, aesthetic references, emotional framing, and character voice/roleplay.

Intent-Based Development: A development approach that shifts focus from the *how* of writing code (syntax, algorithms) to the *what* the software should do. Developers and non-technical individuals describe their intentions and let AI tools handle technical implementation.

Low-Code/No-Code (LC/NC): Platforms that democratize software creation by allowing users to build applications through visual interfaces, drag-and-drop components, and pre-built templates, often without writing traditional code. Examples include Bubble, FlutterFlow, Zapier, Airtool, Microsoft Power Apps, OutSystems, and Mendix.

Minimum Viable Experience (MVE): The minimum holistic experience—encompassing marketing, sales, onboarding, product usability, support, and branding—that must be provided to satisfy early users and effectively validate a core product idea. Goes beyond just functionality to consider how users feel about the product.

Minimum Viable Product (MVP): A product with just enough features to satisfy early customers and provide feedback for future product development. Focuses on core features needed to solve the user's problem and test the riskiest assumptions.

Minimum Lovable Product (MLP): Builds on the MVP by adding elements of design, usability, or features that elicit a positive emotional response or delight from users.

AI Terminology

Large Language Model (LLM): An AI trained on vast amounts of text data that can generate human-like text, complete tasks, and assist with various applications including code generation. Examples include ChatGPT, Claude, and others used in vibe coding platforms.

Artificial Intelligence (AI): Computer systems designed to perform tasks that typically require human intelligence, such as visual perception, speech recognition, decision-making, and language translation. In vibe coding, AI serves as the translator between natural language instructions and functional code.

Natural Language Processing (NLP): A field of AI focused on the interaction between computers and human language, enabling computers to understand, interpret, and generate text. A fundamental technology powering vibe coding.

Generative AI: AI systems that can create new content, including text, images, music, and code, based on patterns learned from training data. Tools like ChatGPT, DALL-E, and MidJourney have become standard parts of startup workflows.

Agentic AI: AI systems designed not just to respond or provide information, but to autonomously plan, make decisions, and execute complex workflows to achieve user-defined goals. This moves AI from an "answer engine" to an "action engine."

Prompt Engineering: The practice of crafting effective instructions for AI systems to produce desired outputs. In vibe coding, this involves creating clear, specific prompts that guide AI tools to generate appropriate code. You can specifically ask AI to "write better code," focusing on security or performance.

Human-in-the-Loop (HIL): An approach incorporating human oversight for evaluating subjective outputs or critical decisions in AI systems. Essential for quality control and ethical AI development.

Data Quality & Bias: The critical assessment of input data for accuracy, completeness, consistency, and potential biases. Fundamental to AI performance and ethical considerations.

Hallucination (AI): When an AI generates content that appears plausible but is factually incorrect or fabricated. A significant risk in vibe coding that can lead to problematic code or features.

Software Development Concepts

API (Application Programming Interface): A set of rules and protocols that allows different software applications to communicate with each other. Essential for integrating services and functionality into applications.

Frontend/Backend: Frontend refers to the user-facing part of an application (what users see and interact with), while backend refers to the server-side logic and database operations happening behind the scenes.

Technical Debt: The implied cost of additional rework caused by choosing an easy or quick solution now instead of using a better approach that would take longer. In AI development, shortcuts like using poorly prepared data or inadequate testing create technical debt that makes future improvements harder.

Agile Methodology: An iterative approach to software development that emphasizes flexible planning, evolutionary development, early delivery, and continual improvement. Generally preferred for AI projects due to its adaptability.

Scrum/Kanban: Popular frameworks within Agile methodology that provide structure for team collaboration and project management.

Waterfall Methodology: A linear, sequential development approach where progress flows in one direction through distinct phases. Less flexible than Agile but sometimes preferred for projects with well-defined requirements.

UX (User Experience): The overall experience a user has when interacting with a product or service. In vibe coding, UX becomes a critical differentiator. Nearly 40% of people might stop using an application if the layout is not engaging and attractive.

UI (User Interface): The points of interaction between the user and a digital product or service, including screens, pages, buttons, and other visual elements.

Regression Testing: Testing to confirm that recent code changes haven't adversely affected existing features. Critical for maintaining stability during iterative development.

User Acceptance Testing (UAT): Validation process where actual users test the software to ensure it meets requirements and works as expected in real-world scenarios.

Business and Marketing Terminology

Customer Acquisition Cost (CAC): The total cost of acquiring a new customer, including marketing and sales expenses. A key metric for evaluating business viability.

Customer Lifetime Value (CLV): The total worth of a customer to a business over the entire duration of their relationship. Important for pricing and business model decisions.

Value Proposition: A statement that clearly communicates the specific benefits a product or service offers to customers. It should be customer-centric, stating who the product is for, the problem it solves, the unique solution offered, and resulting benefits.

Value Proposition Canvas: A framework tool that helps businesses identify and articulate the value they provide to customers, mapping customer needs to product benefits.

Monetization Model: The strategy for generating revenue from a product or service. Common models for AI applications include subscription tiers, usage-based pricing, freemium, token-based, outcome-based pricing, and hybrid approaches.

Subscription Model: A business model where customers pay recurring fees (monthly or annual) for access to a product or service, often with different tiers based on features, usage limits, or user seats.

Freemium: A business model offering a basic version for free while charging for premium features or expanded usage. Effective for user acquisition but requires careful balancing to ensure conversion to paid tiers.

Network Effects: The phenomenon where a product or service becomes more valuable to its users as more people use it. This can create powerful, defensible advantages and drive exponential growth.

Market Validation: The process of determining if your product idea addresses a genuine market need before investing significant resources in development. Encompasses problem validation, solution validation, and business model validation.

Pivot: A significant business strategy shift based on customer feedback or market realities. May involve changing the target market, value proposition, or core product focus while retaining some aspects of the original vision.

Buyer Persona: A semi-fictional representation of your ideal customer based on market research and real data. Includes demographics, behaviors, motivations, and goals to guide product development and marketing.

User Journey: A visualization of the complete experience a user has when interacting with your product, from initial awareness through adoption and ongoing usage. Helps identify pain points and opportunities for improvement.

Growth Hacking: Ethical growth strategies for sustainable business expansion. Includes designing viral mechanics, referral systems, cross-promotion opportunities, and data-driven experimentation for maximum ROI.

Marketing Flywheel: A customer-centric growth framework that views growth as a continuous, self-reinforcing cycle rather than a linear funnel. Leverages momentum from satisfied customers to drive referrals, repeat business, and advocacy.

AI Business Models and Metrics

SaaS (Software as a Service): A software delivery model where applications are hosted by a provider and made available to customers over the internet, typically on a subscription basis.

Monthly Recurring Revenue (MRR): A measure of predictable revenue generated each month from subscription customers. A key metric for subscription-based business models.

Annual Recurring Revenue (ARR): Similar to MRR but measured on an annual basis. Indicates the value of recurring revenue normalized for a year.

Churn Rate: The percentage of customers who stop using a product or service during a given time period. A critical metric for subscription businesses.

Return on Investment (ROI): The ratio between net profit and cost of investment. For AI projects, demonstrating clear ROI is crucial for adoption and continued support.

Net Promoter Score (NPS): A metric measuring customer satisfaction and loyalty based on how likely customers are to recommend your product to others. Indicator of potential for organic growth.

Customer Effort Score (CES): A metric measuring the ease of customer experience, particularly focused on how much effort customers must expend to accomplish their goals.

Time-to-Value: How quickly new users can experience the core benefit of your product. Shorter time-to-value typically leads to better conversion and retention rates.

Key Insight: Language as the New Interface

As Andrej Karpathy noted, "the hottest new programming language is English." This paradigm shift fundamentally changes how we think about software creation, moving from syntax mastery to effective communication with AI collaborators.

Actions to Take:

1. **Build your prompt vocabulary**: Create a personal library of effective prompts that reliably produce the code structures you frequently need
2. **Learn the "feeling-layer of communication"**: Practice

describing the emotional and experiential qualities you want your software to embody

3. **Study successful vibe-coded projects**: Analyze open-source examples to understand how others effectively communicate with AI coding tools

Appendix C: Interviews with Successful Vibe Coders

Introduction

The journey from concept to successful application often looks different for vibe coders than for traditional developers. In this appendix, we share the stories of entrepreneurs and creators who leveraged vibe coding to bring their visions to life without extensive technical backgrounds. Their experiences offer valuable lessons, practical insights, and inspiration for your own vibe coding journey.

Alex Turnbull: Visualizing Success at Groove HQ

Alex Turnbull founded Groove HQ, a customer support software company, despite having no formal engineering background. His approach to communicating his vision visually became key to his success.

When you first started Groove, what was your approach to building a tech product without a technical background?

"I couldn't write a line of code, but I knew exactly what I wanted to build. My secret weapon was visualization. I started with hand-drawn sketches of the user interface and basic workflows. Eventually, I taught myself just enough Photoshop to create more polished mockups. These visual assets were incredibly powerful for communicating my vision."

How did your visual approach help you build your team?

"Those mockups were worth more than a thousand words when recruiting technical talent. Engineers could immediately grasp what I was trying to build. The visuals bridged the communication gap and helped persuade talented developers to join our mission. It showed them I had thought deeply about the user experience, even if I couldn't implement it myself."

What advice would you give to non-technical vibe coders trying to build a technical team?

"Focus on becoming an exceptional communicator of your vision. Learn to speak the language of user experience, even if you don't speak the language of code. Engineers want to build meaningful products that solve real problems. If you can clearly articulate the problem and show a thoughtful approach to solving it, you'll attract the right technical partners."

KEY INSIGHT: Visual Communication

Non-technical founders can bridge the gap with technical talent by creating visual representations of their ideas. Even simple sketches and wireframes can powerfully communicate your vision and demonstrate the thought you've put into the user experience.

How did you approach the development process once you had a team?

"I focused on my strengths while trusting my team with theirs. My role was defining the 'what' and 'why' - what we were building and why it mattered to our users. I established clear roles from the beginning, with me owning the product vision, business strategy, and user requirements, while the technical team focused on implementation and architecture."

What's your take on the emergence of vibe coding and AI-assisted development?

"These tools would have been game-changing when I was starting out. I spent months creating mockups that today could be generated in hours. But the principle remains the same - success isn't about technical knowledge, it's about deeply understanding your users and clearly communicating that understanding. AI can accelerate the process, but the human element of connecting with your users' needs is still essential."

Jodie Cook: Leveraging Existing Assets with Coachvox AI

Jodie Cook built Coachvox AI, a platform that allows creators to build AI versions of themselves for coaching and engagement. With a background in content and social media agency ownership rather than technical development, she leveraged her existing content assets to create a successful AI product.

Tell us about how you developed Coachvox AI without a technical background.

"I had spent years creating content - books, articles, podcasts, and social media posts. When I saw the potential of AI to transform how people consume information, I realized my content library was an incredibly valuable asset. The key insight was understanding that my technical limitations didn't matter as much as my domain expertise and unique content."

How did you approach the technical aspects of building an AI product?

"Instead of trying to become a developer overnight, I focused on finding the right technical partners who could complement my strengths. I was clear about what I was bringing to the table - deep industry knowledge, a valuable content library, and a clear vision for the product. This clarity helped me attract technical talent who could handle the implementation while I focused on strategy and content."

EXPERT PERSPECTIVE: The Asset-First Approach

"Non-technical founders often overlook their most valuable assets," explains Cook. "Before diving into coding or even vibe coding, ask yourself: What unique resources do I already have that could form the foundation of a product? Domain expertise, content libraries, industry connections, and audience relationships can be more valuable than technical skills when starting an AI venture."

Your platform achieved six-figure Annual Recurring Revenue (ARR) before its official launch. How?

"We focused on demonstrating clear value to early adopters. The AI coaching experience we created was novel, but more importantly, it was useful. Early users saw immediate value in having access to personalized coaching that incorporated my expertise. Word of mouth from these initial users created momentum that translated into pre-launch revenue."

What lessons have you learned about monetizing AI products?

"Understand your value metric - what are users actually paying for? With AI products, they're often paying for outcomes, not features. We structured our pricing around the transformation we enabled rather than the technology itself. Also, don't be afraid to charge early. If you're creating genuine value, users will pay even when your product isn't perfect."

Actions to Take: Identify Your Assets

1. **Content Inventory:** List all content you've created that could be valuable in an AI context
2. **Expertise Audit:** Document your specialized knowledge that others would find valuable
3. **Network Map:** Identify connections who could provide complementary skills
4. **Audience Assessment:** Evaluate any existing audience or customer base you could leverage

---

Ambar Shrivastava: Building SaaS with No-Code at Coverdoc

Ambar Shrivastava used the no-code platform Softr to build Coverdoc, an AI-powered platform for job seekers that achieved $1,000 Monthly Recurring Revenue (MRR) without writing a single line of code.

How did you identify the opportunity for Coverdoc?

"I was personally experiencing the pain of creating customized cover letters for job applications. It was time-consuming and repetitive - exactly the kind of problem AI is perfect for solving. The key was starting with a very specific problem that I deeply understood, rather than trying to build something complex or revolutionary."

Why did you choose a no-code approach instead of hiring developers?

"Speed and control were my primary considerations. Using Softr allowed me to iterate quickly based on user feedback without dependency on a development team. I could test assumptions, pivot when necessary, and scale gradually without significant upfront investment. The platform handled the technical complexities while I focused on the user experience and value proposition."

KEY INSIGHT: The Validation Advantage

No-code platforms offer a powerful advantage in the validation phase. By reducing the time and cost to build a functioning MVP, they enable founders to test market assumptions with real users before committing significant resources. This approach minimizes risk while maximizing learning.

What challenges did you face with the no-code approach, and how did you overcome them?

"The biggest challenge was balancing customization with the constraints of the platform. There were moments when I wanted functionality that wasn't readily available in Softr. In those cases, I had to decide whether to find creative workarounds, integrate with other tools, or simplify the feature. This forced me to focus on what was truly essential for delivering value, which ultimately led to a cleaner, more focused product."

How has the emergence of AI-assisted development tools changed your approach?

"It's been transformative. I now use AI to help with everything from copywriting to designing user flows. When I hit a wall with what no-code platforms can provide, I use vibe coding approaches to describe what I need, and AI tools help bridge the gap. The combination of no-code platforms and AI assistance has further democratized software creation."

What advice would you give to non-technical founders just starting their vibe coding journey?

"Start with validation, not building. Before you even open a no-code tool or AI assistant, make sure you've validated that your idea solves a real problem people care about. Set up a simple landing page, drive some traffic to it, and gauge interest. Once you've confirmed there's demand, focus on building the minimal version that delivers the core value. Everything else can come later."

Actions to Take: No-Code Validation Process

1. **Problem Validation:** Create a landing page describing your solution
2. **Traffic Generation:** Use minimal ad spend or community outreach to get visitors
3. **Interest Measurement:** Track sign-ups, email captures, or pre-orders
4. **MVP Planning:** List essential features needed to deliver core value
5. **Platform Selection:** Choose the no-code platform best suited to your MVP needs

---

Charles Thomas: Scaling a Marketplace with Bubble at Comet

Charles Thomas built Comet, a freelance marketplace, using the no-code platform Bubble. Without traditional coding skills, he created a complex application that quickly achieved significant monthly recurring revenue.

What motivated you to build a freelance marketplace without a technical background?

"I saw a gap in how freelancers and clients connected in my industry. Having experienced the pain points firsthand, I had a clear vision for a better solution. What I lacked in technical skills, I made up for in domain knowledge and user empathy. I understood exactly what features would solve real problems for both sides of the marketplace."

Why did you choose Bubble as your development platform?

"After researching various options, Bubble stood out for its flexibility and power. It's visual programming model was intuitive enough for me to learn quickly, yet sophisticated enough to build a complex marketplace with user profiles, search functionality, messaging, and payment processing. The platform's ability to handle database relationships was crucial for the marketplace model."

EXPERT PERSPECTIVE: Platform Selection Strategy

"When evaluating no-code platforms, consider not just current needs but future scalability," advises Thomas. "For marketplace businesses, you need a platform that can handle complex relationships between users, robust search capabilities, and transaction processing. Don't choose based solely on ease of use – evaluate against your specific business model requirements."

How did you approach the learning curve of a new platform?

"I broke down the learning process into small, achievable goals. Instead of trying to build the entire marketplace at once, I started with creating user profiles, then added the project posting feature, then search functionality, and so on. Each small win built my confidence and expanded my capabilities. Bubble's community forums and tutorials were invaluable resources during this journey."

What strategies helped you achieve product-market fit?

"Constant user feedback and rapid iteration were key. We launched with a very basic version and immediately started collecting user insights. The beauty of the no-code approach was that I could implement changes quickly, sometimes within hours of receiving feedback. This created a virtuous cycle where users saw their suggestions implemented, which increased their engagement and loyalty."

How do you approach scaling and technical limitations?

"As we've grown, we've faced some scaling challenges typical of no-code platforms. Our approach has been to optimize within the platform as much as possible, while selectively integrating with other tools for specific functions. We've also begun working with Bubble developers who can implement more advanced customizations. The platform has been remarkably capable, handling thousands of users and transactions without major issues."

Actions to Take: Marketplace Development Strategy

1. **User Personas:** Define detailed profiles for both sides of your marketplace
2. **Value Proposition Mapping:** Clarify the unique value for each user type
3. **Core Functionality Identification:** List the minimum

features needed for marketplace function

4. **Platform Evaluation:** Assess no-code options specifically for marketplace capabilities
5. **Phased Build Plan:** Create a step-by-step plan for building core marketplace components

---

"Excel Prototype" Founder: Lean Validation and Resourcefulness

This founder, who preferred to remain anonymous, took an ultra-lean approach to validating their SaaS concept, starting with nothing more than an Excel spreadsheet as their initial prototype.

Tell us about your unconventional approach to prototyping.

"When I first had the idea for my SaaS product, I didn't immediately jump into building anything fancy. Instead, I created an Excel spreadsheet that mimicked the core functionality of what I envisioned. It was crude but effective—it demonstrated the essential value proposition and gave potential customers something tangible to react to."

How did you use this basic prototype for validation?

"I reached out to potential customers in my target market and walked them through the Excel prototype, explaining how the actual product would work. These conversations were invaluable. They helped me understand what features were truly essential versus nice-to-have, and most importantly, whether people would actually pay for the solution."

KEY INSIGHT: Bare Minimum Testing

The most efficient validation doesn't require even a working MVP—it requires identifying the absolute minimum demonstration needed to determine if customers would pay for your solution. This could be as simple as a spreadsheet, a PowerPoint presentation, or even a conversation about a hypothetical product.

How did you transition from Excel to an actual product?

"After confirming there was genuine interest, I collaborated with a designer to create proper Figma mockups. These mockups gave potential customers a clearer vision of what the final product would look like. With these mockups and the validation data from my initial conversations, I defined the bare minimum feature set that customers said they would pay for."

How did you find technical talent without a big budget?

"Resourcefulness was key. I posted on Reddit and found part-time engineers who were interested in the project. I started small, with very limited hours, and focused on building just enough to get a functional MVP. As revenue came in, I gradually increased development resources."

What advice would you give to non-technical founders on a tight budget?

"Question every assumption about what you 'need' to build. Most founders overestimate what's required for initial validation. Start with the simplest possible representation of your idea, get it in front of potential customers, and be brutally honest about whether they're truly excited by it. Only then should you invest in building anything."

Actions to Take: Ultra-Lean Validation

1. **Zero-Code Prototype:** Create a representation of your concept using tools you already know
2. **Decision Criteria:** Define clear indicators of validation before starting conversations
3. **Customer Conversations:** Conduct at least 10 in-depth interviews with target users
4. **Value Definition:** Document the minimum functionality users would actually pay for
5. **Resource Mapping:** Identify the most cost-effective path to building that minimum functionality

---

My AskAI Founder: Pivoting to Product-Market Fit

The co-founder of My AskAI, with a background in finance rather than technology, built an AI customer support chatbot for SaaS businesses that reached $25,000 monthly revenue after pivoting based on market feedback.

Your journey began with experimentation. How did you approach learning about AI technology?

"I started by playing with GPT-3 when it was first released, building small tools and experiments to understand its capabilities. There was a lot of trial and error. My financial background actually helped—I approached it analytically, trying to identify where this technology could create measurable value for businesses."

Tell us about the pivot that led to My AskAI's success.

"We initially built some simple AI tools that were interesting but didn't solve pressing problems. The breakthrough came when we started talking to SaaS businesses about their customer support challenges. We realized that many teams were answering the same questions repeatedly, which was perfectly suited for AI automation. That insight led us to create a specialized AI chatbot focused specifically on SaaS customer support."

EXPERT PERSPECTIVE: The Pivot Process

"The best pivots come from staying close to your customers while remaining flexible about your solution," explains the founder. "We maintained our focus on leveraging AI, but completely changed our application of it based on real market needs. Listen for pain points that make people say, 'I would pay to solve that problem right now.'"

How did you build the product with limited technical knowledge?

"We started incredibly small—just $99 in initial investment. Instead of trying to build something comprehensive, we focused on one core function: answering FAQs for SaaS products. We used existing APIs and platforms to handle the AI component, while focusing our energy on the integration with customer support workflows and the user experience."

What were the key factors in scaling to $25,000 monthly revenue?

"First, we solved a very specific problem with a clear ROI—customers could see exactly how much time and money they saved by automating support. Second, we made implementation dead simple, with a focus on quick time-to-value. Finally, we leveraged our early customers for testimonials and case studies, which were powerful for proving the concept to new prospects."

What advice would you give to non-technical founders about finding product-market fit?

"Don't fall in love with your first idea or approach. Be willing to experiment, listen carefully to feedback, and pivot when necessary. Also, don't try to build everything at once. Pick one core problem, solve it exceptionally well, and expand from there. The path to $25,000 monthly revenue started with a $99 investment in a very focused solution."

Actions to Take: Finding Product-Market Fit

1. **Experimentation:** Build small, low-cost experiments to test technology capabilities
2. **Customer Discovery:** Conduct problem-focused interviews, not solution-focused
3. **Pain Point Identification:** Look for problems people explicitly say they would pay to solve
4. **Focused MVP:** Build the smallest possible solution that delivers clear value
5. **ROI Measurement:** Help customers quantify the value of your solution in their context

---

Synthesized Lessons from Successful Vibe Coders

Throughout these interviews, several common themes emerge that can guide your own vibe coding journey:

Focus on Problems, Not Technology

Successful vibe coders obsess over understanding specific user problems rather than the technology itself. They use vibe coding as a means to an end—creating solutions to real problems—not as an end in itself.

KEY INSIGHT: Problem Obsession

Before opening any coding platform or AI assistant, deeply understand the problem you're solving. The more specific and well-defined the problem, the more effectively you can leverage vibe coding to create a solution.

Validate Before Building

Every successful founder emphasized the importance of validation before significant development. This often meant creating landing pages, conducting user interviews, or building minimal prototypes to test assumptions before investing heavily in development.

Leverage Your Non-Technical Strengths

Your domain expertise, industry connections, content assets, and user empathy are incredibly valuable advantages. Successful vibe coders focus on what they bring to the table rather than what they lack.

Start Small and Iterate

Rather than attempting to build comprehensive products from the start, successful vibe coders begin with minimal implementations focused on core value delivery, then expand based on user feedback and validation.

Choose the Right Tools for Your Context

The founders interviewed used various approaches—from no-code platforms like Bubble and Softr to traditional development with visual mockups to hybrid approaches combining AI assistance with existing tools. The key was selecting tools appropriate to their specific needs and capabilities.

Build a Complementary Team

Even with powerful vibe coding tools, most successful founders eventually build teams that complement their skills. They focus on clear communication, role definition, and finding partners who share their vision while bringing technical expertise.

Focus on User Experience

The "vibe" in vibe coding extends to the overall feel and experience of your product. Successful founders prioritize creating intuitive, friction-free experiences even when the underlying technology is complex.

EXPERT PERSPECTIVE: The Vibe Advantage

"The most successful non-technical founders I've worked with have an almost obsessive focus on the user experience," notes a venture capitalist who has invested in several vibe coding startups. "They understand that technology is just an enabler—what matters is how it makes users feel and what it helps them accomplish. This user-centric perspective is often their greatest advantage compared to technically-focused founders."

Embrace Resourcefulness

Limited resources forced these founders to be creative in finding solutions, from using Excel as a prototype to finding part-time developers on Reddit to leveraging existing content assets. This resourcefulness became a competitive advantage, leading to more efficient validation and development.

Final Thoughts: Your Vibe Coding Journey

The stories shared in this appendix demonstrate that successful vibe coding is less about technical mastery and more about vision, problem understanding, and strategic execution. While each founder's journey was unique, they all shared a commitment to solving real problems, validating their ideas, and leveraging whatever tools and resources were available to bring their visions to life.

As you embark on your own vibe coding journey, remember that your lack of technical background isn't a liability—it can be an asset that keeps you focused on what truly matters: creating solutions that resonate with users and solve meaningful problems.

The technological landscape will continue to evolve, with AI tools becoming increasingly powerful and accessible. But the fundamental principles demonstrated by these successful founders—problem obsession, lean validation, user-centricity, and resourceful execution—will remain relevant regardless of how the tools themselves change.

Actions to Take: Start Your Vibe Coding Success Story

1. **Problem Journaling:** Document specific pain points you've experienced or observed
2. **Validation Planning:** Design a simple experiment to test

   if others share this pain
3. **Asset Inventory:** List your unique strengths, knowledge, and resources
4. **Tool Exploration:** Experiment with vibe coding platforms that match your needs
5. **Community Building:** Connect with potential users and other vibe coders for support

Your unique perspective and approach may be the foundation of the next success story featured in a future edition of this book. The vibe coding revolution is just beginning, and non-technical founders are at the forefront of this transformative movement.

EXCLUSIVE LIMITED TIME OFFER!

Your Journey Doesn't End Here: Join the Vibe Coding Movement!

Congratulations! You've reached the end of "Catch the Vibe," but hopefully, this is just the beginning of your exciting journey into the world of app creation. You've explored the mindset shift, learned the strategies, and seen the potential of vibe coding to turn your unique ideas into reality.

Reading this book has equipped you with the foundational knowledge and inspiration. But the real magic happens when you start *doing*. Building, testing, launching, and selling your own apps is where the true transformation occurs. And you don't have to do it alone.

Take Your Vibe Coding Skills to the Next Level

To help you accelerate your progress, find support, and connect with fellow creators, we've built the **Catch the Vibe ecosystem** – a dedicated space designed to help you master vibe coding and launch your apps faster than you ever thought possible.

We offer a powerful combination of resources:

1. **The Vibe Coding Community:** Connect with like-minded individuals, share your progress, ask questions, overcome roadblocks, find collaborators, and celebrate wins together. It's your hub for ongoing support and inspiration.
2. **The Vibe Coding Course:** A structured, deep-dive program that expands on the concepts in this book with

video tutorials, hands-on exercises, and advanced techniques to streamline your workflow from idea to launch.

3. **Personalized Coaching:** Get tailored guidance, strategic advice, and accountability from experts who can help you navigate specific challenges and maximize your app's potential for success.

Exclusive Offer for "Catch the Vibe" Readers

As a thank you for purchasing this book and taking the first step, we want to make it even easier for you to join us. Visit us today and unlock your exclusive reader benefits:

- **50% Discount:** Get half off your entry into the Vibe Coding Course and Community membership. – **Coupon Code: vibebook**
- **Exclusive Bonuses:** Receive a suite of valuable tools, including our proprietary **App Idea Validator software**, designed to help you confidently choose and validate which app ideas have the highest potential *before* you invest time building them.

Ready to Build Your Future?

Don't let your momentum fade. Turn the insights from this book into tangible results. Join a thriving community, access in-depth training, and get the support you need to confidently create and sell your own apps.

Visit us now to claim your discount and bonuses:

Launchwithvibe.com[1]

1. https://launchwithvibe.com/

The vibe coding revolution is happening now, and you have the opportunity to be a part of it. Let's continue this journey together and bring your vision to life!

www.ingramcontent.com/pod-product-compliance
Lightning Source LLC
LaVergne TN
LVHW052016200926
848481LV00005B/1506